Born in Ipswich, Suffolk, Wayne has always enjoyed creative expression. Largely, this has been via singing, playing instruments and – following ten years in the Royal Air Force – a number of years joyfully pursuing the performing arts (as a hobby, you understand). There were a few lines of poetry, and a particularly creative rendition of the thoughts that came with meditation, but Wayne had not thought himself to be a "writer". That is, until after a few days of meeting the love of his life, when he knew he was going to write the story of their meeting; and then – he wrote.

Dedicated to Marie-Hélène

Wayne Noakes

MOSQUITOES IN SKYROS

How Truth Leads to Love

AUSTIN MACAULEY PUBLISHERS™

LONDON * CAMBRIDGE * NEW YORK * SHARJAH

A CIP catalogue record for this title is available from the British Library.

ISBN 9781398449930 (Paperback)
ISBN 9781398449947 (ePub e-book)

www.austinmacauley.com

First Published 2023
Austin Macauley Publishers Ltd®
1 Canada Square
Canary Wharf
London
E14 5AA

Special thanks go firstly to Marie-Hélène, who lovingly and painstakingly proofread the first two versions (when there were almost double the words!). Secondly, I would like to thank Lisette King, who provided so much help in the "tweaking" of the final version (well, in truth, correcting the many, many grammatical errors that I had repeatedly missed).

Table of Contents

Introduction

(By the Author)

Mosquitoes in Skyros tells of twelve days on a Greek island circa two months PBR (Post Brexit Referendum – for those still wondering if that event may yet herald the second coming or the slow descent to hell).

The story presents a first-person experience of a combined holiday and personal development retreat which, after the initial few de-stress days develops via two main threads: the retreat workshops and the relationship that "ebbs and flows" alongside them.

After just a few days of writing, it became clear that the story would describe the unfolding of a most special and wonderful experience, however, it was not until a few weekends later, with the main protagonist reflecting deeply upon his life, that the story showed itself to be navigating such experiences as have influenced many lives.

As the words continued to come, I discovered that the act of creating, witnessing/observing something is only one part of the overall experience available and that rendering thoughts into words brings *meaning*, and reflecting on those words, provides for an even deeper understanding of how "things" all fit together, in the jigsaw of experiences that represents (a) life.

At the core of the story is the principle, "sharing only truth", and it transpired that the process of writing became so similarly aligned, with the scope of the story expanding to accommodate *truth* of an unexpectedly deep and beautiful nature.

Mosquitoes may be read as an openhearted romance, the reasoning and process behind personal development, or as offering an insight into spirituality.[1] Alternatively, you may simply find a lovely story about a bloke who a few

---

[1] Or all of the above.

NB: For those with particular inclinations regarding the use of footnotes: there are a *few*. Skip over them if you wish, the story proceeds – irrespective (and it just so happens that the footnotes of *particular interest* are expanded upon in a cross-referenced appendix ☺).

relationships on from a challenging marriage – goes on a holiday with a thought to understanding himself a little better, and finds…so much more.

Flight to Athens
(Not Sleeping)

Searching through the night sky for the first signs of Athens lights, my ears have indicated the aeroplane's descent for some thirty minutes but the window at my right is yet to reveal how close we are to landing. I can just make out some hills and I think a coastline, but not knowing much about the geology of Athens – or anything else much about Athens in fact I am prepared to find that this "coastline" may turn out to be a river or lakeside, or none of the above.

Unusually for me, I have not slept well these last few nights, so although I still feel pleasantly excited at the prospect of the holiday and the retreat that follows (but mostly the holiday) I am already looking forward to becoming acquainted with my bedroom. I use the phrase "still feeling excited" because the "not sleeping" and the general feeling of excitement being *around* me had arrived together, but I have been on other retreats and I've been to far more exotic places, so I remain bemused at this. When I have travelled away like this – to a retreat that is – there has been no such similar problem. Yes, retreats have taught me about life and have revealed things to me that were unexpected (mostly concerning myself), but sleeping has never been much of a problem, and I cannot sense anything around the corner – so to speak, so…(?)

Granted, this retreat is a little different in that we are having a few days chilling-out time before the retreat part gets going: one night in Athens and then a few on the island of Skyros at one location before we relocate to a quieter one to commence the retreat-proper.

Still, I've gotten-off on a reasonable start: I have only left my jacket *and* my glasses in the car back at Gatwick(!) though it was nice to find myself sat: a) beside a window and b) only one row away from the others that are doing the same retreat – which was a pleasant surprise considering we had booked our flights separately.

Upon leaving the air-conditioned arrivals area, the elevated temperature of Athens comes as a surprise, followed next by the sheer noise and the sound of many foreign-tongues within it. Less attractively, as we exit the airport building,

I am met by dense engine fume made thicker by the heat of the night, but all abate the second we are aboard our air-conditioned taxi.

We comprises Madelyn and Renna, and Jo-Anne who is one of the organisers, with Karina – the retreat leader – due to follow in a few days. There are others due to join us from elsewhere in Europe: three coming from (I think) France and meeting us here in Athens, and three others from somewhere else in Europe who are already on the Island.

The sound of a local radio station plays through the speakers and we are whisked at speed along highways and away from the city, into suburbs that feel – well, a little drab and sad to be honest. Then at once, I recall the economic crisis that Greece is still experiencing; let's hope some of the money from this event finds its way where it should.

After ten minutes of cool black leather and gentle 80's pop music, I find myself looking out of the window and into the night – as devoid of lights as had been the earlier view from the aeroplane. As the roving headlights pick out patches of grass and bush in an arid landscape, I am asking myself if we are staying *in* Athens at all…and then I start to wonder again just *why* I might not be sleeping. I have not been particularly stressed of late, and I do not recall much happening in dreams either well not those of a troubling kind, just that one that has repeated over the years involving deep warm water…and lively, lovely limbs swimming somewhere above me in the blue…but I digress.

After another five minutes of staring into the night with head leant against the side-screen, what could be "time to relax" becomes occupied with thoughts of more disquiet including, "so why *have* I come on this retreat exactly?" There is after all only a few days of chilling-out before about a weeks' retreat. "And you know what that can bring…" I mouth quietly. I have had my fair share of recounting childhood and teenage memories and trauma, but I have found great understanding on the way becoming more relaxed and gaining the confidence to explore new relationships. Not that I have found *the one* yet, but I remain hopeful, and just this last year I have been surprised by the amount of happiness arising from new *non*-romantic friendships.

Mind you, with some eleven years and four relationships since my divorce it seems about time. Not that I've *not* had some good times; quite the contrary, and it is almost as if one relationship has positioned me ready for the next. Not that it has felt that way at the time of course, but with me generally taking between several months and a year between relationships, there has been the time for reflection and there always seems to have been goodness: things to be thankful for, and things to learn from for the future.[2]

Twenty or so minutes after leaving the airport, and with my body at rest – even if my head has not quite gathered what "holiday" means the taxi turns and ascends a driveway dotted with low-level lighting to halt in front of a (very) big building – correction – series of buildings.

A large reception area opens out to a bar and lifts, and yet further beyond there appears to be a terrace – or another bar (?) It is really *big,* but it seems well maintained and feels welcoming. Having not eaten since the light lunch back at Gatwick airport, I am minded to freshen-up before investigating the bars (and an empty belly has always trumped tiredness with me). There seems to be some live music in the background; I'd like to find out what is happening there as well.

It takes a surprisingly long time to traverse the system of lifts and long (very-long) split-level corridors, before a sign finally shows my actual room number, but having made easy entry and refreshed using the hotel complimentary soap (olive oil-based – mmm), I am about to exit my room when curiosity draws me to the window. Parting the curtains, I slide the glazed doors open to find some wooden shutters that, following some grappling, part to admit the cool night air. I walk a few steps onto the balcony and look out into complete darkness. I seem to be at the end of the building. There is the hum of the air-conditioning plant below me but other than that, nothing stands out apart from a few dim lights in the near distance – perhaps on other buildings ahead of me. Oh well, if it turns out that I am facing the side of a tower block or something, it is only for one night. Okay, let's go and explore.

After two lifts, and a *very* long wide corridor – none of which I remember having used when looking for my room – and then a detour, and another, I ascend a short flight of steps to find something that looks like the reception. Yes, there is the main terrace, the bars and the music, and on turning left, I find myself looking over to a small terrace, no – actually, it is a balcony. Crossing the polished tiled floor, I pass several tables of couples old and young and families with young children. I suspect, unlike me, these people are not visiting just for the night.

---

[2] Perhaps this is what happens when one decides to hold back and work on ones' self when faced with emotional challenges, as opposed to heaping blame upon another or struggling against the natural flow in search of security.

Negotiating plumes of tobacco smoke on the way to the edge of the balcony, I recall it was not many years ago that smoking like this was normal in the UK. At the edge, I look out, and then to left and right, but there is nothing apart from a few distant lights. Looking straight down, however, I see – about three or more floors below me – a sparkling blue pool. I will leave that until tomorrow; we are not moving on until the afternoon, and the bar I had just passed *did* seem to be serving food.

I finally attract the attention of a young bartender who approaches and offers an enquiry – in Greek (of course!)

"Sorry," I say. "I have just arriv…"

"Oh – English," she says with a wide bright-toothed smile, and in quite passable English she advises. "This late in the evening, there is no normal menu but there is a sandwich of two kinds – meats or cheeses. And they both come with potato chips," she finishes.

I ask for the cheese one and a bottle of mineral water and as I reach for my wallet she says, "Where are you sitting?"

I look out to the balcony to a small vacant table and pointing, I say, "There please."

"*Thank you*," she says with a flourish and another smile.

Sat at said table, I take out my mobile and I log onto the hotel Wi-Fi. I quickly find a few interesting posts on Facebook and then – having told a few people that I was off to Greece – I make a short post that includes the hotel name and location. Within a few minutes, I am surprised by a response which informs me – with various "excited" emoticons – that the responder (a she) has been "there" in the same place just recently, and has only just flown out.

Now that *is* a coincidence!

The idea had been to eat quickly, but when the sandwich comes, I see why the name "club sandwich" is associated with America. There are multi-layered, clean-cut triangles of white bread (hadn't thought of that) – making up three layers of bread and two layers of fillings, held together with a wooden skewer, and a small mountain of potato chips on the side to boot. A white bread, processed cheese and mayo sandwich is not very appetising, but I am hungry and anyway, it will spare the embarrassment of being "the fussy Englishman pulling apart his sandwich".

Sandwich completed (yes, I admit, all of it), I rise to spot Renna and Madelyn over at the bar in happy conversation with one, two – no three others, I think.

That must be *the* others – the French contingent: two ladies and a man. However, there is quite some crowding at the bar so I cannot be sure, and I am already tired; if I say hello then politeness will lead me to stay up longer. No, I have a whole ten days to get to know everyone; I think I should get to bed.

Just before entering my room, I walk the few metres past my door to the window at the end of the corridor and peer out into the night one last time... but no, nothing.

In the room, I am quickly in and out of the shower, then switching the air-conditioning off and leaving the balcony door slightly open for fresh air, I go directly to sleep.

Exploring the Sunshine and Its Reflections

Despite the travel, despite the excitement of new places and new faces, and the lack of sleep on previous nights, this night runs similarly to the previous few: e.g., I wake every two hours, finally giving up about half-five to grab another shower with the aim of encouraging my body into some type of normal morning routine.

On emerging from the shower, I spot some daylight at the window, around the wooden shutters. So now, I will see…wow! Straight ahead of me are a few villas and only a bit behind them is the sea. In the distance is an island, and over to the right where the suns reflections off the water cause me to squint, I see a tiny rock-island just fifty metres or so offshore. Further still to the right, the coast opens into a bay or a river-estuary. Perhaps it runs along beside the hotel; that would be nice. While I cannot see very far round to the right, I can see across the water enough to decide it is probably a bay, and I can see some white houses part-way up a hill that rises ever-steeply to a rocky outcrop – beautiful!

Oh, *thank you* Jo-Anne, for this surprising and uplifting start to this day. I am thanking Jo-Anne, but of course, I do not know who has organised this location or the rooms. It may be that Karina (the retreat leader) has used this place as a meeting point for years. It had been Karina's son who had first tempted me to explore Glastonbury (the town, the Tor etc.) giving me a personal tour of that wonderful place, and then I had spent a week or so with them both on a mystic tour of Scotland, and then last year I attended one of Karina's self-development weekends. In fact, I know quite little of Jo-Anne…therefore, this retreat will be an opportunity to get to know Jo-Anne more, and her, me; and I guess, me – myself, if the retreat does what other retreats generally have.

Having appreciated the balcony: the tiling, the red hardwood chairs and matching table, I spend some minutes moving it all around, making space for a little morning yoga. Using a blanket as a mat, I lay down on my back and commence a routine of slow stretches, bends, flexes, lifts and even a headstand on the balcony (for which I am feeling quite proud). Having realised I have rushed it all somewhat – my mind having drifted onto thoughts of investigating the coastline – I am determined to try at least *some* meditation before heading down to breakfast. Thus, I grab two pillows as a sitting-cushion, and dedicate myself to some "still time" under the suns' gaze, *trying* to let go of all thought…(trying).

Ten minutes later and dressed in a short-sleeved shirt and chinos, I exit my room with every expectation – thanks to last evenings' detours – of finding the desired breakfast room quite quickly. Before I set off, I recall the window that I had seen nothing from last night and set off in a bouncy stride to that very same location. One window is partially open, but with a service-trolley loaded high with white sheets, I have to squeeze past to get a better view. The windows overlook the roofs of many, many apartments and…yes – almost certainly a bay there behind them. The white apartments are all aligned to face the water and beyond there is a garden – palms, bushes and such – that I would assume goes down to a rocky shore(?) This deserves some further investigation – after breakfast, of course.

Down at the lower level and the entrance to the breakfast hall, I am greeted by an experience completely different from that of the previous evening. The corridor is bustling with people – young, old, and in-between – and almost all are tanned and dark-haired and all are heading towards breakfast.

I resolve to locate Jo-Anne who said she would meet us at breakfast, at around eight-thirty – I think, and I am not far beyond that time. Walking into the food hall, I am welcomed by the smiles of the waiting staff. To my right, I see other doors exiting down steps to – I presume – the terrace where I had heard the music last evening. Realising I had avoided meeting people last evening, I feel a different motivation today: one that leads me to seek out the others, including the "new" others as well – if they are here. The big open-plan hall has many tables and wide full-height windows around three sides that let in the morning sun and provide for an excellent view of the bay.

Most of the people having breakfast seem to be having a good – if somewhat busy – time. I say "most" because quite a number – well, those at the buffet tables at least – look somewhat *perturbed*. As I take in a wider view of the several buffet tables, the hot-food serveries, drinks dispensers and all, I can quite understand why. The tables nearest to me present breads of all kinds: white, brown and rye, seeded and sliced, and numerous shapes and sizes of baguettes. I put aside the intention to meet with Jo-Anne for a moment – getting closer to the bread to breathe in its aroma. Then, dodging children and their watching parents, I spy butter and spreads, and different types of honey, jam and cheeses – *so* many cheeses. There are meats: sliced-up and in pâtés, and yoghurts, creams, fruit – sliced, diced, whole and pureed, and this is just this *one* side. Maybe those perturbed few were simply overwhelmed by choice.

I cannot help myself: I return to the aroma of the bread, take an end piece of a dark baguette and devour it with great pleasure. I am glad that this place is so busy because I am not sure that my behaviour was good etiquette on any continent.

Glancing along the other side of the buffet table I see crisp-breads and crackers, French Toast, breakfast cereals, muesli, nuts, seeds, milk (*milks*) and alongside them, tomatoes and salad items – and…oh my! This is a marked difference from yesterday's breakfast, spent alone in my Suffolk home, looking out over the sun-scorched lawn and shrubs. Yes, I am happy to swap yesterday's peace for today's bounty.

Not knowing where Jo-Anne and the others might be sitting, I decide – instead of wasting any further time – to turn back to the fruit section for a "starter". Moving to the only empty table that I can see, I am about to sit when, glancing towards the sea-view, I see Jo-Anne making her way towards me wearing a bright scarf that stands out clearly against her white T-shirt. She smiles and beckons me, the sun backlighting the edges of her blonde hair. We hug. "You must come and join us, Wayne. We are there, over by the window, in the sunshine. Isn't it fabulous!" she exclaims.

"Thank you, and yes, it is," I reply. "And thank you for arranging the exciting view from my room this morning. Now I know why I had such a long walk to find my room last evening."

"Yes, isn't lovely. I thought you'd appreciate that. Come, come and eat with us. I am almost finished but the others are still eating."

Recovering my fruit bowl, I head off in the general direction of Jo-Anne's departure, weaving between the tables and the steady stream of guests until shortly – I see the rear of her sun-lit golden locks. The table is on the farthest side of the room, end-on to the full height windows. Directly to Jo-Anne's right, with back to the sun, is a tanned, happy and healthy-looking older/middle-aged gentleman, dressed in smart casuals, and busy eating.

"This is Henri; Henri, this is Wayne," Jo-Anne says, and we make a short friendly handshake.

"Madelyn, you know, of course," Jo-Anne says, indicating the seat beside Henri.

We nod and smile. "Hi Wayne, did you sleep well?" Madelyn asks. "I know you were tired."

"Actually no, not so well, but well enough – and I'm feeling very good just now," I assure her.

"And this," Jo-Anne indicating the seat just at my left, beside the window, "…this lovely lady next to you is…" (*Mary-Elaine* – did she say?) "She arrived here yesterday afternoon," Jo-Anne continues, "…with Henri, after spending a few days in Athens." We make a small but lingering handshake, not so easily done with her being just at my side, and I take my seat beside her.

Facing the bay and eating my fruit with sunlight streaming in, I try to follow the conversation between the woman next to me and the man opposite. In doing so, I cannot help but glance from one to the other: the smiling man in front of me and the smiling woman sat beside me. She sounds German or perhaps French, but she is speaking English very well, and with a most interesting accent that seems both gentle and sharp at the same time.

At each turn of conversation back to the woman, I use the opportunity to glance at her… and find the act most enjoyable. I find my glances lingering a moment each time: at her, sat at my left, facing the sun; smiling eyes and sunglasses perched atop blond hair – bunched tightly at the back of her head. Henri is not speaking English so well. He regularly breaks into short bursts of French, but they seem to have slightly different accents and – now I look closer – they do appear to be a bit different in age as well. However, where they might come from and…whatever – is no matter.

As breakfast continues, I learn that Henri is Swiss, and that it is possible to get into the sea from the hotel grounds because he and the (French?) woman had gone into the sea late yesterday, and would like to do the same again today. Ah, they must be together then, this Swiss man and…Mary-Ellen, Marilyn (was it?).

The French woman then excuses herself to get some more food. "Not for zo much," she says with her rich accent. "But I must get zome more Greek yoghurt and also more hunnie – it is so good!"

She returns with quite a pile of fruit in her bowl, then proceeds to persuade Henri to take some of it. As she reaches across the table to off-load her bowl, I find myself drawn to her hands, this time observing that her left hand has a very smart jewelled ring and, a wedding band, (I *think*). Upon glancing back and forth between the two people, I observe that there is *quite* an age difference. Lucky Henri.

21

Following the French woman's lead, I decide to make the most of the "all-inclusive" breakfast, going this time to the hot servery where I select some brown toast, mushrooms, tomatoes and scrambled eggs. On the way back, I make a detour to get one of the Greek sage teas Jo-Anne had recommend earlier. Back at the table, in the sunshine, all are happily eating and drinking, with Henri and the French woman laughing together. When they start to talk of the sea, I enquire how I might later get down there.

"Oh, you will swim?" the woman enquires. "You must join us, we – well I – will probably swim again zhis morning. Actually…no, I think I *definitely* will swim there today. Zer water, it was a bit cool last evening and it will be better to be in zer sun. Maybe I will zee you?" she enquires of me.

"Oh yes, I think I will," I reply. "Err, is there a place I should look for, to get down to the sea?"

"No, it is quite eazy," she replies. "You must go out by zer pool and across zer area there and you will find some steps down. You have to be a little care-full, but no – it is eazy, really. So, maybe I see you, perhaps at ten, or half-ten…near the pool? Or if not, I'll be in the sea!"

This all seems very fortunate to me: the chance to swim on my first day out here, and some guidance at hand if I cannot find my way down to the beach – because from where I am sitting, it looks as if it is quite some distance away and beyond a steep drop.

In the conversations that continue around the table, I learn that the name of the other woman I had spotted at the bar last night is Rachel. Both Henri and Mary-Ellene (does he say?) have mentioned Rachel several times now, and in such terms that show Rachel is known to both. I learn from Henri (in broken English) that Rachel decided purposefully not to come down to breakfast this morning because she finds this number of people "just too much". I nod with understanding. Maybe Rachel is all-ready for the relaxation side of this holiday and does not want to get powered-up just to have to unwind again later.

As we all rise to leave, Henri points over towards the entrance and waves. "Ah, there is Rachel."

We weave our way through the bustling breakfast room and out of the sun to where Rachel beams a wide smile at us as she reaches out to share hugs. Firstly with (?) the pretty French lady, then with Henri and then, "Wayne, this is…" Jo-Anne starts to say, but then Henri continues, "Wayne, this is Rachel – my wife."

Rachel is wearing a wide-brimmed sun hat which she holds to her head. As she moves closer towards me, I reach out to her and we engage in an easy and warm hug. As lovely as it is, however, I am not quite fully in the moment, for I am pondering over having just learnt that Henri is with *Rachel*, not with…*her* – the pretty French woman. In any case, it remains that the French woman had been wearing both an engagement and a marriage ring, moreover – what difference does any of this make: I am on holiday and later this afternoon I will be flying onwards to start a *retreat*.

We depart with Rachel and Henri walking out onto the terrace, and me going back to my room to brush my teeth and get prepared for swimming.

With trunks on, shorts and a T-shirt over the top, and with a sun hat and a few Euros in my pocket, I am walking down the corridor when I notice, "Poolside and Changing" on a sign beside the first lift. "Most excellent!" I declare as I push the call button. This section of the hotel-complex seems older, or at least the lift certainly seems old and slow…or am I just impatient to get into the sea? The lift continues down…and down and…stops. Stainless steel doors open revealing a dimly lit corridor. Once at the far end, I descend several steps to a pathway heading towards – well, I assume towards – the pool. Fifty metres or so down the path, I am fast deciding that this is not a hotel-complex at all but a resort centre. Following several more flights of stairs between chalets and suchlike I at-last, see the pool – albeit still some way below. The poolside has chairs, sunbeds, sunshades, picnic tables, drinks bars – the works; and is busy with swimmers and sunbathers. It does not, however, appear that anyone (i.e., the French woman) is waiting, but being uncertain of the time, it is possible I have been too slow getting here, or maybe I had misunderstood, or she has changed her plans – perhaps.

At the far side of the pool, a gate provides an exit through a tall green wire-mesh fence. The gate is attended by a responsible-looking smartly uniformed man (yes, this *is* a holiday resort) and beyond there appears to be the kind of trees and bushes I had seen from the window. Across to the right is a bar and two café/restaurant-like places, then further around, a tiled area has people dancing to "upbeat" music…or is it an exercise class? Behind that is a shop of some sort. Perhaps I will come back here at lunchtime, but for now, I am drawn to the promise of the sea.

Just as I turn towards the gate, I recognise some familiar dance music. It is one of last year's popular Salsa dance numbers and I immediately feel more at home. Looking back at the "exercise class", it dawns on me that in fact a Latin dance class is taking place. "Mmm, I wonder if perhaps a dance might not be out of the question," I say to myself. However, having observed the dancing for a just a short while and the nature of their moves, I see they are doing only beginners' moves. Still, it was a nice thought.

Turning back towards the gate, I am set upon finding out what is beyond, when someone strolls across my path immediately ahead. I say *someone*, but to be accurate, it is a near-naked woman. She is *very* attractive: curved, tanned and complete with a micro-costume that is turning heads – and not just those of the men. I am aware of my eyes' inclination to follow her path, but I resolve not to give in to the instinct…which lasts all of a second because, even while I am still thinking about resisting the urge, I find my head has already turned to the rear-view of the tiniest of thongs and the curviest of behinds – sauntering towards the poolside. Greece may be a Catholic (or Methodist?) country, but there appears little conservatism down here at poolside (I am rather happy to say). Glancing forward to avoid the risk of collision, I see the gate-attendant has had his attention similarly diverted, and following his gaze, I find I am just in time to see the tanned figure dive and the water close around her. As I continue on my way, I cannot help but ponder on just how deeply some auto-responses may be lodged within us – well, within me and within the gate-guard at any rate.

On passing through the gate, I feel decidedly *observed*. With the CCTV camera, it feels like going through airport security again. It is interesting how this feeling of "being watched" leaves me feeling – well, almost guilty or vulnerable…or something. Of course, it could be something to do with the hotel towel I have in my swim-bag, but the feeling quickly evaporates upon taking in the view of the trees and bushes and a glint of the reflected sunlight – that promises much.

The pavement changes to a wooden-slatted walkway between strips of very green, very hardy-looking grass. All of the sunbeds appear occupied. Of course, it would have been a bit easier if I had remembered my glasses; even if the French woman happens to be down here somewhere, there is little chance of me spotting her amongst this expansion of sunbeds, sunshades and sun-worshipping bodies beyond about thirty metres!

The water comes into focus some fifteen metres (?) away, but it still appears to be somewhat lower than the land here (?) – anyway, I *have* remembered my mask and snorkel so all I need now is a place to lay my towel. I suppose I could simply drop all my things on the ground here and get straight in, but everything seems so *nicely* organised; no, it is not the thing to do here. Finally, having walked far over to the left where the numbers of bodies appeared to be thinning out, and having surveyed the scenery along the way – just in case, I, at last, come across a single sunshade two rows from the sea with two sunbeds yet unoccupied. It takes only seconds for me to prepare for the sea, but I then spend a minute or so, carefully placing and covering my belongings and getting my bearings so that I can find my way back.

What I had earlier thought was a rope fence to separate the sunbathing area from the beachside area, turns out to be the edge of a smartly constructed beach-terrace. It has a brick-paved edge and gaps where vertical steps go down the metre or so to the water. Descending the (ladder-type) steps is not-at-all easy, and I start to wonder if British Standards might make such things less difficult and somewhat safer back in the UK…but then again, back *in* the UK no such steps would take me down into a warm blue Aegean Sea.

Swimming with mask and snorkel in such clear water simply and completely fills my senses. There are not many people in the water, but the few that are, are all busily swimming, so I stand little chance of spotting anyone. At the farthest edge of the buoys that define the swimming area, perhaps seventy-five metres away, there appears to be someone swimming with their head down, but even with my mask lifted I cannot be sure whether the swimmer is even a man or a woman.

After about half an hour of swimming, I return to my sunbed and having used my towel on my hair, I lay down upon it. This is *so* good: feeling the warmth of the sun on my body; I have forgotten just how much power the sun has. After just a few minutes, however, I cross my arms over my face to protect my sight. Even then, I can still sense the sun through my flesh-pink eyelids, but ah, there is the time now, to relax. Yes, feeling carefree and relaxed…feeling a bit overpowered by the heat of this sun maybe but…ah, my sun hat, I think it is in the swim bag I have brought with me.

Looking up from beneath the brim of my hat, I can see the dark denim side. This means the light blue and swirly white flower side is facing outward. I do not mind the hat this way around: I'm quite comfortable with the patterned side; it is after-all a good surf-brand – which means it must have at *least* something cool about it, yes? I recall, however, my youngest daughter's embarrassment some years back, when she had observed her close-to-middle-aged father wearing a (rather) conspicuous surfer-dude hat. Mind you, I think I might also have been wearing my bright orange Bermuda shorts that day. (*Dads!*)

Golly…that makes this hat about ten or more years old. *Where has the time gone!* Oh, and I remember now why I had bought the hat: my daughter (same younger one) had asked to wear my treasured Harley Davison cap given me by my cousin when we had been on vacation in America. Within half an hour, however, she had lost it, and so I had bought this one. Initially, I had worn it with the plain denim side outwards, until having turned it inside out by mistake one day, my eldest daughter observed, "Dad, it's a reversible!" I then commenced to wear it with the denim side out when walking and with the flowery side out when on the beach, to which my older daughter (kindly) said, "Cool," and my youngest merely *winced*.

It is nice here, in the hat…in the sun.

It would be nicer still, of course, should I have come across that French lady – or anyone I know for that matter, but perhaps I am better to use this time for myself.

Hearing the seagulls; listening to the seagulls…hearing the gentle whoosh of the breeze across my hat, listening to the breeze and the occasional voices in conversation that pass behind me…

Just laying back, in the sun; feeling the sun warming my face…heating my face…the sun, hot sun, heating my body *and* my face…and thus: all of five minutes into my purposeful attempt at relaxing in the sun, I come to remember I am *not* a natural sunbather. Checking for the time on my mobile phone, I find it is a quarter to twelve. It is just as well I have not rested here much longer. There should just be time enough, however, to shower, change, pack and get to the reception for the twelve-thirty checkout, and then the *check-in* with Jo-Anne to receive the full details of the afternoons' transfer. I guess, after that, I will need to stow my suitcase, find some lunch, and be back at reception ready to leave around three o'clock: not so much of a "restful start" to the holiday then!

Passing by the gate-guard, this time with his back towards me, the thought strikes me that he is looking in the wrong direction. Surely, he should be monitoring the people coming *from* the beach, into the complex? Then, I glance towards the pool, recall the morning, and I fully understand his preference.

Upon entering the hotel, I am met by relative darkness but am thankful for the accompanying coolness. As the lift door opens, there is a tall man and two young children – giggling – looking forward to the pool or the beach no-doubt.

(I recall some similar times…) The man and I exchange a nod and a smile in mutual appreciation of his children's excitement, and the three pace-off down the corridor towards the sunshine.

It is just before one o'clock when I arrive at the reception. About half the group have made it here ahead of me and are busy checking-out and putting their cases in the luggage room, and catching-up generally with each other. Having surrendered my key-card and paid for last nights' club sandwich, I walk to the luggage room. As I approach, the sliding door opens and Renna comes out, "Hello Wayne, are you ready then? Isn't it lovely here…oh, watch the door." Despite the advice, I am only halfway through the sliding door and pushing my suitcase ahead of me, when it starts to close. Surprised, I sidestep then start to fall over some luggage stacked just inside the doorway. In misplacing my foot, I wince as my right ankle turns over and collapse upon other baggage.

Fortunately, the injury seems slight and within a minute my ankle can fully flex and take my weight in the normal way, but deciding it wise to rest, I go over to the picture windows that overlook bay.

Members of the group come and go, sharing a few words, checking their baggage, and paying their bar-bills. From the comfort of a deep upholstered sofa, I am contemplating what might be achieved between now and three o'clock, when the void is filled by the arrival of the French – Mary… (something-or-other). Leaving Henri and his wife to continue to the reception desk, she sits down opposite, smiles and says, "*H'allo!*" She finishes with an attractive rising inflexion that suggests she is feeling quite upbeat. I ask her if she ventured into the sea and she tells me she did, and then asks the same of me. When I confirm I had as well, she says (in steady, ever-so-slightly broken English) "Oh, what a pity, we could have swum in it, together. I was alone. Henri did not join me today. He was with Rachel."

With my best pronunciation, I agree that it had been something of a small misfortune that separated us because I had looked for her and Henri. I added that I had been snorkelling, however, so my head had been down in the water a lot. She tells me she had not worn her mask and so had done quite a bit of swimming. "I do not like the sun so much. I can only do sun-bazing for just a few minutes and then I say *I have had enough*."

I ponder on whether it *had* been her – swimming far out near the ropes. It was not from want of trying that I had not found her, so maybe it just wasn't to be.

Having completed their checking-out, Henri and Rachel join us and proceed to converse fervently, their conversation rich in gesticulations and facial expressions. At a point just after the language turns mostly away from English, the French lady goes over to check out, and I politely withdraw to ponder again on what can be done with the time yet remaining. I recall having seen a toasted sandwich consumed at the poolside and I decide what with not knowing when and where our evening meal will be taken, I might just as well go back down there.

While not professing to be a toasty connoisseur, I do every few weeks or so frequent a lovely "bare and arty" café on the main shopping street in the local town of Woodbridge named The Fire Station. There, the most delicious sourdough bread is served up encasing cheddar, leeks and mushrooms (as an example) accompanied most often by a freshly made salad. The salad is a veritable meal in itself containing such as beetroot, spinach, rocket, celery/celeriac, orange, walnuts, new-potatoes and chives…anyway, this toasty is nothing like those(!) but being served poolside and in the warmth of the Greek afternoon sun, it certainly scores a few points.

The next half-hour passes relatively quickly, and in letting the time pass without much thought, it seems I am beginning to relax at last. Perhaps this stopover in Athens is a *very* good idea, not just as a means of bringing together people from different countries, but also as a means of downshifting a gear or two. As I ponder over my normal routines, it is clear just how busy I have allowed my life to become recently: yoga and meditation before breakfast, then in the week – inspecting construction sites, and perhaps a dance class or two, and at the weekend – busying myself in the home and garden, or walking, cycling, and perhaps a dance party of an evening. I find myself questioning whether *any* or *all* routines may in time become simply another form of entertainment if we are not careful.

With more time seemingly available, I get out my mobile phone and look at the images taken that morning, and then at the message post from last night. As I study the wording more carefully, looking at its various interpretations, the message had – on reading last night – seemed to be implying that the sender had been in *this* hotel. However, upon reading it now, they might only have meant just that they had been in Athens recently, and perhaps the "only just flown back" was a bit of artistic-license. There is much of that on social media: "positive embellishment of sentiment." Still, it could be worth following up when I get back to the UK.

Our departure from the hotel proceeds without issue, although the same air-conditioned comfort of the taxi as last night makes stepping out into the heat of the airport – a small shock to the system. Many people are queuing in Departures: in an assortment of clothing and with an assortment of luggage (and some *baggage* as well, no doubt). Within our group: some of the luggage is being carried, some worn on backs, some pushed and some pulled but without exception we are glad to be on-route. Two of our number appear to be quite jovial in fact, but not all display such similar emotion. One appears tired, two are looking somewhat confused, and another looks to be either deep in concentration – or just a little distressed. All of us are at the airport to catch a flight; we are all subject to the same set of immediate external influences: the environment of the building, the general bustle, the announcements, and things; however, as I look around within the group, it is clear that many are having quite *different* experiences. [3]

Once through security, I hear Jo-Anne call out to Rachel, and then she addresses the French lady as "Marie-*Hélène*" (!) Using far less accent than Henri and Rachel had used, Jo-Anne has sounded the letters clearly enough for me to hear the "H" of *Helene* – not "Elaine" (or *something*).

We collectively decide to take a pit stop at a kiosk, and I choose a bottle of water and a small chocolate-covered nutty-bar (…at least I think that is what the wrapper shows, I cannot understand any of the words). Marie-*Hélène* meanwhile, sits beside me with a yoghurt pot containing some diced and dried fruit. She is conversing with Henri, initially in French (I think) changing to English as she opens the conversation to the rest of us.

Henri jokes about Marie-Hélène's apparent addiction to Greek Yoghurt, which he says had started in Athens a few days earlier. Marie-Hélène tells us how the three of them – Henri, Rachel and herself – had spent a few days in central Athens before meeting at the hotel yesterday evening. When Marie-Hélène speaks, I observe how she drops most of the "h" sounds – saying "*Atens*" instead of "Athens", and I note many of the "th" sounds being completely replaced with soft "z" sounds. This really is the most lovely *badly* pronounced English I have ever heard.

---

[3] Because of the different "baggage" as opposed to "luggage" – perhaps.

An hour before take-off, we all gather our things and amble off to departure gate number fifteen. As we file through the gate, Marie-Hélène and I are required to hand over our (comparatively small) cases; they may be classed as "carry-on" but it seems the aeroplane is not large enough to have the "carry-ons" carried-on. Having walked across the shimmering tarmac, we ascend a few steps to board a (small) twin-engine turboprop aeroplane.

Once on board, I find my ticket has placed me beside the window on the right side of the aisle and before I manage to look up, I hear, "*Allo.*" With that rich-sweet French accent that my ears are starting to enjoy, Marie-Hélène – smiling, it always seems – slips her handbag off her shoulder and sits down.

"May I?" she continues, quite unnecessarily.

"Yes, yes of course." I play-along.

We immediately start to talk about…*stuff*; about our suitcases, about how long we might be in the air for, about how we had *not* met when we had swum, and so on. Marie-Hélène tells me it was virtually dark when she had gone swimming at the hotel the night before with Henri. She explains that they had both wanted – not just to swim – but also to escape the very busy commercial feeling of the hotel. Continuing, she tells me that they have swum together quite a few times and that it suits Rachel because she needs to have the sea very warm before she willingly takes the plunge. We then return to our misfortune of not having met down at the sea. As well as being in the water around the same time, it turns out that we had both spent only a short time lying in the sun before heading back. I find myself wondering how she has such a good tan if she doesn't like to sunbathe. We then debate the possibility that she could have exited the water just after me to have been laid out on a sunbed just some metres away, and that we could have been enjoying each other's company like this, instead of *not-enjoying* the sunbathing.

I confess to my misunderstanding of her name – right up until just in the departure hall, but she brushes it off, advising that it is particularly hard for the English to understand because French do not pronounce the "H", and that her surname also has two "e's" with accents above them (Marie-Hélène), which gives them the sound of an English "a"; the overall sound, therefore, being akin to the English spelling of "Marie-Alaine". We talk about the different airlines we have used and how the service can vary so much, and I recall how every time I get on a small plane like this one – I have a desire for roasted peanuts: having taken four such aeroplane flights in the USA where peanuts had been given out freely each time. Very different, we agree, from some of the low-cost airlines that even seem to begrudge providing tap water nowadays.

I start to feel the aeroplane's descent and as I look out of the window at the growing images of waves and land, it dawns on me that we have been engaged in almost constant dialogue since before take-off.

"I think we must be nearly there," I observe.

"Really, so fast? I zought we would be flying for forty minutes?" she queries.

She looks at her watch. "Oh yes, it has been zat long already. Really, I am surprised!"

On the tarmac, it feels even warmer than on the mainland. As we walk the distance from the aeroplane to the very small airport terminal, I find myself talking again with Marie-Hélène, sharing our first impressions of the island of Skyros.

Following a short delay (baggage handling!), I depart the airport building to see that most of the group have already boarded a minibus. However, a discussion is in mid-flow regarding the fact that there is not enough space for us all – at least not with all our baggage, sorry – *luggage*. Jo-Anne speaks up to assure us that another vehicle is on the way and following a seat count by Henri, he accedes to volunteer for the second vehicle.

The second vehicle turns out to be a Fiat 500, and with quite some humour we observe that Henri, who is probably the largest of us, has consigned himself to the smallest transport, along with a number of suitcases! Fortunately, Henri also sees the comedy in the situation, but it does nothing to reduce our laughter as from the cool comfort of the mini-bus, we observe the image of the small Fiat behind: packed with cases, bags and Henri, and looking every bit like the typical overstuffed family car going on holiday!

The countryside is sparse and dry; no doubt the result of a long hot summer. There are only a few thin trees and some small bushes presenting any form of greenery, and even then, the colours and textures of the leaves tell of *dryness*. The road becomes small and winding with hills rising all around, but within twenty minutes we start to catch glimpses of the sea. We enter a small town with buildings stretched out ahead of us and going partway up a hill. The mini-bus turns sharply into a yard to come to rest within a semi-circle of interconnected white-walled, terracotta-roofed buildings. Most of the buildings are single-storey, with a few two-storey sections rising like small towers.

Getting out of the minibus, the air seems lighter, fresher – and I sense these buildings are all that now separates us from the sea. However, before we can grab our cases, Jo-Anne points out that the family that lives here and who will be looking after us *require* that we are introduced. Accordingly, our happy-faced dark-haired hosts appear from nowhere and line up to greet us. We, in turn, line up and walk past them all, Jo-Anne relaying our names as we each shake hands and say hello. The scene reminds me of some TV stately home drama (but less *stuffy*). A few faces stand out to me: that of a young man who speaks some English and that of the grandmother who is neatly attired and offers the widest of smiles.

One at a time, we are led off and down a short passage between the buildings. Being the last, I have the company of Jo-Anne together with the young man, and the grandmother as I am led down the passage, and out onto a wide terrace looking to the sea and a big blue sky. My room is immediately on the right, in the corner and – I am told – in the oldest part of the building, which in turn is one of the oldest buildings in the bay. I am also led to understand that the room is one the grandmother uses when it is empty, so I am assured of both its comfort and its setting.

It *is* a lovely room. With a sheltered porch, a cushioned bench, a table and chair out front, a dark wooden door opens to a pleasantly attired room and a double bed and semi-reclining chair – both with pleasant light-purple throws. I am advised that the rooms are never usually locked by the family because everyone feels quite safe here, however, there is a key *there*, in the lock, if I should want to lock the door. I offer my thanks, but as soon as they have departed, I take the key and my suitcase, park them swiftly inside the doorway and exit to explore.

The terrace has light-grey paving slabs and a slightly raised middle section of some more-ornate tiling upon which, set out in seashells, is the word "Welcome". The first few metres of the terrace have a gazebo overhead supported by whitewashed pillars. It has palm leaves and vines forming a cover from which hang the last few remaining bunches of dark over-ripe grapes. I pick a few; they taste very sweet but with rather tough and acetic skins. Around the edges of the gazebo, the foliage has been allowed to drop about half a metre or so, giving some additional shade and probably providing some privacy when viewed from the beach. There then comes a largely open section for about five or six metres, dotted with raised planters containing various bushes and evergreens. There are also some olive trees and a few shrubs – flowers now all but gone. There is a raised planted area along the right side, and there remain some orange and deep terracotta-coloured flowers on the bushes – now half-closed, perhaps in sympathy with the approaching sunset.

Central to the far edge that overlooks the beach, is a stand-alone gazebo – about four metres square, also with dried/tired-looking palm leaves over it. Underneath, there are some tables and chairs. Immediately to its right is a larger circular raised-planter with a few green bushes and one central pedestal bush laden with large semi-exotic red blooms, stamen projecting boldly into the cooling evening air. These are perhaps those species that stand the proudest all day long, and then die. Over to the far left of the terrace and at the end wall is another gazebo, this one having large couches beneath that are strewn with cushions. Despite the temptation of this luxuriant feature, I instead go to stand at the far edge of the terrace, to absorb the complete view for the first time.

We are in a large bay that in turn is part of a very long curved section of coastline that opens out to the left, but curves for miles to the right until almost straight ahead, vast rolling grey hills drop to meet the sea. Directly to the right, several hundred metres away, the beach stops at rocks and becomes cliffs not far after. At this point, the hill inland has many white buildings that stretch almost unabated to the high rocky top, but with the angle of the sun already casting long shadows, little more detail is evident.

Where I stand, the beach has fine sand and slopes gently down to the shore about twenty metres away. The sea is undulating slowly and reflects beautiful shades of blue from silvery to dark-denim. The waves are small and break very quietly in long rolling sequences that my eyes follow as they run along the water's edge.

There are only a few people on the beach. They look as if they might have had their fill of the sun and sea for the day, but are not yet ready to let go of the experience entirely.

Turning to look back at the terrace, there are several rooms at ground level – five or six perhaps; and there are two – two-storey sections to which a staircase leads. There are, I presume, a few more rooms up there, one of which appears to have a small dark-wood balcony that must offer quite a stunning view of the bay.

Jo-Anne has said that we will be joined later by Milos our island guide for the retreat, and then our hosts will serve us dinner here – on the terrace. This will be a lovely place to dine.

Then, quite suddenly, there are three "new" faces on the terrace – all three having come from the same area in Mid Europe. I recognise them most recently from a weekend spent in Glastonbury but also from their occasional attendance at London meetings, and I recall their names: Angelica – "Angel" for short, her daughter Beryl, and their close friend Doris. Now we are *all* here.

Glancing towards my room I see that the grandmother has occupied the seat outside my doorway. She looks so very much at home that I'm guessing it might be her usual evening resting place. I smile at her as I pass by. I sense she has seen this all before, and many times: greeting new guests, showing them their rooms, and then reclaiming her space once the visitors have gone.

Getting out my mobile phone, I return to the terrace to take a few shots and a short video of the first views. I do not expect to be using my phone much here, so if I take a few shots now I should avoid the sometimes-experience of returning home after a great time – but having taken none.

I turn back to my room to find the grandmother is still there. I gesticulate with my phone to seek her permission to take her photo. She sits upright and smiles; (I think the answer is "yes").

Knowing it is some while before dinner, I take my time in unpacking. Having laid most of my clothing out on the bed, however, I realise there is not much cupboard space, and I return half of my things to the suitcase leaving just shirts and long trousers that I then hang in the modest wardrobe. Having shaved and dressed in trousers and a long-sleeved shirt for the cooler evening, I exit to the terrace to join those already seated at the tables laid out for dinner under the central gazebo. No sooner than I have been greeted, the last new face arrives in the form of Milos, our island guide. As I look around the table, there is just one space that appears to be untouched – there being one other empty chair just around the corner from it that looks to have been claimed by someone but temporarily vacated. The "someone" returns, smiles and says, "*Allo.*" Marie-Hélène sits down; I sit down; this seat is just fine.

Fast-fading daylight is augmented by terrace lighting, and our hosts emerge to spread a vegetarian feast before us including stuffed peppers, jacket potatoes and cold bean salads – home-cooked and looking very, very tasty.

During the meal, the turn of conversation goes to Milos and he tells us something of his history. Being Dutch by birth, he explains how he had adopted the Island as his home some twenty or so years back, and now hardly ever leaves the place.

Jo-Anne then tells us about the plans for the next few days. There will be optional sunrise meditations and yoga on the beach first thing each morning, breakfast and lunch will be served here on the terrace and evening meals elsewhere. The proposal for tomorrow night it that we dine at a beachside restaurant just a little way down from us, and for Tuesday evening it is suggested we go into the local town to eat. There is also the option of a town-tour on Tuesday before the meal – to be guided by Milos, and at breakfast tomorrow we will discuss it all further.

Dusk gives way to the night, and with our meal and the conversations thereafter having lasted something close to two hours, most now begin to depart for their rooms. I go to the edge of the terrace again, to listen to the ever-present gentle rolling waves, and I try to make out their white foam as I breathe in the cool night air. Turning back to the terrace, I notice several people have congregated outside one of the more-central rooms. I join them and we share light-hearted recollections of the day. It seems we have all enjoyed the company, and having now shared our food, our space and our time on a few occasions, it feels like a sense of the group "us" is forming.

As if to an unspoken plan, we move naturally from one to the other, sharing hugs and saying goodnight. I like hugging and, fortunately, Henri seems comfortable with hugging as well, for not all men are so inclined.

Turning next to find the pretty French Lady, I say, "You know, I am not sure I actually got round to greeting you with a hug this morning – what with breakfast and all, so I must wish you an especially warm 'good night' with this one."

With Marie-Hélène looking a little hesitant, I take a moment to connect with her arms before moving into a hug. It feels good, especially good – actually. I guess I am feeling quite uplifted from the day's experiences but even so – that was a *nice* hug. Having spoken so much already, I guess, a sense of *familiarity* is part of this good feeling, and besides that, she is a very pretty woman. All the same, it is a *particularly* nice hug.

I pull away, but for a second – just a split second – she remains as if my arms were still around her. I feel concerned. Maybe because of my dancing, I am somewhat over-confident with the close proximity of another, and maybe she is not so much? Maybe I was a bit too close or…? All this runs through my mind in a split second and then a moment later, it is gone.

All are with smiles and saying "*Good-night*" and variations thereof, and then we go each to our rooms, to bed, to sleep.

Good Morning Skyros
(A Truly New Place)

It is…well – *early* in the morning on the fifth day of September and my second day on the Greek Island of Skyros. The main retreat does not begin for a few days, so I should be relaxing in this – the holiday part; so why, therefore, is this already the second time I have woken and why *so* early?

From the window beyond the foot of the bed comes a soft light that penetrates both the lace and the cream cotton curtains and it gives just enough light to find my travel-clock on the bedside cabinet. However, there is not enough light to read the time so, with the clock in my hand, I crawl down to the end of the bed and move its face at various angles to the window until I find just enough light to see – that it is (*humph*) five-twenty.

Oh well, I have certainly woken up early in worse places than this and I am after all – *on holiday*. I might only be having three or so hours of sleep in a stretch these last few nights, but when I wake, I do not feel particularly anxious about it. I have been content with the relative stillness and warmth, and with a general feeling around me of excitement/expectation – or something. Maybe I am looking forward to the snorkelling more than I thought. It probably won't be like some other places I have snorkelled – such as the Philippines, Australia or the Red Sea – but being in clear warm water and observing the sea life and the myriad reflections of blue usually brings me great pleasure.

Finding my swimming trunks, and putting on my dark-blue linen trousers and a light terracotta T-shirt, I venture out onto the terrace. At the end-wall overlooking the beach, my attention is captured by a staggered line of pink-hued clouds which my eyes follow to a point over-head, before tracking back down towards the sea where the clouds stretch out in a line just above the horizon. We were invited to meet on the beach at sunrise – I know – but I feel inclined to consider some meditation right now. The breeze outside, however, is just a little *too* cool and so returning to my room, I tidy my bedclothes and place two pillows, one on top of the other, and sit on the bed. Seeing my pendant by the bedside, a small metal cross (of-sorts) (…that's interesting – having not remembered to put it on earlier). I take it in my hands for a moment and then fasten it around my neck. The cross resembles two cylinders notched together at right angles, with wire wrapping around the joint, binding them together. The shape of it does speak somewhat of the Christian icon but I see the shape as representing the interconnection of the physical and the spiritual more than the Crucifixion. I accept (what I see as) the core truth regarding the Christian story, but I have not adopted the whole belief system and in fact, do not subscribe wholly to any scheme that requires – *assumes* – the complete acceptance of another persons' personal experiences, as would seem to be at the core of most religious scripture.

Life, it seems to me, is of most value when it involves *experience* rather than belief. When a person of ancient times has written down or has had transcribed on their behalf, (and in ancient tongue) what they can recall of *their* experiences, only to have it translated one or more times, and then have it extracted from, expanded, dissected and paraphrased, to be applied selectively by a third-party to suit those themes as may be forefront to the society of the day or sometimes just to suit a third-party's specific interests, well, sorry that does not seem a good basis on which to form an understanding of the world in the richness and reality with which it presents itself *today.*

It is apparent to me that there are some conditions or more accurately perhaps *processes*, that can be placed under the title of "natural law" – as some scientists would seem to be working to understand. Principal to these is the "currency" of energy, its permanence: meaning that energy is never lost – only transmuted into different forms, and another example is the interaction between what we perceive as time and space. Furthermore, many religious texts, wisdom-based traditions and ancient and modern-day gurus would seem to speak in the same general way on a surprising number of topics including: the continuity of life, the importance of truth, and the general interconnectedness of life. This all lends further support to the idea that there may be something, or several "somethings" that one might be forgiven to interpret as being constants, rules – or if you like "truths" that have always been a part of life.

I also recognise "the supremacy of love": the particular aspect of interconnectedness that I sense as universal life force energy or more simply: *Love*. In my use of the word "Love", I mean something more than the emotional state that is conventionally linked with romance, and as a signpost to its meaning, I would offer the example of the ever-enduring Christmas story, where Love becomes rooted on the earth in its purest form – through the birth of Jesus.

My first deep love-energy "awareness" came through the practice of Reiki, and because of that personal experience, I *believe* in Love. Whilst this means I cannot find myself wholly "anti" any religion/belief system that recognises Love at its core, I am, however, very aware of how *that* which *may* be true for all of us, has *so many times* – been repackaged, managed and manipulated for the good of some, and sometimes for the suffering of many.

In summary, the "cross" that is my pendant is okay with me because of the Love connection I associate it with but besides this, there is another very meaningful connection I have with this particular cross and one of a very experiential nature. I had received the cross as a pre-show good-luck gift from a fellow member of the cast when I had been in a production of the musical Godspell, back in the 90's – staged at the Wolsey Theatre in Ipswich. The cast member concerned had been on holiday and brought back several gifts/tokens that fitted the theme of the show. Mine was this cross, and since the director declared it a "permitted piece" of jewellery, I began to wear it on stage, taking it off after each rehearsal. The "experience" when it came was quite a surprise. We had reached the point in the rehearsals where we had to act the crucifixion scene – that is, to act it fully and not just walk and talk – and we all quite-unexpectedly found ourselves becoming very emotional. It is usual to experience feelings related to what is being portrayed, but in this scene, the show seemed to take on a life, an energy – all of its own. As the rehearsals continued, most of us became familiar with the emotions that attended the crucifixion scene, but when it came to the dress rehearsals and performances, the feelings intensified to the point where the scene led to real tears on stage, *every* night. (After the show, it was revealed that some of the backstage crew had also found themselves regularly and so-similarly moved.)

Anyway, that's how I came across *the cross*. As to why I wear it now: well, knowing I have become very sensitive to the energy of crystals, this relatively dull metal object – whilst holding much meaning for me – is less likely to have intrinsic energy than a crystal, and so I feel I can reach for it and wear it without needing to be particularly mindful of any effect it may have on me. Just now, however, as I recount the story of the cross, I remember something new: the cast member who had given it to me had been on holiday in *Greece*. The cross has come home!

I look for the time again: six twenty. It is time to go for some yoga on the beach. I think Jo-Anne had said sunrise is to be expected around six-forty.

Outside it is decidedly lighter and warmer than before – positively welcoming in fact, and where there had been pink hues, it is now very-much golden and concentrated in a particular section of the horizon. Thinking that the sand might yet be a bit cold and damp, I pop back to my room to get a thin blue foam mat out of my suitcase.

Down on the beach, I lay my mat clear of the debris washed up by the nights' waves, and at such an angle as to have me facing the sun when it comes up. I start with a short standing exercise: connecting with the universal life-force energy and visualising the golden light entering me from above, then I lie on my back and work through a selection of my morning routine poses and moves.

While in process, three of the group come onto the beach with Jo-Anne and sit down – just to my left. They are politely quiet so as not to interrupt me, but I stop anyway: I can do this alone anytime.

I listen as Jo-Anne offers words to welcome the sunrise, to introduce us to the day, to accept whatever it may bring… *"As the sun rises this new day, it brings all that is needed,"* she offers. Then we are given some guidance on a series of poses known collectively as the sun-salutation. It seems Jo-Anne has a similar understanding as I: that these poses vary from one school of teaching to another. She therefore invites us to vary them to suit our own needs; very wise – and just as well for me as I am unable rush these things and am soon lagging the others. When at last we sit at rest, the clouds are on the horizon so it is not obvious that the sun has actually risen. Therefore, we sit patiently/longingly until the sun comes out fully, after which everyone (else) leaves the beach. I, on the other hand, feel the need to search for the type of deeper peace that seems to have eluded me in the excitement of the last few days. All I find myself able to do, however, is a few more yoga poses, but at least this enables me to complete what I had started earlier.

As I prepare to return to my room, I am pleased to see Marie-Hélène approaching with Henri. Ah, Marie-Hélène had said yesterday that she and Henri often swim together. I watch as they both walk quickly straight into the water. Oh yes, why did I not think of that? Can I be so chilled as to *not* think about having fun? Let's change that. Trousers off, and in the sea – yes, this is a *good* idea.

I make my way to where Henri and Marie-Hélène stand and thank them for providing the incentive, offering that I might well now do this every day while I am on the island.

Following showering and changing, I head out to the terrace for breakfast.

I sit in the same position as last evening, but so has Marie-Hélène so there is no complaint from me. Laid out before us is the first course: a selection of sweetbreads, fruit and honey that are just so tempting to the eye and the pallet that they may yet constitute my whole breakfast on their own!

A particularly interesting observation then befalls me: that Marie-Hélène is no longer wearing any rings. When the opportunity arises, I check to see if she has rings on the corresponding finger of her other hand – just in case I had mistaken one hand for the other: but she has not. I am *sure* there had been rings on her finger at breakfast yesterday…not that it is anything of my business at all of course – but still… Jo-Anne updates us regarding dinner this evening and we all confirm our interest to meet at the restaurant down the beach as previously proposed. She then reminds us that part of the purpose of being on the island, is to retreat from normal living for a while, and proceeds to introduce the concept of "ECOS". ECOS (we learn) encapsulates a way of coming together and sharing as a group and Jo-Anne tells us that we will be encouraged to follow this scheme every morning. It includes sharing plans and aspirations for the day, and as in recent years, it is suggested we include guided visualisations. I hear Jo-Anne, but instead of *listening,* I have drifted into my own thoughts on the lovely situation I have found myself in: the island, the beach, the sea, and days of sunshine and swimming with…lovely people. Jo-Anne meanwhile, has continued to talk about ECOS and (I think) what the individual letters stand for, but by the time I am tuned in again, all I catch is that she (Jo-Anne) will now start us off with the first visualisation. It is no easier to stay focussed during the visualisation, but when Jo-Anne concludes, I do at least "come back" immediately…just in time to be met by complete silence and Jo-Anne's gaze, but only for a moment. She continues looking around the table (as I release an out-breath) and offers that Rachel might *volunteer* to open ECOS tomorrow morning, to which Rachel smiles and says, "Ooh yes!" Jo-Anne then continues her "lighthouse" gaze, finally bringing her eyes back to me. "And Wayne, would you like to close ECOS tomorrow?"

I am somewhat surprised, and unsure what it might involve but – still, why not. "Yes, yes, I will. Thank you," I reply. (Thank you?) As I begin to ponder on what I might have just agreed to, almost to the point of worrying, another train of thought arrives, and coming out of the still place I had drifted into earlier it offers, "*it will go well, it will all go well – just let it happen.*"

Back in my room, I busy myself – brushing my teeth, only to deduce that I have no plans for what to do with the rest of the day. Maybe I should get into the winding-down process a bit more with some reading or a gentle walk on the beach…or – *yes,* snorkelling!

On walking the few steps down from the terrace to the beach and heading for the foreshore, I notice Rachel standing just a short distance to the right. She smiles and comes over to me. "Henri and I are about to take a walk down the beach – to help our breakfast settle a little. Would you like to come and join us?" She continues, "Henri has just gone in to get a sweater for me in case the breeze makes me cold. I feel the cold so easily, even in this climate, and…" (still not pausing) "…by the way, Marie-Hélène is joining us too."

I feel persuaded that a walk would be good for me after such a big breakfast, and with such company… I'm sure I can hold off snorkelling for a while. "Thank you, that sounds lovely," I reply.

"Alright, good," says Rachel, still smiling sweetly.

As I turn back towards the terrace, Henri and Marie-Hélène are at the top of the steps, and I stand aside to let them down. "Hello again," I say. "I think I might be joining you on your walk shortly."

"Oh, you are going, here – with us?" Henri enquires, as he indicates the general direction of the right side of the bay. "*Okay!*" he says happily.

The French Lady moves gracefully past me; hair tied back in a tight bunch, with large dark sunglasses perched upon high cheekbones. "*Allo!*" she says, smiling. I watch the two of them descend the last few steps down onto the sand (though mostly I watch *one*), before asserting, "Yes, I think a walk right now would be just fine." Accordingly, I take-off up the steps two at a time to deposit my unwanted swimming and snorkelling gear.

Back on the beach, Rachel is on the foreshore, waiting for me, but the others are not. "They have started walking already," she points down the beach. "They always have so much to say. I thought I would wait for you so that we can walk together."

"So," Rachel continues, "we have known Marie-Hélène for quite some time now. We have a villa on the Cote d'Azur quite near to where she lives. Do you know the South of France?"

We walk slowly as Rachel tells me of how they came to meet and be friends, and of some of their travels. She tells me how she had introduced Marie-Hélène to spiritual development about a year back at a retreat centre in Glastonbury, and how they had gone to a meeting in London earlier this year. This is of particular interest to me because it was this year's Easter meeting in London that I had missed – the *one* seasonal meeting I had missed in about the last five years. Could Rachel be talking about the same meeting? That would be a bit of a coincidence.

Marie-Hélène is evidently happy in Henri's company. Even at this distance, I can make out her laughter and see her wide hand gestures and her head shaking and nodding with laughter. Meanwhile, Rachel enquires how I came to be on the retreat, and if I have been with Jo-Anne or Karina before. She seems interested to hear that I have been on several retreats in the UK and abroad and have been involved with the same (it would seem) London based group for some time. She learns that I am single, that I have two grown-up daughters, a steady professional career, and enjoy walking, cycling, travel, music and dancing – particularly Salsa. Rachel happily informs me that their son-in-law is a musician – a percussionist, and plays a lot at dance events particularly involving Salsa. "Henri will enjoy telling you more – he is so proud of him."

Rachel is kind, sensitive and very outgoing and it is very easy talking with her, partly because she so clearly enjoys talking, but also because she is skilled in maintaining a two-way exchange. There is quite a pattern to it in fact: she imparts information about herself and Henri on a topic, often quite detailed information and then politely and directly, asks similar from me. Nevertheless, it is all good; I'm confident enough to be part of this gentle interrogation – if that is what it is – and besides, she does keep feeding me nuggets of detail concerning Marie-Hélène.

Looking up, I see that Henri and Marie-Hélène have stopped walking. In fact, they have had to stop because they have run out of beach and now face a near-vertical rock face. Upon joining them, we all immediately turn around and set off back towards the villa. As we begin to walk, I find myself beside Henri and having referred to what Rachel had said about their son, I mention my interest in Salsa. It transpires that Henri and I both work as consultants in the construction industry, he in design, me in safety and health.

With Rachel and Marie-Hélène having set off at a faster pace, they are some way ahead, and stand with bare feet in the surf, waiting for us to catch up. I am interested to know why they now wait for us, and I wonder if a particular question or piece of local knowledge is about to be delivered. However, Rachel simply smiles, reaches for Henri's arm and – urging him on – starts engaging him in French, leaving Marie-Hélène and me alone.

Talking with Henri had been pleasing – but somewhat difficult, and talking with Rachel had been – well, certainly most pleasant, but I cannot help feeling she had been actively managing our conversation somewhat. As I talk with Marie-Hélène however, it feels to be so much more easy, natural, free-flowing and balanced. Due to the combination of her accent and her occasional mispronunciations, I listen quite intently when Marie-Hélène speaks, and I suppose she must be doing the same careful listening to me. She asks if I know much or any French, to which I answer, "… 'Oui', 'non' – that's about it really," and we both laugh.

Marie-Hélène asks about my work and as I start to tell her she interjects to tell me of Henri's work as an architect – also in construction. When I inform her that I had just been talking of that with Henri, she says, "Ahah. I see you know *all* about us already. And, may I ask, what did Rachel tell you, of me?"

Her question is, of course, offered in jest – I think – but when I mention what Rachel had said about spiritual development and the like, Marie-Hélène willingly expands on it. She tells me that she has also been to Glastonbury, also with Karina, and – as it transpires – close to the time of year that I had gone. The conversation then leads us to discover our associations with the *same* London group, and how, with a slight change of circumstances, we would have met in Glastonbury last autumn *and* at London this Easter!

The thought that I might invest some time in exploring a friendship with this person is quite uplifting. As we continue to talk, I observe how the sun lights up her hair and reflects off the brim of her sunglasses in several miniature starbursts each time that she lifts her face to receive the breeze.

We talk about our experiences of previous retreats: how a retreat can reveal so much of ones' past, even bringing to mind events not previously recalled. We discuss how the burden of carrying painful memories can be relieved upon finding the words to describe those memories in the "now", and how relief so often comes just by using the wisdom we have *now* to give more clarity on the "back-then".

We discuss how, in reviewing our memories and sharing them openly within the safety of a supportive group, and with guidance from experienced facilitators, the troubled-emotions that have arisen in connection with those deeper memories, can be better understood, processed, and then often – released. Next, we confer on how, sometimes, some source of inner wisdom seems to participate, helping us to form a better understanding of past pain, and assisting us towards a more meaningful and complete emotional healing. Before we leave the subject, we agree that whenever we have attended a retreat or a development workshop, we have ended up with some deeper understanding of our lives and have often found greater happiness.

At this point, we are standing still and gazing out to sea in silence, pondering (the past – perhaps). Then our attentions return simultaneously to the here and now, and the sights and sounds of the sea remind us we have both brought snorkels and masks to the island, and we agree that we should put them to good use, and together – soon.

Back at the villa, we present our plans for snorkelling to the others present, but it turns out that only we-two has brought such equipment. Subsequently, a few minutes later, it is just us two, standing on the beach, surveying the water.

"May I suggest we head out to the left, towards that little harbour first; towards the shallow end of that line of rocks?" I propose. "It will also help me get used to snorkelling again – having had quite a break from it. Then we can go along the rocks to the end and after a little look around, come across the deeper water back to here."

"That is a good *edae*," Marie-Hélène agrees. "You go ahead. I do not see so good underwater. Maybe you will find zer way better – yes?"

"Yes – sure," I say, happy to be given the initiative. With mask (me) and goggles (her), we acclimatise to the water and set off to the left. After only a short while, it is clear that Marie-Hélène has done quite a lot of swimming because she has overtaken and is already some way in front. She is also, however, now veering towards a course taking her straight out to sea! I take off in hot pursuit, but within a minute, I start to *feel* just how long it has been since I last swam like this. However, just as I start to wonder if I will ever catch her up, I see her just ahead – chasing a single slim sand-coloured fish. With her continuing to turn to the right I make another correction in my course, but this time I keep my head up and an eye on her position. After just a few seconds, however, Marie-Hélène stops swimming and starts treading water. She lifts her goggles, smiles and shouts, "Sorry – there was a fish! It's the only one I have seen and I got carried away."

I spit out my mouthpiece. "That's okay," I reply. Then, having lifted my mask as well, "I saw you peel off to the right but I couldn't catch you up."

"Really! Oh, I go swimming a lot at home; every day when I can in summer," she informs me.

"We're actually close to heading back the way we came now," I advise. "Which is okay, we can go the other way if there might be some fish there… because there's not so many here."

"Yes, I know," she says, and when we are close enough to talk at a normal volume she continues, "No, it is alright, I think what you have said before is true, that we might find fish over there," pointing over to the line of rocks. "Go on. I will follow this time." She smiles.

Partway to the rocks, I spot a small shoal of fish moving slowly. As they sense my approach, they peel off to the left, towards the shallows. I pause, turn and point towards them, hoping that Marie-Hélène may catch a view of them, but they have gone. Lifting my head, I say, "There was a shoal of fish there," (pointing) "did you see anything of them?"

"No. Were they big?" She asks. "No, just little ones."

"Okay, so – shall we go on? Or we can go back if you like. Maybe there are some fish back the other direction; back where we walked – were walking – this morning?"

"No, that's okay, I would like to explore some more. I am enjoying swimming. I haven't been in warm waters like this for quite a while."

"Oh yes, of course. Zhe English weather." She says jokingly. "I know it well!"

Upon reaching the shore-end of the line of rocks, I find Marie-Hélène has kept to her word and is close behind. As agreed, we head along the line of rocks in search of – well something, anything really. As luck would have it, the colours in the rocks and the seaweed make pleasant viewing in themselves and then, at last, we see two more fish. Only two though, and similarly sized to the one Marie-Hélène had chased out to sea, but that does total three proper fish sightings now. The fish are travelling slowly and so I fall back intending that Marie-Hélène may get closer to them before they are frightened off. Just then, a sound arises from within the water. It is a swirling-plinking sound and it stands out sharply. I look up to see – at a distance – a slow fishing boat running an outboard motor. It is coming in from beyond the other side of the harbour. It is white, and perhaps three to four metres long, but before any more detail is seen, it goes behind the rocks at the harbour mouth.

We continue toward the end of the rocks at a gentler pace where we find the water is about four metres deep, and that we now have a view of the harbour. There are several small boats – fishing boats most of them I guess – not much more than three to four metres long. A few are bobbing up and down on the waves; some are up on the beach.

"Back now?" I enquire.

"Yes – you lead, I follow," she replies, but even as she speaks, she is already ahead of me, looking very comfortable in front crawl. A minute later, and with me no closer, I realise that she may have just previously set me up for a less-than-subtle joke.

At the midpoint between the rocks and the villa, the water is about five metres deep and – yes – there are still no fish. I am happy nonetheless, knowing the exercise will help my swimming for the rest of the holiday, and besides, it is enjoyable to be swimming with this attractive lady – even if I can only *just* keep up with her. Once in the shallows near the villa, we stand up and lift off mask and goggles. We remain surprised at not seeing many fish, but we agree there is yet more of the coastline to explore, and plenty of days to do it over. We also agree to catch up with one-another after lunch and try snorkelling in the other direction.

"*After lunch*," we had said, but lunch is not scheduled to arrive until about one o'clock. I am not hungry – as in, my stomach is not feeling empty – but all the same, I do feel ready to eat. It turns out that the shade of the gazebo is quite a necessity because it is nearly an hour later before our food finally arrives, but no one has voiced impatience, and sitting in the same corner of the table as at breakfast, I find myself quite happy…simply watching *her* face. I watch her mouth as her pronounced accent moves her lips through those expressive shapes required of the French language. I do this for quite some time, until noticing that Rachel and Henri – sitting just the other side of Marie-Hélène – would now seem to be watching *me*!

The food may have been late, but it is all very fresh and – as Jo-Anne tells us – "is all locally sourced, if not indeed locally produced," and if it is not from the Island itself, she continues, then it is almost certainly Greek if it is to be found anywhere. "It has to be," she confides. "They simply cannot afford to import much because of their poor economy."

Big, ripe, and deliciously red tomatoes decorate the table. There is fresh bread that smells *so* good and lots of olive oil, cheeses, and in particular of course – Feta. There is also that yoghurt and cucumber dip – I think – called Tzatziki, and plenty of mixed leaves and – new today – a cold butter bean salad and a potato bake which along with beans and tomatoes, also contains something like aubergines (are they?) Whilst basking in the experience of the food, I cast my eyes across the table, observing the smiles being exchanged as the food bowls move around. Appreciating the beach and the sea, the suns' dappled shadows on the white tablecloth and the faces of those around the table…and on the face of Marie-Hélène.

I do not know precisely how much time is given to talking, eating and laughing, but it eventually settles into a comparative calm at a point that seems to correspond with the last portions of food disappearing from the serving plates. After a further period spent simply sitting /reclining at the table, people start to filter away to eventually leave Marie-Hélène and me alone.

"So, would you like to try some more snorkelling this afternoon?" I ask. "Perhaps we could head out towards the other end of the bay where we walked this morning, towards that little island of rocks?" I continue, pointing in that general location.

"Yes, I would like zis," she replies. "And perhaps zis time we shall find some fish."

"That would be nice – yes," I say rising to move. "I'll just get my mask and snorkel."

"Okay, I will meet you back 'ere in five minutes," she concludes. Within three minutes, I am back on the terrace. Fifteen minutes later, Marie-Hélène arrives.

"So how about we swim down to the left side of those rocks," I offer, "and see what we find when we get there?"

"Good *edae*," she replies and immediately turns to walk down the steps to the beach. Marie-Hélène drops her towel at the point where the sand changes colour and the beach steepens, and she continues without hesitation into the water. I meanwhile, have folded my towel, placed my sunglasses inside and have laid the neat package down near to Marie-Hélène's towel. I next proceed to fumble a while with my mask strap – remembering that I had been aware of it being too loose in the morning. By the time I am actually *in* the water, Marie-Hélène is already swimming quite some way away, head down. Has she found something?

As I join her, she rises, "Zhere is nozing 'ere eizer – no fish! Shall we go – where you 'ave said? You go ahead and zis time I will try not to get lost chasing fish."

I set off, but by about halfway I am already wondering where my swimming partner has gone; she does swim well. Changing my aim to where Marie-Hélène seems to be heading, I ask myself whether she may have a sense of where the fish are located, but shortly afterwards I see the rock island is at quite an angle to us and is considerably closer on the right. Realising that my current trajectory will set me *directly* behind her, I seem to find myself picking up my stroke. A minute or so later, and quite a few more fast strokes than I had estimated, Marie-Hélène is in clear view straight ahead. Long elegant limbs, slow, efficient, deep-reaching strokes – she does cut a fine line through the water. No longer concerned with fish or even determining our direction of travel, I simply enjoy *following*.

I am just beginning to enjoy this new human component of the Greek seascape when I notice that the seabed is hastily rising towards us. Next, I see some dark hazy shapes ahead and I gather we have reached the island.

A few metres back from the rocks we both come to a halt and start to tread water. I lift my head to find that the island is different from what I had expected. Comprising many individual rocks and boulders it does not feel natural at all. Surveying the shore and seeing that the cliffs have buildings right at their top edge, I deduce that this island is in fact, a wave-break. I spit my snorkel out, "How are you doing. Did you enjoy the swim?" I ask her.

"Oh yes, it was so good to swim zis long way," she replies. "Have you seen much fish; I haven't?" I ask.

"Just a few, nozing special really," she says.

"Same here. Maybe we will have to wait until we are at the next place. I hear it is quieter there and even more beautiful," I say.

"Yes, maybe; but you know, I am starting to wonder why I came all zis way when I could have seen so much more fish at home." I can tell she is joking, yet I can also tell that like me – she is rather deflated by our findings so far.

"How about we swim around it and see what's on the other side?" I suggest. "Yes, yes let's do zat. Which way around is it you want to go? I don't mind," she offers.

"How about we go to the left, out to deeper water first, and then come back on the shallower side in case we are tiring a little by then?"

"Why? Are you getting *tired?* We can go back anytime if you wish it." I am sure that she is pulling my leg, at least slightly. "No, I am fine," I assure her. "I guess I always tend to consider practical things from the point of safety…not just because of my current job, but also because safety was drilled into me while in the Air Force. Actually…" I continue, after ejecting a mouthful of water from an unexpected wave – "actually, I did quite a lot of deep-water snorkelling when in the Philippines a few years back, working from a motorboat a mile or so out from shore around a small island much bigger than this one. It took about three-quarters of an hour to swim around it."

"Oh really!" Marie-Hélène exclaims.

"Yes," I reply, and then partly to reassure her of my capabilities and hoping to impress her, just a little: "Yes, we had hoped to see some whale-sharks, but never did. A bit like today really, only with smaller fish-expectations," I laugh. "There were just lots of jelly-fish filaments like ribbons, that we had to keep dodging and swimming around and under. Luckily, we have nothing like that today."

"Oh yes, they can be bad." Marie-Hélène adds, "I was fired by jelly-fishes very badly in ze sea where I live. I still have the marks on my arm from zem."

Clearly, Marie-Hélène has had quite some adventures of her own. I must take care not to make assumptions. I am finding this beautiful woman to be ever-more interesting.

"And you, you were in the Air Force; on aeroplanes? How interesting. My father, he flew in aeroplanes. He was a pilot."

"*Really*. I would like to hear more sometime," I exclaim, realising I must now put any thoughts of point-scoring aside.

"Oh, I will be 'apply to tell you more another time. Oh, we do have zome things to talk about."

"Yes, another time – for sure," I agree, happy to now have several reasons for approaching and talking with Marie-Hélène *another* time.

There is no discussion of who goes first this time; something tells me that Marie-Hélène will either stay behind or go ahead – just as she chooses!

Accordingly, with snorkel mouthpiece inserted, and blowing out twice to clear the tube, my head goes down and she is already gone.

There is nothing much new to look at, and there are no fish: no fish at all. When we reach our new target, we surface. "Okay, what shall we do? We swim around it yes – if you are okay?" Marie-Hélène proposes.

I appreciate the way that she is thinking of me, but the beach is only about seventy to one-hundred metres away and I have not felt any currents so far, so there's not that much risk – even if I do get rather tired. "Yes, this exploring is good fun. Let's do that."

This wave-break looks about the same size as the last, so I'm guessing it won't be much more effort to swim around this one as well. Actually, I really would like to push on; and so, with mouthpiece back in, and targeting the far end of the rocks I set straight off (behind Marie-Hélène). Just around the end, we find there is yet another wave break island ahead. This time, however, there is no discussion required – just a nod, and we presume to go on.

"Yes, you go ahead," Marie-Hélène says confidently – almost too confidently for my liking (/ego). I think she may be watching out for *me* now. It feels good to sense someone's concern for me in this simple-meaningful way; I am not used to that. Of course, me getting tired: this just might yet happen!

The next stretch of open water has surely been the same distance as the last, but as we draw close to this third wave-break my arms begin to tire, and my legs feel like they are virtually flapping around behind me.

I resort to breaststroke, partly to have a final-hopeful look for fish, but mostly to make it easier on my muscles. Yet still, there are none. We briefly discuss our continued surprise at the lack of fish and then decide to push on and around the end of this (last?) one – yes, surely this *last* one. Before setting off, I offer that I am feeling a little bit tired, and suggest we might swim directly around this next rock…whatever – and then go directly to shore and walk back. "It will give us a chance to talk easier, and for me to rest my muscles so that I don't over-strain them on the first day," I declare. It is agreed.

This next wave-break *is* the last, and thankfully so because the coolness of the deep water is taking its toll on me.

Marie-Hélène comes up alongside then – upon receiving my smile – proceeds past me and on towards the shore. I slow significantly as I get to the shallows, but as the orange bikini-clad bronzed figure of Marie-Hélène exits the water in front of me. I have a flashback and my tiredness seems to evaporate: I recall the James Bond movie where on some golden-beach island, Ursula Andress saunters out of the water towards our Scottish hero. (Or Ursula *Undress* – as I would call her as a boy). [4]

---

[4] The colour of our respective hair is perhaps not so dissimilar to those icons of film, and nor is Marie-Hélène's figure any less attractive from this angle, but to compare me any further is perhaps stretching it somewhat!

Out of the water and with masks and goggles off, we look back upon the wave breaks. They no longer hold any intrigue or mystery for me and instead appear quite grey and barren. There remains, however, one mystery yet unsolved, which is: "where have all the fish gone?"

The sun is on our backs as we walk slowly along the beach towards the villa. "So, you were on aeroplanes in England – how you say – the air-force?"

Marie-Hélène enquires. Before answering I notice her face remains marked and indented by the goggles she had worn. In this light and after all the swimming, she looks understandably "well-exercised". She is perhaps a little older than I had first assumed back on the mainland yesterday; mid-forties perhaps but oh – what a lovely smile, and such pretty blue – correct that – blue/grey eyes.

"Yes, I was in the RAF: the Royal Air Force, for ten years."

"Really. That is quite a long time. And did you fly?" Marie-Hélène asks.

"No. I had wanted to be a pilot when I was young of course, and I had achieved good O-Level results, but I had no interest in staying longer for A-Levels and I knew nothing about the university system. So – no, I just wanted to get on and leave education and my somewhat-unhappy memories of childhood behind."

"So, what did you do in the RAF?"

"After a three-year apprenticeship I got my first choice of working with the Phantom Jet, a fighter-interceptor, a plane I had idolised as a boy."

I tell her how while in the air force, I had visited places like Spain, Iceland and Sardinia also the Falkland Islands, and that the squadron I was serving with went to Cyprus for a month each year where in fact I had first tried snorkelling. "And what did you do after the air force?" Marie-Hélène politely enquires.

Not wanting to spend too much more time on my past, I hastily summarise the key roles in my civilian career being: factory manager, quality assurance manager, then a change to health and safety, an expansion to include environmental management, and working from home when a buy-out by an international concern resulted in the head office moving to Bradford. Nonetheless, my career flourished. I rose to a non-executive position on the board, and my new Italian employer began talking about a potential Europe-wide role. However, with much travelling and regular nights away from home adding further challenges to an already tense marriage, I tell how I took the decision to turn around and down-size, working from home for a small consultancy business to give more time to family and home-life. As it transpired, the marriage was not saved, and a few years later, I separated and then divorced, but the same job has continued to serve me well.

For a while there is quietness. It strikes me that the talking has been mostly from me. Marie-Hélène has been very attentive, but the exchange has been rather one-sided. "So, you said when we were swimming, that you swim near where you live?" I prompt. "Yes, in Mandelieu-La Napoule my apartment is about five minutes' walk away from three beaches. And zhere is a castle there and in the summer – oh, I am so lucky…in the summer I try and swim there every day, around the bay and across the front of the castle. It is really very beautiful."

"So where are you on the south coast? Not that I know any of it myself, but I have heard of some of the famous places of course," I say, making quite light of the fact that I fact I know virtually *nothing* of France – let alone the South of France.

"Oh, yes there is Nice and Cannes, Saint-Tropez, and Monaco – I'm sure you and everyone has heard of those places. Monaco is where they do the car racing – you know?" she says lightly and almost off-hand.

"Yes, I have heard of those places."

"Well, I am not far from Cannes you know of that from the film festivals?" I nod. "Well, I am just four or five kilometres away from zhere." I am impressed. Not that I know what it means to live four or five kilometres from Cannes, or any other place on the south coast of France but still…

"Oh, before you start thinking," she says, laughing as she talks, "'Oh I know Cannes; she must have lots of money', no – I do not and in fact, I live very near the centre of an old village that is nothing like Cannes. Do you know Cannes?"

"I know nothing of Cannes," I reply. I can suppose however, how un-real life might feel if one is totally surrounded by the trappings of image-focused, status-driven lifestyles. This is what I am *thinking*, but what can I *say* that is sincere but not too assuming?

"I know a little about the Cannes film festival and the Grand Prix from watching the TV but of course, I do not honestly know what it might feel like to live in the South of France."

"Cannes, huh! I hardly ever go to Cannes, especially in the festival season and in the summer. It is too much *bling* there: people and life – it is not so real there you know?"

Here is she: dripping with tan, beauty and elegance and yet she distances herself from the rich-and-famous imagery born of the area from which she hails – the "bling" as she calls it. This beautiful woman is becoming quite intriguing.

"Oh, but the area, it is so beautiful. I can walk in the mountains, the Esterel, or near the Pre-Alps in the morning, and be swimming in the sea in the afternoon. Ah, I am so lucky – really." she says, almost as if reminding it to herself as much as informing me.

"That does sound lovely," I agree.

"Yes, and you know, one of, my favourite things in the wintertime, to be in the sea and be looking at the mountains with snow on them. There is a place on the beach when you can see the sea, and the castle of La Napoule and the snow on the mountains – very beautiful."

I have been sold the idea. ("Take me there," I think, jokingly.)

"But, you know, I say *winter*," Marie-Hélène continues, "…but it is not the winter for me that you have in *England*."

"Yes, so I hear," I concede. "But England is not always so cold and wet; the East Coast where I live has one of the highest sunshine figures in the UK and I often swim in the sea until October without a wetsuit."

"Oh, really!" she exclaims, but we continue to joke about the English weather and she goes on to tell me that even in winter she goes swimming regularly, and doesn't even *own* a wetsuit.

By now we are walking quite slowly with towels slung over opposite shoulders and mask/goggles and snorkel-tubes dangling from our hands. During our conversation, I have observed that Marie-Hélène uses her hands greatly when expressing herself. Even now, she keeps moving her goggles from her hand to her forearm so that she has both hands free. Then the goggles begin to slide down mid-sentence and she slides them up again before continuing – almost as if her hands and voice are interconnected. To think, it was only yesterday morning when I had first caught sight of her and we had first – just briefly – talked over breakfast with the others, and when I had caught sight of her rings and…oh yes, I hope I can find a way to approach that subject soon; there is something I need to know.

"So, you say you were married. Do you have any children?" Marie-Hélène asks.

I am gob-smacked. It is as if she has just been sensing my thoughts…or maybe it was I sensing hers. "Er…yes," I stumble. "I have two daughters, well –

grown-ups now, really. They are three years apart and both have partners and their own houses. The older one married last year, and the younger one bought a house with her partner just over a year ago. Actually, no…nearer two years ago. Gosh, time goes fast."

"Ah, I have two boys, men – I should say, but they will always stay my children. And there is three years separation between them also. *'Too – also'*? Should I say 'too' or 'also' what is right, please?"

We then conduct a short discussion concerning the English language in which I offer my understanding of the use – inappropriate or otherwise – of the words "too", "to" and "also".

Just before arriving back at the villa, we pass the fish restaurant where we are due to be dining later. Our reservation is for seven-thirty and with neither of us having our phones, and Marie-Hélène not wearing her watch, she asks me to guess the time. I look around as to gauge the suns position, and I put my hand to my chin in the pretence of deep thought. However, my foolery quickly concludes, and I make an honest attempt to *feel* the time. "Ermm…let's say four-forty," I offer.

"No, really?" Marie-Hélène exclaims. "So late, you think? Surely, it is only just four or something?"

"Well, I do sometimes seem to be quite good at guessing time, so I will stick with it: four forty."

I reconsider asking the "ring" question, but it is not the right time. (All the same, it would just be nice to know.) Then, two of our group come out on the beach: the two ladies that have come together. One goes into the sea and the other stands and watches. They seem close friends or perhaps even partners – seeing they are so attentive to one another.

"Okay, I will go and check the time. Wait up 'ere please," she says as we complete the steps to the terrace. Marie-Hélène exits with a flourish.

Marie-Hélène returns, (with a flourish) and with her watch in hand and with a big grin says, "Hah-ha! You are wrong, but it is later than I thought. It is a-quarter-to-five if that is how you say it? Hah. You said four-forty!"

I laugh with her but at the same time, I am privately quite impressed by how close my guess had been.

"So, actually, you were really quite close," she says, almost as to mimic my thoughts. "Like I said, I sometimes seem to do it fairly well." Becoming quiet, I suddenly comprehend what a positively lovely afternoon it has been; and how great the morning had been and, in fact, the whole day.

"Thank you," I say looking directly at her, her blonde wet hair pulled back over her right ear, her light blue eyes smiling at me always smiling.

Then I observe in her a change of expression. A moment of hesitation, of inquisitiveness – or doubt, but I continue, "Thank you for your company. It has been lovely talking and walking and sharing swimming with you today, even though there were no fish."

"Yes, I agree," replies Marie-Hélène. "It was good, even without the fish, though I am wondering if I did know better – if I had *known* better – if I would have come here to find less fish than at home. No really, it was good, and I liked talking with you too, but now I need a shower. So, I will see you tonight, yes? We can talk some more perhaps."

"Yes. That would be nice, yes," I reply without hesitation.

"See you *later*," she says, leaving her words floating in the air as she turns; or, is it me who is floating…anyway, she turns and, still smiling, goes off to her room.

"Lucky shower," come the words in my mind as I turn towards my room. From within me, I sense something warm and meaningful starting to form – asking for my attention. The feeling starts as a shimmer, then begins to spread outward, and as I give the feeling more attention, it surfaces to the point that my face breaks into a wide smile. This really has been a lovely day, and yet even as my smile still lingers, I feel almost given to write-off the day to experience, as a time now passed; as a one-off. Except, her parting words then return to me anew, my smile revisits me, and I am brought to recognise that something very meaningful is happening and is by no means finished. The lovely experience that *was* – continues, because Marie-Hélène has already invited me to spend more time with her this evening.

Time for my shower too (/as well).

Shaved and dressed for the cooler evening temperature and wearing some aftershave, I am impatient for the evening to begin. I am concerned that I may have been displaying my appreciation of Marie-Hélène slightly too much, because truth be told, I had spent so much time just in the moment of it all, that I really cannot remember what my behaviour was actually *like* this afternoon. Feeling progressively uncomfortable with not having many memories of how I had behaved during the afternoon – during the whole day even, I ponder on whether I should prepare for the possibility that Marie-Hélène may have reflected differently on the day and could decide to give me some space this evening…woooh (double-take!) Do I *usually* monitor myself this way? If I do, it must surely distract me from being spontaneous and responsive. On the other hand, has it been that I have simply felt so comfortable, so accepted, that I have not felt the need "check" myself; that I have simply *been* me? I feel the smile return, but – of course – I will have to wait and see. In the meantime, I shall try to approach the evening with the same general mindset as when I woke this morning: *life is good and I shall be open to receive all manner of goodness – if that is what is to come.*

At six o'clock I go outside to mingle, but no one else is there. I walk to the edge of the terrace. The sun has set far beyond the hills behind me, beyond the town. The beach is deserted, but I can hear the gentle background Ibiza chill-out type music that is constantly played from the bar to the left. The beach umbrellas over to that side of the beach have been tied up and the sunbeds re-set square to the shoreline. With time feeling to be going too slowly I go back to the room to occupy myself…and out comes the mobile phone. There follows an interlude in which I set about reviewing and moving photos between directories, deleting those that I can let go of, and experiencing memories that arise with those I keep. (I have many photos…)

Soon enough, it is nearing seven o'clock and lifting my head from the phone to feel a slight stiffness in my neck…I wonder if I may have in reality, started to nod-off (!)

At the door, I look out to find the terrace populated by half a dozen or so of the group. Having had *enough* use of the phone, I turn back to hide it under some clothes in my suitcase, and with my mind unfocused and open to whatever the warm evening may bring, I stride out – pulling the door closed behind me.

Once in the middle of the terrace, I turn to find Marie-Hélène sat outside her room, looking down at *her* mobile. Maybe she has been outside a while and I could have been out here talking with her some more instead of getting lost within my phone. Rachel and Henri come out from their room. I exchange a few words with Henri and then as he leaves, I talk a little with Rachel – who asks about my afternoon. I tell her I had spent the time swimming around the rocks with Marie-Hélène and Rachel nods knowingly and smiles all the way through, voicing the occasional "oh, lovely" and "good" and other such affirmations. Then Rachel departs and Marie-Hélène comes over. "*Allo!*" she says to me. "So, you are *hungry*." (Apparently an assertive comment, but in finishing with a very slight upward inflexion, I understand this is French for "*are* you hungry?".)

Jo-Anne comes down from her room and suggests we go down to the beach and start to make our way to the restaurant. Marie-Hélène and I walk the short distance until we reach the narrow steps up to the covered terrace. All at once, I feel self-conscious of the attention I am giving – have given – Marie-Hélène, and how it might appear to others. Accordingly, I step aside before going up the steps and turn to regard the rock-islands out at sea. They are decidedly grey and stark in the fast-fading light, but they are enough to take my attention away from the self-doubting thoughts of a moment ago. Leaving the cold rocks behind, I turn back to ascend the steps…to be met by the scent of a certain citrus perfume, and all doubt and attachment to grey rocks and cold concern vanishes.

I want to sit with Marie-Hélène but she is someway away, and the seats either side of the long line of tables set out for us are already being claimed. My intent is going to be obvious, but ignoring such concern I lower my eyes and am beginning to push my way through when…looking up I see Marie-Hélène making her way towards *me*. "So, where shall we sit?"

"Oh, shall we sit at the end of the table there?" I suggest, pointing towards the end of the long line of white-clothed tables where they stop at a low wall overlooking the beach. "Good views and a nice fresh breeze."

"Yes, good idea, but I hope – not too fresh a breeze. You English will find it warm tonight, but for me, this weather is almost a little cold – you know," she says humorously.

I look to the menu and am relieved to find that there are descriptions in English. The choices are virtually all fish, which is to be expected I guess, but even written in English there are some descriptions that escape me. What with being in a different country and all, I feel like trying something different tonight. Drink orders begin to be placed and Marie-Hélène asks me if I would like to order anything in particular. "Perhaps some wine?" I reply, continuing that I do not usually take alcohol, and she replies that she is thinking of having some sparkling mineral water herself and invites me to join her. "That would be nice," I say. "And what about a starter?"

"A starter?" I think out loud – looking around at the bread and oil already on the table. "I'm not sure. I don't think I have truly felt hungry before any meal since that first breakfast in Athens."

"Oh, I know exactly what you *mean*," she agrees. Then from elsewhere, I hear, "A plate of Greek salad to share, and some Feta – oh, and some Tzatziki!"

"Aaa yes – okay, yes to that," I concede (after all, I *am* on holiday).

"Yes, for me too." chimes-in Marie-Hélène, then turning to me, "That Tzatziki I like it *sooo* much!"

Returning to the menu, I am wanting for something new…aahah cuttlefish; now *that* would be different. I place my order and reach out for a (another) piece of baguette. Stretching out towards the oil I find it too far away, so I engage Marie-Hélène to reach it for me. "So, *olive oil*: what is olive oil in French?"

"Huile d'olive," she says, "with oil being spelt h-u-i-l-e."

"Ooole," I say back.

"No – '*ooui-le*'," she repeats. "You know French, it is not so easy, and we do not say our h's very much at all."

"Ooiell?" I try again. She just laughs.

"You must practice, every day – this," she says still laughing, and I join her.

Our mineral water comes and Marie-Hélène breaks the seal and pours for us both. In seeing her left hand presented, I notice again – no rings, and none on the other either. I suppose she just might have forgotten to put them on, or she just doesn't wear them often. She has been married, and I now know she has had children, so perhaps she occasionally wears her rings out of respect. Then again it is not my place to judge; I know very little about her life and what she has lived through.

Perhaps, the rings are worn to feign a status of marriage to put off would-be suitors – or something; she is very attractive, so maybe she finds it easier in public places. However, if the caricature of the Latin man holds, of course, a mere ring or two would not hold them back. They might even see it as an interesting challenge. All I can be sure of is that she is not wearing the rings this evening…oh – *this thinking must STOP.*

I thank Marie-Hélène for the water and take a sip, then reach for a third piece of baguette; then more oil and Feta and Tzatziki, and a bit more salad…and I am wondering if I should have ordered a main course at all!

When at last it arrives, I find the cuttlefish not as big as expected, but it is quite thick and with tentacles – which I had *not* expected. It tastes much like squid, so it's not too much of a challenge, but some number of mouthfuls later on however, I am starting to find the taste rather bland. I reach out for some Feta and Tzatziki; it is not the way of fine-cuisine perhaps, but I want to enjoy what I am eating.

"I thought you were not feeling so hungry," Marie-Hélène says, in jest (I *think*).

"Do please try some if you like?" I offer.

I do seem to have a "thing" about clearing my plate. I am not sure if it is from my childhood or if it was also re-enforced when I tried to encourage my daughters to eat-up when they were young, but that old program is weighing a bit heavy just now; a bit like the fish in fact.

"Oh, thank you," she replies, "…but no, I do not like what it tastes…like – you say *like*? Normally I would enjoy sharing things, but I am really starting to feel a little full up. But you should try some of my fish, please – go on," she encourages, pushing her plate closer to mine. "You will help me finish this; it is just too much for me."

It seems only *polite* to try some of hers as well, and it looks more appetising than mine. "M'mmm – yes, that *is* good," I confess, "…but your fish was a smaller than mine to start with, I think perhaps it should be up to *you* to help *me* eat mine," I assert.

Marie-Hélène has one fork-full of each, I have one of hers and then two more mouthfuls of mine, and we both give up.

The fast-fading sunlight has been progressively supplanted by a string of overhead lanterns. The off-sea breeze has now dropped off somewhat, but the evening air feels a little cool – which moves Marie-Hélène to reach for her light-yellow cardigan and wrap it around her shoulders. As the material settles upon her, the herb & pepper of my cuttlefish is replaced by the much more welcome notes of citrus. I feel strangely tempted to reach across and put an arm around her in a protecting/warming gesture, but immediately I catch myself (…where did that thought come from?) I hope that in my, "living in the now," I have not committed any other inappropriate act this evening…but there I go *again*: another misplaced notion. It has not been since my marriage that anyone has complained about my manners in any such way…marriage (?) Could it be, that I have carried this sensitivity towards being accused of poor behaviour, *that* many years? Well, it might explain why I have sometimes not found it easy to relax with others – especially in groups. Yet this morning and this afternoon with Marie-Hélène, I was *so* relaxed that I could have willingly told her all and everything about – well, all and everything, and without any fear of being judged or misunderstood or… (spooky!)

Chairs scrape across the terracotta floor and we commence to reach for our purses and wallets amidst comments and compliments declaring, "How good that was," and, "How full I am," and, "How lovely and warm it still is," (for those hailing from middle Europe that is).

Milos (our island guide) is saying his farewells to our hosts. "Kalinychta," I think I hear him saying, which I guess must be "goodnight", and a few of us try to mimic the same sentiment with varying amounts of success.

Going down the steps to the beach, I see Marie-Hélène a short way ahead – arms linked with those of Rachel and Henri either side of her, their heads sporadically coming together in laughter. I talk with Renna, who offers her respect for my "brave" choice of the cuttlefish, but recounting how I had eventually been beaten by the combination of its size and blandness, I propose I may have been a little too over-enthusiastic in my choice. We do however wholeheartedly agree: we are full in our stomachs and our hearts – having been delighted with our first full day on the island.

I glance ahead…yes, I am happy.

Marie-Hélène waits at the bottom of the steps leading up to the villa and as I get closer, I realise she is looking directly at me and smiling. *Allo* she says. "So, I am feeling quite tie'erd, I think I will be sleeping well tonight."

"Me as well – at least, my body feels tired, my mind, however, does not quite feel ready to turn-in yet. I think I may have missed my launch-pad time, so I may just wait-up a while for my sleep-cycle to come back around."

"Ah, you are so funny!" she says. "I have never heard anyone say – speak, of their body that way before. Hah!"

I invite her out of politeness, of course – to take the steps ahead of me, but I am soon thankful for my good conduct as I now observe her ascent. On the terrace, we are all met with a most pleasant surprise, for our hosts – in our absence – have lit tea-lights and placed them on each windowsill and table.

"I will just stay outside here a while, I think," I say, at some risk of repeating myself.

"Okay, perhaps I go to my room now. I think I shall sleep well," she replies. "Okay, well – sleep well," I say, trying to maintain my lightness but feeling like the end of the evening has arrived too soon. As she departs, she turns, smiles (always smiling) and then goes into her room pushing the door – almost – closed.

She switches her bedroom light on, pulls the curtains across the window, and…I become conscious of the fact that *I am watching her*.

Henri and Rachel have also made themselves at home in their room, putting their lights on and drawing their curtains, but Henri now exits and moves over to their cushioned seating. He nods waves and smiles at me. I return the same friendly general acknowledgement that could mean both "good night, see you later" but could also be used for "hello, how it is going". (*Men!*)

Looking for something further to do I turn to move towards the cover of the gazebo at the edge of the terrace. I lean my weight on the arm of a chair and gaze out to sea – trying to make out the white of the rolling waves as they break. As I move around a chair with a half-thought to sitting down, I catch sight of Rachel emerging from her room. She goes over to Marie-Hélène's room, knocks on the door and enters straight in. Changing tack, I move towards the left side of the terrace from where I might avoid the light and see *the waves* better. Gazing out to sea, I open my chest – pulling my shoulders back, rolling them up, over and back-down a few times – to take in a cleansing portion of the night air. Recognising my repeated attempts to stretch the night out further, I then find some quite different thoughts arising… *"This day is already 'good'; sleep now and let it go; wake tomorrow to another new day"*.

Yielding to my own unexpected demonstration of wisdom I set out on a diagonal route directly to my room, but then, upon hearing voices and footsteps I slow. With head forward, but looking sideways, I see Rachel walking back into her room and then the backlit figure of Marie-Hélène exiting hers. With a bottle of water and a glass, she strolls over towards Henri. Henri gets up and offers his cushioned chair to Marie-Hélène, and she moves to sit, I find myself on a somewhat adjusted course that takes be beneath some grapes – conveniently ready to be eaten, and thus providing a pause long enough to make eye contact, though (hopefully) without it looking quite as contrived as it surely is. "Not so tired yet?" I ask to Marie-Hélène.

"Rachel is not ready to sleep. She came and talked. I thought I would take a little water." Henri waves me closer. "Come, come – Wayne, and sit here with us," he says getting up and heading towards Marie-Hélène's room. He takes one of Marie-Hélène's, sets it down just opposite Marie-Hélène. "Come, sit join us," he repeats warmly.

Rachel comes out and moves the candle from their window to place it beside the one already in the middle of their table. "There," she says. "That's better," and sits next to Henri, snuggling into his side.

"Wayne, now wasn't that a lovely meal," Rachel continues, and with flickering lights across happy faces, there begins a lovely ending to a most lovely evening – indeed, a most lovely day.

Some thirty minutes later, and having seen the others into their rooms, I contentedly stroll the short distance to mine to find the door quite securely closed – and locked! What to do about it? I could wake up Jo-Anne, try and get a spare key from our hosts perhaps…or I could just go directly to find them. Heading for the front of the buildings to see if the family are still up, I head down the darkened narrow passageway dividing my room from the others. On reaching the front courtyard, I see no lights at any window. There are several doors, but which one should I knock on? Deciding it is too late and not particularly thoughtful to start knocking randomly, I turn towards the terrace to find Madelyn sitting outside her room. "Hi Wayne," she says. "Is everything alright?"

With nothing to lose, I tell the story of how I came to lock myself out of my room. However, on reaching the part of the story where I explain the door had previously been open for ventilation, it dawns on me that the window may also yet be a-jar. With a new plan beginning to hatch, I reach into my pocket for my phone so to use the torch on it – and ah…oh, no phone. Just as I turn back to Madelyn with a mind to ask for her phone, I notice the tea light on my table. Holding the flame close to the window, I shield my eyes from the reflections and – aha, yes, the window is still ajar. I manage to slip my fingers into the narrow gap around the window, and then slide them down and along the bottom edge just enough, to flick up the stay, and gently… it opens.

The built-in seating immediately outside the window offers relatively easy access to the opening, but not wanting to risk the excitement of a fire adding to the proceedings, I return the tea light to the table. Peering into the darkness, I'm guessing the floor to be around the same level as the terrace here, and so standing on the seating, and turning, I dangle my left leg in behind me. My foot finds what *might* be the edge of the glass-topped table, but it does not reach the floor, and since any imbalance could find my weight bearing down onto the narrow window ledge via the general area of my groin, I resort to the tea light again. With the lace curtain held well aside (!) I hang partly through the window with the tea light in hand to confirm the exact table-edge, then (replacing the tea light again) I climb and pull both legs up underneath me until I am squatting in the window frame, head jammed tightly to its underside. Jiggling myself around sideways through the opening (thank-*goodness* for yoga), and bracing myself tightly for balance, I pull my head down, under and through, and I can just about…just about…wiggle/slide my foot sideways enough to clear the ledge and…find…the table. Seeing my foot to be well clear of its edge I transfer some weight slowly to the table to ensure the glass does not slip or break…then, "Hey, I'm in!" I whisper out to Madelyn. "Oh, good. Well done. Goodnight, Wayne."

"Goodnight."

Still Not Sleeping, But Really Living

I have been dozing for some time, not asleep but not completely awake either, and this is the second time I have been in this 'not sleeping' state since going to bed last night. However, just like yesterday, it is only now that there is enough light to see anything much, and therefore, just like yesterday, I look towards my trusty travel clock…and the large LCD digits that show the time as…five…something (just – like – yesterday).

Not thinking much, sort of meditating in fact, I am trying to find some sense of myself within this experience that is 'Wayne not sleeping'. I look to the dawn light at the window and try to picture the terrace and beyond that, to sense/connect with the beach and the sea. This will just be a phase (I'm sure) this "not sleeping"; there is bound to be some reason for it. There have now been five or six nights of broken sleep, but after all, I remain happy enough, and last night was…was so lovely. The afternoon was good as well – what with the swimming, the walking and then the meal, and Marie-Hélène of course…

If I were at home now, I would be getting up within an hour, so I conclude I might as well just get on with the day. Turning to locate my yoga-come-camping mat, my sight instead falls upon on the bedside cabinet and my pendant laid there. Dropping all else I take the cross and with an end in each hand, I turn towards the window, towards the sun, "…be in my head, and in my understanding." Almost immediately, I sense the tingle of energy between my palms. Offering my silent thanks, I fasten the pendant around my neck.

Upon opening the door, I am met by the view of the terrace and a thinly clouded dark blue sky, with traces of lighter blue in the distance. Walking until the sea comes into view, I now see traces of pink just above the horizon where – I assume – the sun will later appear. With no one else about, I go down the steps to the beach to a spot just clear of the tide-line and lay the yoga mat. I start to work through some yoga poses and transitions, but after only a short while I become attracted to the changing nature of the light which has now brought tinges of pink and purple to the edges of the few clouds that have formed. I speed back to my room, rifle through my suitcase for my mobile phone, then making a grab for my blue swimming bag and finding it already contains my deep-red sitting-shawl, I pop my phone in beside it and return with both post-haste.

I take only a few photographs, but it is difficult to break from the spectacle of dawn to return to yoga. Thus, with the colours in the sky and clouds changing by the minute, I take out the shawl, float it around my back and with crossed legs settle down to watch. Watching turns to sensing and then to feeling as, with its warming glow on my face, the sun begins to rise.

Others come down to the beach and settle to my left, but experiencing quite a deep peace I do not break my gaze; no offence intended, and none taken. More of the group arrive and in my left peripheral view, I notice a white figure settling upon the sand: Jo-Anne – all in white save the flash of a turquoise scarf around her neck. As the sun begins another transit across the sky (*or so it seems*) Jo-Anne gently offers words to welcome it, and us, to "this new day". She then invites us to join her in Sun Salutations – which I start to follow closely at first, but in recalling how difficult I had found it to keep in time yesterday, I soon yield to my own slower pace. Taking the time to connect with each breath and each stretch, I set aside the idea of completing any set number of repetitions so that when Jo-Anne ends the group movements, I come to an immediate rest. In time with the group now, I join their stillness and it becomes *our* stillness as collectively we engage with this – our – peace, and offer it towards the goodness of this new day.

After everyone else has departed, I spend a further ten minutes on my own, finishing a few most favoured/beneficial poses for back and shoulders. Having ascended the several steps to the terrace, however, I am taken by surprise, for virtually everybody is out – doing yoga! Marie-Hélène is present, Rachel as well, and the only person not engaging in this gentle art this morning would appear to be Henri. It is warming to see so many, considering of course that everyone is on holiday.

Feeling rather peckish and most-certainly ready for my morning tea, I retrieve the small plastic bag containing my dried lemon verbena leaves and walk down the passage to the other side of the villa: the family side. There, I find a large white-clothed table containing a range of dishes – some full, some empty, and to the right a low doorway into (*aha!*) the kitchen. Entering, I find a beehive of activity, with the grandmother (who we now know goes by the name of Ya-Ya), her grandson and I presume – his girlfriend, busily preparing what would seem to be a veritable feast. There are aromas of freshly cooked bread, pastries, and coffee, but although tempted otherwise, I make a hasty exit to minimise their disturbance.

Ya-Ya comes out behind me and stretches her arms to me for a hug, which I willingly accept. She says something in Greek which I receive as "good morning" and I return the same in English. However, I do not escape so easily: she holds me in her gaze and then carefully and slowly mouths the Greek words to me once more – encouraging me to repeat them. I try, and she receives my efforts charitably with another big smile, then in surprisingly clear English she says, "Did you sleep well?" (!)

"I am feeling very good today, thank you," I reply. "I enjoy the sunrise and it is so warm here already," I annunciate slowly, gesticulating upwards and around in a general fashion. Ya-Ya smiles again, then turns back to the kitchen.

I pick up a glass from the table and with the (excuse) of looking for some hot water, I re-enter the kitchen suspending the glass and waving my bag of verbena leaves ahead of me to pre-empt any misinterpretation. The grandson reaches for the kettle switch. "Just a minute," he says. "You prefer a cup?" he adds, looking at my glass. "No, thank you," I reply. "I find the taste is better in glass."

Ya-Ya exits past me, then re-enters, but as I begin to step aside, she stops before me and takes my hand – leading me back out. Just as I start to think maybe I'm getting in their way, she halts at the table, takes a piece of freshly cooked flatbread, dips it into honey and offers it up. "You are hungry? Eat!" she says through her smile. Looking at the bread and honey suspended just in front of my face, I reach to take the tasty morsel from her hand, but Ya-Ya does not allow it and instead waits patiently, intending to feed me! I open my mouth and she places the morsel directly in, and in that one simple act, she has me feeling at-home. Casting my mind back to childhood, such "happy family" experiences have been relatively rare, so this means much to me. Ya-Ya would also seem to be pleased with the result because before going back into the kitchen, she hands me a plate and gesticulates that I should continue.

"Hey, Wayne!" I hear from behind me, and turn to see the grandson holding a steaming kettle. Ya-Ya offers a comment to her grandson, and with similar smiling sensitive brown eyes to his grandmother, he continues, "Ya-Ya says she likes you." He then pauses, looking from the table and to my plate before continuing, "Ah – yes, I see *why*," and proceeds to smile all the more deeply. Conscious that such simple warm-hearted exchanges do not take place so often in the western way of living, I cannot help but smile back. Here in Greece, it would seem that people have/take/give the *time* for such pleasantries.

Our 'brunch', as I think one might best describe it, involves the eleven of us sat around the square of white-clothed tables under the palm-leave gazebo, filling our senses with cheeses, fruits, honey, yoghurt, and bread: rustic, savoury, sweet, seeded, white, brown, sliced, torn and toasted. I am sat facing right once again, with head to the left to regard the sea and the sun…that is, until I am joined by Marie-Hélène, who sits down immediately around the corner from me whereby my head would seem to prefer a different lean. Marie-Hélène immediately takes in the sea-view, lifting her large dark sunglasses and perching them atop her sun-tanned face. Her smiling eyes would seem to be connecting quite-often with mine, and the attention I occasionally offer her would seem only to widen her smile – although it could also be something to do with the fruit, sweetbreads, yoghurt and honey…

At around half-past ten, we quieten and Jo-Anne reminds us of the ECOS process that starts today – passing the baton then to Rachel who with calm confidence leads us directly into a visualisation. With eyes closed, a gentle breeze on our faces and with soft words falling upon our ears, we contemplate beautiful vistas in our minds' eye: lights, crystals, feelings of connection; pathways to the source of Love, channels through which that Love can be received, bringing peace within us today and forever…

There is a pause while we all re-find our place, adjusting our eyes to the light, and then Jo-Anne thanks Rachel on our behalf before moving us into the middle section of ECOS where we are invited to talk about anything on our minds: events of yesterday, hopes for today etc. Two of the group tell us of a walk they took down the coast to the left, to a small chapel and an old windmill – passing a derelict lighthouse on the way. Marie-Hélène and I look to one another and – with no further exchange – we understand our mutual interest in exploring that same route.

Jo-Anne then tells us of the loose plans for the rest of the day: lunch around one-thirty, then in the evening there are two events: a guided tour of the local town including a visit to the hilltop monastery, and then another group meal in town to follow. She continues that Karina – the second retreat leader – is expected to join us at the meal, and we are informed that Madelyn has volunteered to receive our payments for the town tour and our contributions towards such as bottles of water and any other consumables we may have taken from the group provision bought previously. Finally, *I* am reminded that it is my turn to lead the *closing*...

I invite all to close eyes, to feel the suns heat on our faces and on our bodies, and to *know* that the sun exists to light, warm and nurture our world each and every day. I invite all to feel the blessing of being here in this space, on this island, where we do not only receive the sun directly upon our skin, but where it also heats the ground and the sea to give rise to fruit such as figs, and the grapes that are yet suspended on vines around us. Knowing that the sun will always be here for us, we should walk forward into this day, feeling and sharing in that warmth, *knowing* that light, and the love that goes with it. ("*So be it*.") Smiles and quiet words of appreciation are offered me, and with ECOS declared complete for the day, the group begins to disperse.

Marie-Hélène and I remain at the table. She tells me that Rachel and Henri are going to a shop down the road to get some water and fruit and to have a general look around, and that she is going with them. I am wondering if I should bring up the idea of the walk to the lighthouse instead, when... "And, maybe you would like to join us?" she invites.

(YES!) "Yes, I also would like some water, and some fruit."

"I am just getting my sunglasses. We can talk about the lighthouse later. I will see you back 'ere in a few minutes?"

Oh yes! I am thinking, as she turns without waiting for my answer and walks confidently to her room.

In my room I am fussing around for some money in my wallet – not the normal one with UK money, but – ah there, the one with Euros and credit card. Then, out on the terrace... "Oh, but I will need my sandals." In my room once again, I am waiting for my eyes to accustom to the relative darkness...and then, I take off my sunglasses (!) "A few minutes," Marie-Hélène had said, so there should be time enough to find my sandals, but I do not want the others to set off without me. Out into the sunlight again with the sandals, then back in *again* for my sunglasses, finally exiting with the thought that I should make an effort to at least *appear* to be relaxed and...oh – there she is, waiting for me, in the middle of the terrace, looking my way – smiling.

"Rachel and Henri 'ave gone ahead; only a short while ago," she says. "Zo, we can easily catch zhem up if we want."

Heading left, we go out the side of the terrace via an interconnecting door that takes us directly into the adjacent premises – which looks like a coffee shop and/or a bar. Out on the other side, the sand is already hot and – childlike – I find myself walking purposefully "toe-heavy" so that my feet push into the warm soft golden ripples as I go.

Reaching a kiosk, Rachel exits a side door and advises that we might wish to carry on towards the main shop by ourselves because, "Henri is looking to buy some flip-flops and it could take some time." However, Marie-Hélène says, "No, it is fine. We will wait," and turning to me continues, "If zhat is okay with you?"

"Yes sure, no hurry," I say, but immediately after I feel some regret as to the effect any delay might have on the lighthouse walk. Henri and Rachel are sifting through the racks of coloured foam-plastic footwear when Marie-Hélène remarks, "At these prices, I might also buy some – just to use on holiday and zhen leave zhem here." Flip-flops are chosen – white ones, after which the four of us walk along a dusty road passing the white low-walled gardens of successive beachside villas. My mind returns to pondering over whether we will *ever* get to go on this walk when, only some twenty-five metres further on, we halt outside a storefront.

Sometime later, we exit from our air-conditioned shopping spree, with me carrying bottled water, fruit and almonds. Proceeding back up the road, Henri and Rachel go ahead leaving Marie-Hélène and I to take our time walking and talking. We discover we both have had quite full lives: we have both been married and have two children: Marie-Hélène two boys, and I two girls. We find we have four years separating our ages, and four years difference between us and our respective ex-spouses, which leads us to realise that we are each the same age as our ex's. I tell of how I had separated in 2004 and divorced in 2005, and that I have had a *few* meaningful relationships in what seems – as I look back – to have been quite an extended period of self-discovery.

We both stop walking, and then we stop talking – having found ourselves already back at the villa. We agree to change directly into our swimwear, grab our masks and snorkels and some water and get straight back out to find the lighthouse.

Once enroute, we share our recollections of the information given us earlier: that we have to set off to the left and go some way past the little harbour we had seen yesterday. We do not know precisely *how* far but "no worries": we will eventually come across a chapel and a mill and who knows – perhaps we will find some good snorkelling as well. "No problem," she says, smiling and setting her dark sunglasses upon her bronzed face and re-gathering her hair into a small bunch. (Yes, no problem at all.)

Having stepped down onto the beach at the base of the steps, Marie-Hélène takes off her sandals. "Ooohh," she says. "It is nice and warm, but not so 'ot – not *too hot* – yet." She makes a good "h" sound, and a fair point; I follow suit, taking off my sandals to be greeted immediately by the same sensual warmth between my toes.

"Marie-Hélène –sorry," I say. "I am afraid I will have to ask that you slow down a little. I cannot experience this lovely sand and walk so fast. You know, I am getting a bit more like that each year: not getting any slower in my body, just wanting to take more time to 'enjoy the journey' that bit more."

"Oh, yes" she replies. "I know what you mean, but you have to forgive me, I have zhis *hot* sand every day I go swimming at home in Mandelieu-La Napoule, so it is normal for me." When she speaks the words Mandelieu-La Napoule, they feel to describe some exotic place I cannot yet imagine; but for the moment I am happy in my ignorance because the words seem perfectly made for listening *to*; when Marie-Hélène speaks them, they present such a mix of Latin vowels and consonants as to be like a stream of poetry upon my ears.

She slows her pace to mine. "Go on – *enjoy*," she invites. "I know you are not very used – to it, do you say? I know you do not have zhis hotness in the UK very much." She is right of course. We have already exchanged quite a few such jovial observations; gentle leg-pulls upon the differences re "you French" and "you English" based on the themes that would seem to run through both our societies (and the climate of the British Isles is of course always fair game). I am coming to appreciate the way Marie-Hélène speaks warmly whenever she lays her humour upon me. More to the point, what I like just now is the way she is walking so close and gently colliding with me as we drift side to side on the uneven sand.

"So, how did you come to separate, you and your wife? You said you 'ad changed job and tried to work it out? It seems so reasonable. Why did it not work out?" Marie-Hélène asks.

I tell her how both my ex-wife and I had been unhappy for several years. We had tried two periods of joint counselling but found it did not resolve things sufficiently. It had taught me some finer skills of communication, such the type of active listening that enables me to really *hear* the other, and learning how to accept another's expression of feelings without taking it personally, jumping to judgement, or trying to fix things etc. However, I started to become frustrated when my wife no longer wanted to continue practicing these skills. We had also both read books like the "Women are from Venus…" one and "Feel the Fear and Do It Anyway" but in each case, applying the lessons didn't happen equally with both of us.

Despite having the opinion, however, that many things *making* me unhappy would seem to be within my wife's ability to change, I could not avoid the fact that many things in life were still open to my control or at least, open to my interpretation. I had also begun to understand that many conditions that had found me feeling unhappy "with" my marriage, seemed to have been a repetition of things that had first occurred *before* marriage. Therefore, accepting responsibility for doing something at least with *those* aspects of my life where my wife's behaviour had less influence, I decided to seek out some personal counselling.

Marie-Hélène had been listening intently and without interruption, and as I pause, the thought comes: "*don't enjoy sharing the past so much that you forget the now.*"

The moment finds me standing with Marie-Hélène in quite a new place (both within and without). Beside us is the small harbour we had seen whilst swimming yesterday. Seeing the sand giving way to rocks just ahead of us, I put my sandals back on, and Marie-Hélène assents with, "*That* is a good idea. My feets, foots – feet, my *skin*, is quite rough from walking like zhis, on the beach in La Napoule. I should look after mine better too. Is that correct: feet? And, have I used the '*too*' correctly? I would like to speak better my English – you will help me, yes?"

"I think you speak very good English," I reply. "But yes, you could have said 'mine better *as well*'."

We go on to discuss (again?) the forms of *too* and *to* and the optional *also* which I suggest are regularly confused by those speaking English. "Yes, you will 'elp me improve," she says.

"Okay," I respond. "And you'll help me learn French," I say jokingly.

"Yes, of course!" she exclaims, both of us playing with this somewhat fanciful idea. A few minutes after, we come across what appears to be the remains of an old building. It is circular and only about half a metre or so high now, but being only a few metres from the shoreline, it appears likely to me that this is *the* lighthouse. We politely disagree on this point however, and over a fresh bottle of water, we discuss the idea of this perhaps having been a windmill, (even if it *is* in an ideal position to be a lighthouse).

"Yes, please…thank-you" she responds, to the offer of another mouthful of water. "We will use dis first then we can have mine," she says patting her large handbag slung over her shoulder.

As I look further along the coast, I see a few large and isolated rocks – perhaps two metres tall – projecting out of the beach, and beyond them a cluster of rocks of varying sizes. They would make a nice photograph (I think,) and accordingly I get my mobile phone out to take a few. We walk on.

"You know," says Marie-Hélène. "Rachel, yesterday 'as said to me about you: "that man has something to teach you." And you know," she continues. "I feel she is right."

"Oh yes?" I offer, as a humorous response. "I'm not sure I should ask anything further about what that might mean!"

"Oh, what do you mean?" she asks, feigning "serious" just perfectly.

"Sorry," I say. "I'm joking. I really have *no* idea what she was thinking of."

"A-ha," she says, "zhis is ze English humour no?"

"But you know," I say, rather more seriously now. "I feel there is much meaning in our meeting. It feels like we both have something to teach each other."

"Oh, I don't know about that. I think you 'ave been doing this spiritual zing for much longer than me. No, I am sure – it is you that will teach that to me," she says through her smile.

"That seems a little unfair but, okay then," I add, seeking to add to the humour. "So, what is it you can teach me? Oh yes, you are going to teach me, la French!"

Once more we laugh together, but then she trumps me yet again by simply saying, "*Okay!*" She stops short of offering another word, as if she may be about to reveal something further…but instead, she takes to walking close by and bumping into me a few times before continuing, "*So,* you say you know *no* French. How can this be? Our counties are so close?" she taunts.

"Okay, so maybe I am being a little disingenuous – I…" I begin, but I am interrupted.

"Stop, what is that you said that word *disgenurous* was it?" she enquires.

"Sorry," I reply. "I should be more careful with the words I use."

"No, no please do," she implores. "My English must improve, tell me what the word means?"

"But I understand everything you say. You are being too hard on yourself," I retort, fearing that the correction of Marie-Hélène's English might take away the delights of listening to her accent and her delightful "mistakes". "Well, okay, so…" and I explain the word disingenuous by likening it to "somewhat-misleading". Then I inform her, "In actual fact, I do know a *little* more French than just yes and no. I know un, deux, trois," knowing my pronunciation is very poor. "And I know deuce, oh and chocolate, and soison-neuf." I say, waiting for a response, knowing the last to have been a little "risque" but, sadly, knowing not a lot else. No immediate response is forthcoming.

I am presuming that my delivery of "sixty-nine" was either aimed too wide, or it had completely missed the planet, but then I wonder if I might have caused some offence, and now I start to regret saying it at all, but no – I *will not* let it worry me. Trying to reduce my apparent ignorance, I proceed: "Actually, perhaps I do know of a few famous French songs," rushing on to say, "…you know the one: '*Je-tem*', from the sixties I think, and also there's that song from the musical "Moulin Rouge", also from the sixties as well I guess, which does leave me feeling somewhat *old* right now!"

Being uninterrupted, and in pursuit of improving my image (!) I continue: "I realise that the lyrics of the musical-one are probably a little bit naughty," I continue, and then pause…

"Go on," she says, "no, do go ahead, oh you must tell me! You cannot build me up to zhis and then say nothing!" she declares.

We look at each other and we both know that this is going to be funny, and whatever transpires it is already *okay,* whatever happens.

"Okay," I say. "And look, I know that it is probably in an American song, but it is in French, and it is the longest string of French words that I know, and so…"

"*Vouller-vous coushae avec moir – sus-soir, vouller-vous coushae avec moir,*" I sing out with good tunefulness, but questionable accent.

Marie-Hélène bursts out laughing, "No! Really! You say zhat! And you only just meet me!"

We laugh loudly together; me because I can see that she really did find it funny, and her because she actually *knows* what I am saying, and she knows that I clearly *do not*.

Still laughing heartily Marie-Hélène says, "So, you tell me zhose words, yet I zhink you do not know that they mean?"

"You're right of course. I do not know exactly what they mean, but I know it is something about going to the bedroom at night time."

"You just have *said*..." and she pauses to laugh, "...You just *said* you wanted to take me to bed tonight!"

"No," she says. "No actually, it says more than that, but *that* I cannot say," her laughter preventing her from completing a whole sentence now. "Ah, it's so funny!" she continues, now almost in tears. Almost bent double with my laughter, I know that this episode has just concluded a most beautiful and meaningful step in "getting-to-know-each-other", and that my innocent/ignorant mistake will never be allowed to be forgotten.

As our laughter subsides, we find ourselves walking in complete silence for perhaps the first time. It dawns upon me that only a short while before I had been talking about "the end of my marriage". How do we keep drifting so easily between "serious" and "joyful" and...is it wise to tell her more: to tell her so much? We continue to walk in silence until we find ourselves stood opposite an outcrop of tall yellow-beige rocks, weather-worn and sea-sculptured like veritable pieces of art. Thoughts of my life story now give way easily to the admiration of the scenery and the discussion of the various rock-shapes.

Upon deciding to push on towards what we hope will be a chapel and perhaps even some snorkelling, we once more fall into quietness. Straight away, my thoughts return to the question of whether I may have already said enough about my past, but it seems that Marie-Hélène has noticed my inner disquiet, because she momentarily slows and comes close to my side and says, "I think it is good for you to be talking about your marriage and things".

"You sure we shouldn't stop?" I ask. "This seems a heavy subject to be chatting about, with us only just having met and all."

"No, it is important for you, I can tell," she says. "And I am finding it interesting. You speak – you explain such zhings – so clearly. I am learning zhings too so, please go on. You were saying about some private counselling?"

I recount how in the counselling, I had found that some of my behavioural traits had been taken on unconsciously from my parents, and some had been taken from society at large. The counselling also helped me to understand how I had unwittingly continued to apply those behaviours without even realising I had a choice. I learnt that when faced with an emotionally charged problem I could now *choose* to pause and review the situation before responding, and then respond differently in ways that might assist understanding – or at least not inflate things further. On looking back, I can see how the counselling had changed me, but my wife seemed not to have joined me on that journey.

"And yesterday, you mentioned that you had been offered a big career change. You did not take that?" Marie-Hélène queried.

"I was so desperate to save the marriage and to avoid my children establishing such unhappy memories as my childhood had given me, that I willingly let go the career opportunity to try and put everything I had learnt into practice."

"But, if the marriage had not been working as it was, then something needed to change and there could have been so many possibilities if she had of supported you," Marie-Hélène very accurately put it. "Did she not see all the exciting possibilities for you and her and your children, perhaps moving to Europe?"

"Wow!" I exclaim. "You know, in all these years, no one has ever put it in that way to me. Actually, the eventual career change to work more locally and with less over-night stays turned out to be good for me personally, but it didn't save my marriage."

I went on to say I had tried my best in the subsequent four years but it hadn't worked out. Having been subjected time-after-time to the closing argument: "Okay, then we will have to get a divorce," there had come a day when I simply – surrendered. Whereas I had previously felt fearful and had always stepped 'back from the edge', usually agreeing to further responsibility for bringing about a change to appease my wife's unhappiness, on this occasion I simply said, "Okay," to her threat, and that was that; decision made.

Now and again, Marie-Hélène follows up on aspects of my marriage-story with some similar experiences of her own, taking care not to take over the storey with hers, just sharing her similar experiences as a means of showing her understanding of mine

Just ahead of us now, where I had thought was a small white building on the headland, turns out to be a small white building on an island just offshore. We discuss whether the building we are looking at *is* the chapel that we were expecting to find and if so, how the others could have got to it.

Walking only modestly further, it becomes clear just *how* far the island is away from the mainland and then, just as we are about to question the matter further, we spot another small white building – onshore. It stands quite isolated, and must surely be the chapel that our friends had referenced. Just four metres or so square, and barely three metres tall, we walk its exterior in a matter of seconds. There are a few small darkened windows and at the entrance a small heavy-timbered door – very dark, very ancient.

Marie-Hélène enters, and I follow. Waiting for my eyes to become accustomed to the low light levels, I find a strong aroma of incense. Looking around for the source of the aroma I see none, but I suspect every surface of this diminutive refuge is coated with fine particles from years of incense burning such that this heady-aroma is never lost. Marie-Hélène and I exchange only a few words, and those in hushed tones. The deeply stained walls are full of pictures and paintings, wall hangings and shelving displaying religious icons and plenty of such other stimuli towards prayer/meditation/inspiration. Marie-Hélène finds an unused tea-light and enquires if I might join her in a dedication. Using the flame of a candle already burning, and with eyes closed, I go within to find some words: "May this special space continue to provide a sense of relief for those that may come burdened, and a sense of purpose for those that come already blessed with well-being, such that all may be moved toward peace."

I look up to see the face of Marie-Hélène in the flickering lights, and (silently) add a further most-private wish of my own, upon the completion of which Marie-Hélène lifts her gaze to meet mine in a fleeting, gentle smile; then turns to exit.

Outside the chapel, my senses are accosted by the increased heat and light, while at that same time a stout breeze acts upon my face and legs. Having not thought once about taking photographs of the chapel we had just exited, we both cross over to the rocks at the water's edge and take a few shots of the island now just a short stretch of water away. With photos taken, I turn around to be met immediately by a view of our final tourist objective for the day. It had been obscured for the most part due to the route we had just taken, for at first glance we have found just another mix of whitewashed buildings. However, in moving position to photograph the island, we can now see – at the far end of the new buildings, and only another hundred metres ahead – a most unlikely shaped tower that can only be an old mill (minus sails).

After more snaps are taken, seen and compared – deleted, reframed and taken again…Marie-Hélène offers me an inviting smile and I sense she is waiting for me to continue my story. However, not wanting to taint this lovely walk with too much "pain-now-past", I resolve to fill in the remaining gaps with some brevity, for – after all – life has generally improved for me (and would appear to keep being so.)

In life-after-marriage, everything seemed to be about accepting the necessity of change as a natural part of evolution emotionally, mentally, and even physically. Once I had started looking forward with some hope, life seemed to turn and to meet *me*, presenting many exciting opportunities for celebrating, and learning. I started sensing that the changes of emotion state within me came and went like waves; that when the downward wave inevitably bottomed-out, there would always come the upward wave, and in their wake, I started to realise that the process always offered me something important to learn. Furthermore, I found that once understood and learnt-from, most of the emotional challenges never came back and that instead in their place, came visiting for a while – a new perception: my first real mindful sense of *peace*.

In the months that followed I purchased a place of my own: a much larger place than I could ever have foreseen thanks to the help of a good friend who lent me some money towards the deposit. Yet still, the waves came. I found challenges at work with the worst employment-related stress in my life to date, and it coincided bizarrely with a rising wave in my most fulfilling hobby: amateur dramatics. I was expecting that one "wave" might balance the other, but instead, I was left feeling washed-out; washed-up high and dry in a strange, complicated and unknown territory. This brought an entirely new lesson, showing me that too much apparent "goodness" can take one so far from one's identity/self-image that even amid maximum achievement – all sense of joy can seem quite distant.

It was then that I saw an advertisement for a Mind, Body & Spirit event in the local town of Woodbridge. Remembering I had been to such an event there before with my ex-wife, I found myself oddly drawn to attend. I recalled before, there had been treatments and therapies on offer to help relieve stress and worry, and quite honestly – I was starting to feel desperate for any kind of help. When a chair at one particular stall became free, I took it – telling the therapist how I was currently experiencing *some* stress. For five pounds I received a Reiki energy treatment lasting fifteen minutes, from which began a most amazing change. Within just five minutes in her chair, I felt a heat and sensed a golden light coming upon me, just as if I was under a spotlight on stage. Moreover, a few minutes afterwards, I was aware of knowing – not just thinking, but *knowing* – that everything would turn out alright.

In the months that followed and having experienced my first Christmas alone, I started working on the divorce papers and even made the first tentative steps towards meeting others. By the time my divorce came through, I could already sense a future unfolding before me – the divorce now simply part of the natural process of change; simply "the next step". Eventually, with a greater sense of confidence and stability and sensing the opportunity for much personal growth, I realised I just *had* to find out more about this phenomenon called *Reiki*.

Finding myself returning from yet another incursion into my past, I see that as before, we have at some point stopped walking. I look across at Marie-Hélène, who stands still and attentive, and seemingly quite at ease despite my repeated out-pouring. I have been recounting some of the most sensitive and poignant experiences of my life to someone I have only just recently met, and yet I feel so very content.

"Wow!" she says. "You have just told me so-much. I do not zhink anyone has told me so much before. I am not so sure that I understand it all really, my English is not so good, but I think I understand it enough. Thank you for being so very open and sharing it to me; *with* me," she concludes, still without the faintest sign of any concern or complaint.

In the process of my last sharing, we have travelled just some fifty or so metres, and are at the tip of a headland. We begin discussing the small white building – now at the other end of the island, and in debating its attributes we conclude it is indeed another chapel, but as for why it should be there… (?)

We take out our phones once more to take photos: of the island, mill and rocks (etc.), me taking particular care to get the occasional photograph with Marie-Hélène in-shot, just by chance – of course. Looking for a place to swim, and agreeing upon an area where the rocks and the water depth should give us the chance to enjoy some good snorkelling, we begin to remove our shorts and tops. Marie-Hélène reveals an orange bikini that deserves a photograph of its own, but in comprehending I am again at risk of ogling her, I divert attention by asking her where she thinks we might best enter the water. She does not have an answer, however, and returns the question to me.

"Over there then, I think," I say. "Where the rocks seem to go into shallow water and the waves are smaller." As I take out my mask and snorkel, Marie-Hélène laughs. She says the mask reminds her of a gas mask from the war. I admit that it is probably twenty or so years old – perhaps even thirty, and that I had bought it in Cyprus during one of my visits there with the Royal Air Force.

On closer inspection, I see the headband is starting to crack and is losing some elasticity, so I doubt it will last much longer.

We bunch our belongings together at the foot of a large rock and walk to the place I had suggested, only to find it is in fact a rock shelf that has accumulated sand and pebbles. Entering the shallow water, I find the rocks slippery, and upon seeing some seaweed and then some sea urchins I offer a hand towards Marie-Hélène. She takes it and we steady each other until we are clear of the hazards. With the edge of the rock shelf just a few metres away and the water about half a metre deep, we both set-down flat and then launch off – Marie-Hélène first – over the edge, and out.

The seascape is *lovely*: so much better than what we've seen elsewhere. There are also a few more fish here. The most enjoyable part of it all, however, is simply the swimming…well, more precisely the swimming *together*. Being in deep choppy water and being mostly submerged seems to pose little challenge to our communication, as with nods, glances and gestures and occasionally a few touches, pulls and pushes – we proceed very well.

Having swum clear around the rocks ("around the rugged rocks…" I should perhaps have had Marie-Hélène rehearse) and at the narrowest point between the headland and the island, we find ourselves in even deeper water. Fortunately, it is also calmer water and so we both make our way through and around the corner with little difficulty. With there being no currents of any appreciable degree, we remove our snorkels and start to discuss what we have seen in terms of fish and such. We are both pleased by the rock formations and the contrasting colours and forms of the seaweed and the sea urchins, but we cannot be pleased by the absence of fish. As we talk, we realise that there is, in fact, a slight current, and that during our talking it has moved us a few metres further on. Accordingly, we head closer to the shore, towards rocks. Once beside the rocks, we find them to be a metre or so above our head, thus offering no route of exit. I then spot some rocks just below the surface and nearby, and not knowing if Marie-Hélène has seen them, I place myself in between them and her and indicate their proximity. She acknowledges me, but makes no effort to move away. The combination of waves, currents, and the need to tread water leads us into bumping into one another one or two times; and then once or twice more. Then, from my efforts to stay upright and keep us both off the rocks, the occasional touches that ensue seem to linger a while – or at least to me they do; and then they linger some more. I am not sure where the responsibility lies for the lingering, but I am enjoying the closeness and Marie-Hélène does not appear to be concerned; thus, the lingering continues. Pointing out the buildings further down the coast, I suggest that the longer section of sandy beach there might be a nice place to visit another time. Marie-Hélène turns in the water to look in the same direction, and in doing so she turns her back to me and places herself – considerably closer; close enough that our legs and torsos now occasionally touch. Without turning she tells me she agrees about the coast further down, and that we might perhaps go there *another* time.

Marie-Hélène continues to float – there, just in front of me – so close that her back is just a few centimetres from my chest, her wet blonde hair just in front of my mouth. In setting out together today, I fully expected to get to know her a bit more, but I had assumed that the snorkelling and general exploring would be the main focus. The "beautiful French woman" has already shown herself to be a kind, open, and jovial companion, but just now, I feel my perception of her is changing further.

Replacing my snorkel, I swim around to the front of Marie-Hélène, and as my face goes under – just for a second – I see the first full-coloured fish so far. Instantly I am excited and I rise again to inform her hurriedly. I return promptly below and start to follow the fish's path – pointing it out to Marie-Hélène in the hope she might see it as well (/also ☺). After a minute or two of the most-hopeful swimming and the most-purposeful gesticulations we both surface, and I ask Marie-Hélène if she was able to see the fish. She *thinks* she did but admits that with her eyesight, every fish is a bit blurry and multi-coloured underwater. Our laughing starts-over again.

As we continue to tread-water, the occasional touches again begin to linger, and when on one occasion the wave puts us one-against-the-other, Marie-Hélène makes no move to change her position; no move at all. Am I imaging this? Is she just being friendly, or does she know what…what it means, to me? Moreover, what does it mean to her?

I am not sure what to think, and even less sure what to do.

I dive under, going deep enough so that I can turn over and look up at the beautiful patterns of light and the bubbles of air rising to the surface. I fully expect to see her above me, but when I do – I freeze. It is as if I am seeing something "known" and at the same – wholly *new*. Marie-Hélène has begun to swim back, and the view of her swimming above is of a nimble and confident, beautiful aquatic-creature, and with her slow strong strokes, it is a sight to behold. However, there is something more, and rising quickly for air before returning still deeper, I swim ahead and beneath so that I might turn over and gaze directly up at her. I sense the voyeuristic nature of my actions, but for some reason, it *feels* important that I do this. Then, and all of a sudden, something strikes me – not physically or mentally, but *emotionally*, but the effect is so strong, it is almost physical. The view I have – looking up at this beautiful woman swimming on the surface – takes me back to *that dream*. The dream that I have recalled being repeated over so many-many years, is now something I am seeing *in reality*. So many times, this same vision has appeared – has *floated* – into my consciousness upon waking, and it has been accompanied by a memory of warmth and tenderness and connection; in the water, just like – this.

The sudden realisation causes me to release my breath and I hastily surface. I was not expecting anything like *this*: reality fulfilling a dream. I recall the feelings of joyful anticipation "around/about" me – as had accompanied my interrupted sleep of late, and I sense that the range of thoughts and mental/emotional states that I have visited these last few days are – together with the "not sleeping" – all a part of something *bigger*; and that they should be investigated – clarified.

Marie-Hélène clearly, has not had any such similar notions disrupting her stroke and is well on her way back to where we had entered the water. Catching her up seems unlikely, so I contemplate a small detour via deeper waters to at least help settle my breath and compose myself. However, while I have been *contemplating*, Marie-Hélène has reached the rock-shelf where we had entered and is pulling herself out. Once there, however, instead of proceeding to exit, she stays in the water and turns onto her back, looking out and over towards me.

Now *she* is observing *me*, and I am feeling both somewhat excited and a little anxious. Knowing I can make better progress underwater and *suspecting* that Marie-Hélène might just catch me disappearing from view, to see me rise "purposefully from the depths" (…) I decide to make the most of it. Deep I go – well two metres or so, and it takes just a few full-strength strokes to get me to the vertical face of the rock shelf. As I start to ascend, I spot a coloured fish swimming among the weeds and then some red sea urchins and just before I break surface, I offer a silent appreciation for that beautiful vista. I assume my next view will be of Marie-Hélène awaiting my emergence, but it is not. Instead, she has made her way into the shallows and is resting back on her elbows, goggles and snorkel in hand and basking in the sun with eyes closed. Upon reality taking hold of me, quite apart from feeling disparaged – I feel relief. She appears to be content and not anxious to get away, so perhaps she does not suspect she is being so blatantly *pursued.*

Pulling myself half onto the rock-shelf, I avoid direct eye contact with Marie-Hélène. Sliding further onto the shelf and keeping my head down in the water, I pull myself along to the point where sand and shingle (and skin) start to come into view. By now, the water barely covers my back and I have to accept that staying underwater is now a lost cause. Putting my elbows down and feeling a bit like one of those half-fish, half-reptile creatures I lift my head and continue to float/drag myself along until I am about two metres beyond Marie-Hélène, and about as far past as I go without leaving the water entirely.

My amphibian-like avoidance tactic may have worked, but with the next sensible and proper course of action being to stand and walk out, it comes to me that I am about to leave this beautiful woman here on her own. I'm feeling a bit awkward and unsure of myself, and, what if she has been there in the water – waiting for me to join her?

I turn over onto my back and push my mask onto my head, raising myself on my elbows to match Marie-Hélène. It feels a bit silly: staying in the shallows this way, but it feels the *right* thing to do – although, what next? Do I move a bit closer to her? Am I too close to her already – maybe? Could she be waiting for me to get up and go past her, just so she can then walk out without being stared at?

Then, the events themselves mitigate my situation because Marie-Hélène proceeds to stand, walk across the slippery rocks and then sit back down in the water only a little bit beyond; virtually *beside* me. This is the time *not* to worry; this is the time *not* to be thinking of what might go wrong. This is the time to engage with the moment and act for once – just as I *feel.*

"That was good," I say. "I am so glad we came here; it was so much better than near the villa."

"Yes," she says somewhat hesitantly. "Though, where I live, the water is clearer, and there are so many more fish. It is not so good here."

"So – you are right near the sea where you live then?" I ask.

"Yes, my place is near the old village centre and I can walk to the sea in a few minutes. In the summer I like to try and swim there every day or so." She then laughs to herself and continues, "Hah, it is funny: I pay to come to a holiday in Greece only to find the swimming is better at home!"

She says it without remorse; it is "just so". I respect her ability to reflect this way and to find humour out of the unexpected outcome.

Feeling rather more relaxed now, I rest back in the water, my head just short of Marie-Hélène's midriff. She lays back slightly further into the water, resting on her elbows, smiling alternately between me and the chapel opposite.

Slipping my mask further up and off I turn to face the same direction as Marie-Hélène, but with it being a little bit deeper where I am, the next wave washes over my face and makes me splutter. We both laugh at my misfortune and I push myself a bit further up the shore – more alongside Marie-Hélène.

We share some further small talk, but despite the cooling breeze, neither of us makes a move towards getting out. With the waves rhythmically soaking our torsos and occasionally wetting our shoulders, our necks and our…*chests* (doh!) I'm looking *at* her again; but she is smiling at the sun, then towards the chapel, and then at me. Is she waiting – perhaps? Then, it dawns on me: she *knows* I am thinking about her; she knows I have been looking *at* her.

I move a little closer to her. "I really was not expecting all this," I say. "Yes," she says, almost as if she knows what I am alluding to.

"I mean – not just the sea, the sun and this walk today, I mean really – I did not expect to find myself talking and revealing so much of myself to someone – anyone; to *you*. Sharing the experiences of swimming and snorkelling, and – well, everything really; we talk so easily about everything including emotional and spiritual things. It's just all so easy, so comfortable."

"Yes," she says again, simply, honestly. "I am feeling it too."

"I'm just, well surprised, delighted, taken-back. I…"

"We should just enjoy this," she says. "Enjoy this sharing. This feels so special to me."

We are silent for a while, admiring the view ahead, the view to our sides – every second feeling to be so rich in meaning. "I am not sure I want this to stop," she continues, "…just to go back to the villa."

The waves continue to splash us both, rocking us side-to-side in unison and I move closer, turning to half face her. Looking at her openly now, her face lifted to the sun, I gather she must be feeling cooler – what with the goosebumps all over her tanned skin and (…) and yet she chooses to stay-put, beside me. The waves rock us some more, our adjacent arms and legs now brushing one-another. With the next wave I give in to the urge to steady her against their slow rhythmical beating, and I extend my left arm behind her.

It starts to feel like the typical teenage cinema experience: one where the boys' arm is placed nonchalantly across the back of the girls' seat on their first date – *obviously* and uncomfortably. It feels so very natural to have my arm around her; a bit clumsily to begin with, but with the next wave and her agreeable countenance, I adjust myself further; closer now.

She turns her head to observe me. That is how it feels: like she is looking *upon* me – simply looking, and taking it all in. Perhaps like me, she is trying to make sense of this lovely feeling of closeness, of trust, of connection, and perhaps like me, she is sensing a certain excitement as well.

She turns her head forward, giving me scope to *look* again – appreciating her face, her wet hair, the rivulets of water running off bronzed skin. I look to her light blue eyes and follow the line of their contented gaze out to the chapel on the island opposite.

We take turns now in gazing at each other and looking away. We are both quite clearly getting cooler but neither of us is going to disturb this delicate balance of witnessing, offering and receiving each other's non-verbal but very clear expressions of appreciation.

My mind is interrupted again, this time by a memory of a movie-scene. It is that big 1950's romantic film-scene, where two love-struck beautiful people are being washed around on the seashore, and then end up in a passionate embrace. (Where do these sudden interruptions to my attention stem from?)

We are quiet, quite close. The skin of her thigh is against the skin of my thigh and her hip is now against my hip. Another wave comes and my arm moves to steady her further, pulling her closer still. Marie-Hélène looks at me and smiles. She smiles with her mouth, with her beautiful blue-grey eyes, with her blonde eyebrows, with her high cheekbones and then, my eyes fall upon her lips. No longer are we simply observing each other; we are *with* each other – no longer separate. Another wave and now our bodies are completely alongside and all I can feel is skin upon skin. We accept one another's further closeness, our faces now being the only parts of our bodies not touching until…our foreheads touch, and we stay like that for – what seems an age.

I feel something sharp at my elbow and I look to find that my efforts to maintain our proximity have pushed aside the shingle, leaving a rock now pushing into my flesh, into my bone, but this moment holds something so beautiful, so precious, that I do not want to disturb it – the stillness, the mutual appreciation of each other's presence, each other's energy.

Another wave comes and our lips at last touch; but they *just* touch – that is all, although it feels *everything*. The sense of stillness deepens and at the same time the sense of energy increases. We stay like this for wave after wave, with no other measurement of time having meaning. Wave after wave with lips just touching, sensing the trust between us and knowing that this is not heralding an ending, but moving each of us towards a *beginning*.

The stillness gives way to gentle movements and lips feel lips – feel the heat of lips, the breath from lips, the parting of lips – the gentle rhythmical moving of lips. Lips feeling the moisture of lips: feeling the moisture of mouths, the moisture of tongues. Tongues venturing forward but then pausing: tongues sensing tongues but patient – tempting, tantalising playing. Her cool wet body curls slightly towards and then into mine. I curl mine further with my legs tucking under hers, her legs now lifting and draped over my thighs. Our bodies instinctively move to accommodate one another, wrapping into and around each other towards semi-foetal positions.

Knowing that this is the start of something, but something that must not be rushed, our kissing now moves beyond stillness into a quiet passion. Our kisses become something we dwell-over, float-within – a precious treasure offered, received and shared – and still the waves come.

My arm takes my attention again and sensing my discomfort, Marie-Hélène moves to take some of her weight. As I look to my elbow still perched on the rock, the water around it is pink from bleeding. I feel the chill of the water and I am sure Marie-Hélène must now be feeling it as well, and so with a last gentle full-mouthed kiss and with big smiles, we part.

As we stand, our arms reach out and we stroll hand-in-hand over to where the rock shelters our clothes. Marie-Hélène gets out her bright pink Super Dry towel and I offer my hands: "May I?" I say, and knowingly, she gives me her towel and immediately receives it around her back and her shoulders. I move to get out my towel but she says, "No, come 'ere please," and I turn to find she has a corner of her towel in each hand, her outstretched arms inviting me to join her. I move to her – close to her. She wraps the towel around us both and there is a short witnessing-pause where we are just gazing at each other: taking it all in. Then, our eyes close and our lips meet once more.

We share gentle, slow kisses and the kisses are sublime, but more astounding still is the sense of closeness and trust: a sense of presence and peace that holds us both. Pulling my head back with a bit of a giggle, I confess, "I am afraid I'm finding all this a bit *exciting*," and I nod downwards. With the towel and Marie-Hélène's arms wrapped tightly around me however, there is no space for manoeuvring. "What do you mean?" she asks, smiling and feigning innocence.

I make a more assertive downward glance – as if it is not already patently clear to us both what I mean, but she just rocks from side to side and says, "It is alright. Just stay here; get warm. Stay in my arms. Just a few minutes," she continues. "Until we are warm and dry together."

("Just a few minutes…")

My hands come from beneath the towel and move to caress her face and cup her head and we kiss again. When my eyes eventually open, I see hers are yet still closed – our lips still sealed upon each-others, and my attention is taken by the wind and by the sun shining on and through her wet blonde hair – matted and platted now by my caresses.

Our lips part. "I think we might need to dress," I say, observing the goosebumps on her shoulders. We part, and I reach down to adjust myself, but I can do little to hide my rising passion. Unusually for me, however, I feel quite relaxed about it. Even as we gaze openly at one another's bodies, at the signs of mutual arousal, neither of us seem to have any inclination to hide or be shy.

I get my towel out and start to rub my hair. The rest of me seems dry enough already – what with Marie-Hélène's towel and the heat generated by our closeness. Quite nonchalantly, Marie-Hélène removes her orange bikini-top and reaches for her bright pink vest. Pulling it down over her tanned torso, her body gives quite some shape to the garment and the cool breeze just adds to the purpose. As Marie-Hélène turns and starts to divest herself of her bikini bottoms, I figure she is bolder in these situations than me, and I politely turn away to put on my clothing.

Clothed and beginning to feel the warmth again, we approach each other and exchange a series of short, soft pecks. Turning away to finish drying our hair, we soon turn back again for another kiss, then away to pack our bags, and then together again for another kiss – like we are on some sort of emotional elastic. In another full embrace and still kissing, Marie-Hélène pulls me towards her most-purposefully and shuffles us backwards into the shelter of the rocks. Our embrace – it must be said – leaves me slightly breathless.

"Wow!" I exclaim. "What is this?"

"It is something special, I know it," Marie-Hélène replies, with confidence. "There's such passion," I continue, "but with such tenderness too; and a stillness – have you sensed that…when we were first kissing back on the shore there?" I turn and nod where we had kissed in the waves. "Did you notice how first we just stayed close with our lips just touching? There was such a feeling of power and stillness at the same time; a feeling of such presence."

"Yes," she almost-whispers now. "Something very special, very important – I feel it."

Parting and reaching for our bags, we take out our phones in unison to check the time. While still bending over, I stop suddenly as a sense of something new comes about/within me. In addition to the sense of anticipation and excitement that has been around me for nearly a week now, there is now a sensation of…a "space" opening up before me. Without shape and without anything being within it, this *space* feels like…a sense of – *future* (?)

Being nearly two o'clock we agree – even allowing for Greek timing – we really ought to be heading back. We continue talking about how we are feeling: how in a way, we – neither of us – want to leave this oh-so-special place, but at the same time, there is a confidence about our coming-together on this island that is important in itself. Something amazing is happening and it must be allowed to *breathe* here, on the island; not be repressed.

Despite the time, we walk without urgency and as soon as we find our pace, our hands again find a hold. We agree that even if we get back at two-thirty, and *if* lunch has already started, it will probably go on for about an hour, and if we don't get to eat anything – well, have been eating so much recently that we are hardly likely to starve.

During a pause in our conversation, I find myself drawn into thought once more: *two days*. It is only two days ago that we had first met, yet I feel I can trust this woman – almost like I have known this connection before. In any romantic novel this bronze-skinned, fair-haired, blue-eyed, gorgeous Latin lady would have surely fallen from the heavens; however, this is happening – now, and for real. It feels like *all* and *everything* that romantic films and stories could ever promise, and it is here, and now. It all feels so natural, our talking about ourselves and our pasts, and even talking about the notions of "us" in future. "And we are on a retreat – do you *believe* that," I announce quite suddenly. After the giggling that follows my unprompted exclamation, we return to talking, and agree: "this is not the sort of thing one *does* on a retreat." We also agree that with the speed of everything, there is nothing yet that needs to be shared with anyone else, and even if something is revealed – we are adults and are not obliged to seek anyone else's approval. Having agreed all this, however, it still feels that there is some aspect not being addressed – not being witnessed/understood, and so we continue to explore our feelings. There is something so powerful, so strong, sensitive and so wonderful that still seems to need expression. We don't know what it is right now, but whatever happens today, tomorrow, next week – whenever – we both must stay with this feeling; we cannot ignore its persistence, its presence – *now*. Something great will come of our meeting, and at the very least we should expect a friendship for life. "I *know* this. I have no doubt," Marie-Hélène asserts.

I tell Marie-Hélène that I have been seeking the path of authenticity for quite some time and that I have found being truthful – living with truth – always seems to resolve in understanding. Marie-Hélène agrees, and we decide here and now: we will seek to share only truth.

Realising that my life-story had probably filled the greatest part of all our discussions so far, there only seemed one possible direction for our conversation. "So, how did you come to be here; how did life lead you into marriage, and then to a retreat in Greece?"

Marie-Hélène takes her turn in describing the highs and lows that had brought her to this place: from her birth into the nations' Catholic tradition in a town just south of Paris, to her family's move to the valley below the picturesque mountain village of Gourdon in the far south-east of France. She continues with how her early memories of isolation were later supplemented by being boarded in a military academy back near Paris, moving on to studying law at university and gaining her Masters'. How a finishing school ball led to the love-less relationship that was her marriage, although it had at least brought her back to the South of France – albeit for her husband's self-serving reasons. Bringing me up-to-date, Marie-Hélène tells me how the need for income after her inevitable and costly divorce had found her using her law knowledge and her diplomatic skills at a real estate agency for some years, until another encounter with unbridled male ego – this time her boss – led to her second painful and costly "separation": giving up her work. Overall (Marie-Hélène tells me) she has a comfortable lifestyle that includes so many of the things that (now in my words…) *that society professes as heralding happiness.* All the while, however, there has been a force that has drawn her to find…something else.

There have been some *interested* men, and some have figured more significantly than others, but none had been interesting enough to tempt her into trying another live-in relationship. Marie-Hélène has practised yoga quite a lot (though not so much in recent years) and has been on several yoga retreats. Also, and particularly interesting to me, she has studied and practised Reiki – though again, a few years back. Marie-Hélène finally reflects on how an "ex" had introduced her to Rachel and Henri, and that – still looking for answers – she had succumbed to Rachel's gentle persuasion and joined her on a spiritual development course last year. The course then led to a few others – including one which entailed a regression to a past-life in Scotland. "I must tell you more about that some time! Oh, it was very *powerful...*" she digresses, before returning to tell me how she had subsequently been invited to attend a certain spiritual meeting in London earlier this year – and then this retreat here on Skyros.

Before we get within view from the villa, Marie-Hélène reveals something quite unexpected: that her ex-husband had later died in a light aeroplane crash whilst at the controls. She feels – she hopes – that the event has not left much of a scar on her, but she worries over what long-term effect it may have had on her sons, and particularly her youngest son.

As we approach the villa, we look down to see our fingers still woven around each-others; then we smile once more, loosen our grip, and let-go. It feels like I am "letting go" of something, and as we walk the steps up to the terrace, I cannot help but reflect upon one particular word I recall having used quite a few times when we had been talking about our lives: *love*. It is a bit of a shock to find myself considering this word, and it is clearly not the time to talk about…"*this*" to Marie-Hélène; yet if truth is to be told, it does not feel like I am falling in love at all, it feels more as though I am remembering I am already – have *always* been – in love!

"You know, I feel I am going to be writing about this – about our meeting here on Skyros," I announce.

"Really, you already know this?" queries Marie-Hélène.

"Yes, something is already telling me that this is important, that the story of us will be important," I respond. I had been concerned about being late for lunch, but I need not have worried because even my most generous estimation of the Greek time-scale was well short of the reality: an hour later than the programmed time of lunch, we are all present and *still* waiting for lunch.

By in large, everyone has adopted the same seats as used previously, therefore we again find ourselves just around the corner from each other. All the same, I find myself leisurely scanning the faces around the table to see if there are any knowing looks or smiles. Then all at once, lunch arrives in a flurry of movements and a large number of serving plates, and our *now* becomes occupied with another (but less leisurely) experience of Greek dining.

At around six o'clock, having enjoyed an after-dinner coffee brought from the café next door by Doris, having showered off the residues of seawater, and then having spent the last hour or so lazing around on the couches at the shaded side of the terrace – sort of hoping to see Marie-Hélène but without being *seen* with her – it is time to prepare for the evening. The tour of Skyros Town is meant to depart at half-past six, and I am looking forward to the walking as much to help me digest as to explore.

In my bedroom, I freshen with some aftershave before dressing up (in much the same clothes as last night) and strolling out of the room (*with* my key). Our island guide (Milos) has arranged to meet us in the middle of the town, and because four of our group have done the tour on a previous retreat, there are just six of us now. Exiting the front of the property, we turn left and find ourselves on a dusty tarmac road. The road is lined with white walls and wire fences beyond which there appears to be private residences with gardens, small orchards, and vegetable plots. We have been given some directions and Henri and Rachel have explored in this direction, so upon reaching where Milos had described the ascending route turning into steps, and seeing Henri and Rachel going up – busy in conversation, I am confident all is well. During the walk into town this fine Grecian evening, I have occupied myself with trying *not* to get too close to Marie-Hélène. Thus, I hold back at the steps, politely waiting for all to go ahead. Recalling that lunch had finished not so long ago, to aid digestion I decide to ascend – two steps at a time. If I had thought it through, I would have concluded that I risked closing the gap to Marie-Hélène, but having not indulged in such thoughts, I instead suddenly find myself directly behind and almost on top of her. Fortunately, Rachel hears my approach and pulls away from Henri to walk with me, leaving Marie-Hélène to be escorted by Henri who almost immediately manages to say something in French that makes Marie-Hélène laugh. I smile at Rachel, who smiles back. Does she know what is happening? In an effort to divert attention (mine at least), in the time-honoured way, I offer my arm to Rachel, and we carry on up the steps together.

At the top, the footpath is absorbed into a small street between lines of old but recently whitewashed buildings. Looking up we see balconies with hanging flowers and small pots overflowing with ancient-looking shrubs. There are also vines/climbers and small trees – a number still bearing fruit. Some of the overhanging branches have masses of pink blossom, many of them fallen – the petals scattering us as we walk.

Soon enough we approach the fork in the street with the café that we presume Milos had spoken of. A man is sweeping and an elderly couple is sat sipping coffees at a small circular table, talking with a man on an adjacent table and occasionally gesticulating towards the person sweeping. It feels as if the people here might be doing what they do every evening: sitting, exchanging thoughts of their day, reflecting on the weather and: "How it was fine today…but that a chill can be felt now in the evenings," and, "look some tourists, we should welcome them." The lady gets up from the wooden-slatted seat, smiles and moves into the shop (it is hers?) The man also rises and gesticulates as to offer the prime position for our use. Milos arrives on cue and we exchange hellos and rearrange the seating to accommodate all. Milos suggests we might buy water or a Greek coffee, and then he converses with the locals with some affection. Not yet seated, I look around to where I might best place myself (for obvious reasons) but find my indecision has left me no choice, and I sit directly beside Marie-Hélène. Unfortunately, I am so close that I cannot see her unless I make the clear effort to look straight at her – which I do not. All I am left with is admiring the scent of her perfume and glancing upon her legs…occasionally.

Out in the main street there approaches a short rotund man, in his fifties or sixties using a walking stick – a local I am sure, with tanned skinned, dark hair, dark eyes, and a smile worn all over his face. By this, I mean there appears to be no part of his rounded face that is not taken up with folds of skin that accentuate his wide infectious, and near-toothless grin. In point of fact, his smile looks somewhat overzealous – a little unreal. His smile remains stuck to his face all the while he ambles, his stick moving ahead of him in short measures. It is as if he is waiting to find a comfortable place or perhaps to have one awarded him. "Smiley" – not perhaps his real name, and not perhaps as old as I had first thought – exchanges a few words with the man still sweeping, then his slow ambling comes to a waddling-halt just across from where we are sitting. For a few moments, his face displays a series of grimaces, before he returns to that oh-so-wide, and slightly inauthentic smile. A few more words are exchanged with Mr Sweeper but it seems to me that Smiley is not being engaged – not being ignored exactly, but not entertained either. He launches (I suspect) a few well-used opening lines at the gentleman on the adjacent table, but – although politely recognised, he is then passed over. Mr Smiley rests, apparently at ease with his failed attempts to enter into conversation, his face now frequently flicking back and forth between smile and grimace. I cannot help but smile back at him; his smile may be well rehearsed but there is an inner-warmth to it. Still, I wonder what he is *doing*. Oh, is something being passed hand to hand – almost covertly – between Mr Sweeper and Smiley? A few coins, some loose change perhaps. Perhaps Mr Smiley is a local "special-cause" out on his regular evening round; too young to be an elder but not able to qualify for regular work. Suddenly I feel like "the voyeur" witnessing what may actually be quite a mindful and respectful interaction between someone experiencing hard times, and a person who knows what it is to "go without".

We are interrupted by the arrival of drinks and a tray of delicacies – wafting sweet odours across our noses. This so well practised presentation, produces an oh-so sweetly effective olfactory response that perfectly characterises "arriving in a small Greek town". Milos converses in Greek and then conveys that we are invited to sample these special pastries, challenging us to guess their ingredients. Wheat and butter are in the mix – agreed – but then, is that apple, or cinnamon, or…almonds? And, honey – there must surely be some honey in there as well. We stop talking to eat and drink, and so that Milos can proceed to take us on the tour.

Departing the café, we wave goodbye and attempt to copy Milos as he carefully mouths short Greek phrases to our hosts, who smile and say words (feeling like) "Come again. You will always be welcome."

Milos moves ahead and describes the approximate route which will end – literally – at the top of the town with a visit to an old monastery. It is *hoped* we shall arrive before the monk closes the doors at eight o'clock. Milos seems to have a well-practised rapport and as he encourages us up the street, he tells us of the story of Achilles from Greek Mythology: Achilles' mother Thetis, it is said, had learnt from an oracle that her son would not come back alive if he joined Agamemnon in the wars, and she had therefore brought him to Skyros and disguised him as a woman. Having heard that Achilles – being dipped by his ankle into the mystic river Styx – had become (mostly) immortal, Odysseus set out to look for Achilles. Having constructed a ruse where upon hearing a false attack-alarm Achilles – instead of fleeing like a woman – had taken arms and revealed himself, Odysseus then convinced Achilles to depart the island – it is said – from a small port that still today is called Achilli, and together they proceeded to fight in the much-fabled Trojan wars. [5]

We continue to head generally upwards, weaving left and right through small streets, alleys and passages, sometimes with views and vistas, and generally back and forth as one might on an alpine pass. Rachel, Marie-Hélène and Henri are ahead. Up to now, Marie-Hélène and I have exchanged only a few meaningful momentary glances, but with more boldness, Marie-Hélène now stops immediately ahead of me and I halt beside her. With arms hanging down, the back of our hands connect for a moment, and when I move away it is as if a magnetism, some soft adhesion, causes our arms to lift slightly from our sides and have them slide one against the other: elbow brushing forearm, wrist brushing hand, and then with no one watching: fingers touching, sliding and – just for a moment – linking. Then, I catch sight of Rachel who seemed just to have looked away. She walks on with a (knowing?) smile.

We are brought to a polite halt and Milos asks if we have noticed during the tour that there are pots of basil outside many properties. We are told that the herb is considered as a guardian when placed at the entrance to a home and – because of the level of almost religious-reverence this belief receives in Greece – it is quite rare to find basil being used for cooking here. I find this quite astonishing – myself having a small pot of basil almost permanently on my kitchen windowsill specifically *for* cooking purposes.

We are next invited to note the rather whiter-than-white colour of the building that now stands beside us, and are asked if we had noted the wooden crosses over many doorways and in alcoves, or the candles or flowers elsewhere in their such similar places. It transpires we are standing beside one of many private chapels.

It transpires that the chapels are nearly all private here – it being the tradition that families that build a chapel receive a higher social status. Despite being family-owned, we learn that the chapel we are standing beside is often held open for visitors and so if we are respectful, we may enter; and of course we are, and of course – we do.

---

[5] Please see Homer's *Iliad* for the whole of the story.

I am looking at paintings, icons, carvings and such like, and my initial feeling is of there having been much dedication/reverence in those who had created this place. However, there then comes a *sense* of quite a contradictory nature: that the impetus to establish such a monument is more symptomatic of adherence, manipulation or perhaps even oppression…and once again I wrestle with the conflicting perceptions that stem from the subject of religion. [6]

…And there she is again: at the corner of my vision – Marie-Hélène, and in observing her presence I am brought back to the now.

Exiting the chapel, and minding our heads as we step up and out and then down, we turn left to follow Milos up the streets that wind ever-up towards the monastery. A man approaches and stops – greeting Milos in a friendly fashion. Milos breaks his conversation, telling us that this man is a sea captain whose work has him travelling for months at a time, but that even though he has the choice of places around globe, he makes his home – the island of Skyros.

We have just one last turn now, and here the street widens and presents, straight ahead of us now: a terrace-with-a-view. The view is overhead of the town and across to the beach and villa, the rocks we had swum around yesterday afternoon, the island chapel, the old windmill and the rocky headland that witnessed *our first kiss*.

Marie-Hélène comes beside me and we take a few photographs. The fading light means the shots themselves will not be so good, but I know that they will always be so very much imbued by the fondest memories of this day.

Going through the ancient, heavy, dark wood doorway of the monastery (just in time) we come across an excellently manicured potted-garden. It almost feels out-of-place – the whole of the inside being nothing like the bleakness suggested by the external walls and gatehouse. As we ascend the final wide and immaculately clean staircase leading to the chapel, we find two elderly gentlemen reclining in wooden chairs on the adjacent balcony; ah, and there is the monk (or at least, a man in monk's robes).

A younger man emerges from a doorway to the left and ushers us in. I suspect he is the caretaker who does the actual locking-up each day because his overall countenance is of one who has been waiting. He is pleasant enough in his demeanour, but I suspect he is looking forward to his evening meal.

---

[6] See Appendix II: "…and once again I wrestle with the conflicting perceptions that stem from the subject of religion."

The inside of this building is – well – very ancient, very ornate – *very religious*. It has large wooden beams, small-high decorative windows, lots of gold-leaf frames and hanging objects, paintings and icons. An ornate wooden candelabrum hangs from the centre of the high ceiling, and – similarly to the chapel encountered earlier – there is a space sectioned off to the rear, more private, more – select. However, and very unexpectedly, I get no sense of *deeper peace* within this place. There is an energy here, but it feels somewhat disjointed and incoherent, not altogether harmonious – unlike most chapels, churches etc. As I turn, I notice the caretaker is standing at the door – *waiting*. I don't suppose his demeanour adds anything to the tranquillity just now.

Out on the balcony, we look again upon that immaculate petite courtyard, and I have just enough time for a few more photos before we are shown down the staircase and through the ancient gatehouse towards the exit. The ancient wooden doors close firmly behind us.

As we head back down towards the heart of the town Marie-Hélène and I find ourselves hanging back (for some reason). Once back down in the street where we had met an hour or so earlier, Milos leads us through the – quite unexpected – crowds of shoppers and diners. The old town has livened up considerably and I am jostled and nudged as I attempt to keep an eye on the quickly disappearing Milos, and (of course) Marie-Hélène – who is currently interrogating a cash machine. There are countless visitors and evening merry-makers, an occasional cycle and motor scooter and then an old commercial vehicle arrives to navigate the crowds. People are pausing at shop windows, chatting with their partners/friends/relatives, pointing out this and that, and suddenly this feels to me like any and every shopping street.

There is a chemist looking just like a chemist anywhere in Europe, complete with a flashing green cross outside. At the counter, a man stands aside while a woman is being attended by another in a white coat. Perhaps she is seeking guidance regarding which medicine is best for (these symptoms) and the man with her – yes, definitely her partner – does not really *want* to be there. He starts glancing around and then slowly paces around the shelves of skin-care, hair and personal hygiene products, no doubt trying to fill time and avoid the more intimate details of what is being discussed behind him.

Rachel, Henri and Marie-Hélène file off right, into a jeweller's shop. I stay outside for a while but – starting to tire of the bustle – I also enter and make to investigate what next has captured their attention. All around the walls are glass displays protecting and presenting fine precious metals, precious and semi-precious stones. "Rachel, Henri and I are zinking we might like to buy a gift 'ere for Jo-Anne," Marie-Hélène says as I approach her. "It is 'er birzday soon and I would like to get her a little somezing. Jo-Anne is quite special you know; so lovely."

I do *so* love hearing her accent! Her lips move through the soft gentle vowels – removing the H's, softening the R's and occasionally dropping in a few crisp-bright consonants – oh…she is waiting on my reply (!) "Yes, of course – yes, I am sure that colour would suit her."

Feeling just a little embarrassed at my state of disconnection, I just hope to have answered appropriately – Marie-Hélène having just pointed to a bracelet of semi-precious stones in shades of turquoise. Marie-Hélène moves on to join Henri and Rachel, and I feel quite a sense of relief; perhaps the same as befell that man I had observed in the chemist earlier. (I wonder how often it is, that we might cast aspersions on others, simply for displaying those characteristics we would deny as existing in ourselves.)

So many people are here – and so much *stuff*. All this buying; these hopes and expectations, worries and concerns about trying to choose the *right* thing; hoping it may be received with thanks; hoping not to be judged on the thing itself – by the time taken to choose it or the money spent on it or what it shows of one's knowledge of (likes and dislikes of) the recipient. So much…*stuff*. (And, once again, perhaps this reveals more about me, than those I observe.)

As we approach the chosen dining place, Milos comes down the short flight of tiled steps to welcome us. Filing respectfully past diners seated in pairs and fours, we find ourselves on a relatively secluded terrace surrounded partly by bamboo blinds that admit just enough air from the on-shore breeze to make it feel like "outside". I close my eyes and find a picture within my mind of waves rolling gently onto *our* shoreline, opposite the little island chapel, now lit by moonlight – and I turn to find Marie-Hélène directly behind me. We look to the line of tables mated by white tablecloths and head towards two seats at the end.

Milos introduces the owner and confides that the weather is expected to be somewhat cooler this evening; that otherwise we could have sat up top – and he looks and gestures towards a wooden staircase. Milos continues, "I am told, there is a lovely view from the terrace above. The barrier you'll find across the staircase there is only to guard against anyone coming straight in and disappearing up without the staff noticing."

Several conversations take place simultaneously, many containing short excited sentences such as, "Who is yet to come," and, "Has anything been heard of Karina as yet," and, "How come there so many empty seats?"

I go to the staircase and ascend the several uneven steps to leave the hubbub of the world behind. Arriving at a subtly lit rooftop decked out with tables and chairs, I find views on every side looking across the town, across to the hills with white dwellings picked out by the soft streetlights, and to the sea – where I can just make out the dim lights on beachside properties in the area of our villa. I have an idea, a romantic one, and I accordingly turn to make my way to the stairs but am met by Henri and Rachel. I smile and stand-aside before continuing to the bottom of the stairs, where I am stopped again – by Marie-Hélène.

"So, is s'ere anysing to see, can we go up?" I catch myself watching her lips (again) but not finding any words I simply nod and stand aside. Then, my words arise: "May I come up with you?" I ask.

"But of *course,*" she answers, from halfway up the staircase – turning and smiling down to me.

Watching her ascent, and still feeling her smile washing over me, I catch my breath. If love is an emotion, I have never felt one stronger. If emotions are signposts, I have never sensed my course so clearly set before me, and there is energy enough to fill me to bursting. I follow her up two steps at a time – relatively expertly, but then tripping at the last step and steadying myself only just short of falling on my face – this contributing nothing to the ambience of the rooftop terrace. As I catch sight of her again in the half-light, well truly I cannot deny the physical attraction as she gracefully turns and offers yet another smile, but – oh my… *am* I in love?

Moving nonchalantly (trying to) between the tables, I approach Henri and Rachel and share opinions on the lovely views, how lucky we are to be dining here tonight, and how kind the weather is being to us…

Finally, I make my way to Marie-Hélène who is standing in the furthest, most dimly lit corner of the terrace. My head turns to the sound of footsteps descending the staircase, then, coming close to Marie-Hélène, I place a hand at her waist. Directing my attention slowly from one finger to another I sense both tautness and pliancy beneath the fabric. Her head lifts slightly and she braces herself as my face rubs gently against her hair, taking in her light-citrus perfume. As my cheek brushes her ear, I recall the saltiness of our first kisses, and as my lips now touch where the soft skin of her neck blends into her shoulder, she turns and tilts her head back, catching the moonlight on her face. There is no smile now; she is just being present – beholding *us*. Marie-Hélène slowly turns, and we close our eyes as our lips meet – softly, oh so softly. There it is again: the stillness, a sense of timelessness, of power within peace. Remaining still, we are transported by the moment itself to a *nothing* place, to somewhere that is no-*thing* – outside of space and time.

I feel her lips curling up at the edges and we come apart, both now smiling. "Wow," I say. "Here it is again: that deep sense of peace."

"Yes," she says. "It is wonderfurl."

If I am not *already* in love, then in every-way and with every-thing this beautiful woman does and says, I will be there soon. She lowers her chin; our foreheads meet and we need to do nothing more; we just bask in the moment. Together, we lift our faces and turn towards the staircase because we know this is not the time and place.

Just as we sit at the table, Angelica with daughter Beryl, and their close friend Doris, join us, then closely followed by Jo-Anne. We rise to exchange hugs and hellos, and the newcomers become absorbed in the continuing conversations. "Has Karina arrived yet?" someone asks, and just as they do, she does: Karina walks in to receive the warmest welcomes and most joyous hugs one could wish for.

Menus are passed around and we all decide to share a feast of entrées, salads and feta and – of course – Tzatziki. The menus then get circulated *again* when we realise that *some* have yet to choose the main course, and so we (okay – *I*) review the various combinations of pasta, chicken and fish. With all the retreat participants now assembled, and with all having had a full day of sun and fun-filled experiences, much conversation now ensues. I do not find myself as engaged with talking as most (*okay* – as much as Marie-Hélène) would appear to be, and during a pause I find myself wondering why there should be a spare seat to my right…just as Karina rises to introduce the lady who plans to join us at the next location, offering massage and other nurturing therapies. Having worked her way around the smiles, hugs and handshakes, our new participant – accompanied by her little dog – comes back around to my side and having processed her menu options, she settles beside me.

When, in true Greek fashion – the food *eventually* arrives, Marie-Hélène and I enjoy sharing not only the starters but also each-others main dishes. We talk with each other and around the table – but mostly with each other. We would seem to be constantly seeking a physical connection, and just now, it is by leaning gently against each other with both shoulders and knees touching (which is not so easy with two table legs in between). But then…what is that brushing against and around my foot? Rubbing gently over my feet and (*ooh*) my toes? I look briefly towards Marie-Hélène but receive no feedback or acknowledgement. There it is again! Moving my foot, I look again towards Marie-Hélène but no, nothing. Becoming rather inquisitive I am about to break into Marie-Hélène's conversation with Milos…the lady to my right reaches under the table, and addresses her dog!

As soon as I get the chance, I tell Marie-Hélène about the dog and this time she does respond – by reaching under the table and taking my hand in hers. We stay much like this for the rest of the evening: close together, often with our arms down under the table. Eating together, laughing together, both reaching and gesticulating with our one-free hands (and no one notices?)

After lots of tomatoes, Feta, olive oil, pasta, chicken *and* fish, and after lots of smiles, there comes a small chorus of "Baklavas!" from the middle-Europe part of the table. Accordingly, just as I thought the eating had ended (just kidding) plates of that honey-bathed Greek *delicacy* are distributed down the table.

Eventually, we rise. There is no particular rush to leave the taverna, with everyone moving around the table to share hugs and sentiments with everyone else (at least once). Particular attention is given to Milos, the massage lady and Karina who announces she is looking forward to her bed – having made the whole trip from the UK in just a single day. The party then splits into those taking taxis and those who have opted to walk back (no guessing).

In fact, the same six of us who came together now depart together down the streets and alleys of Skyros Town. There are fewer people here now, but the main street shops are still surprisingly busy. Very soon, and having kicked our way through the pink blossom, we reach the top of the long flight of steps. Marie-Hélène and I had ascended these separately, but as Rachel moves forward to catch up with Henri and the others, Marie-Hélène and I choose to go *just* that little bit slower. We take the time to look at the distant hillside and the buildings lit with soft yellow street-lamps – which slows us down some more. Finally, out of "fine gentlemanly conduct" I pause to offer my arm to Marie-Hélène (just to assist with the descent, you understand).

It so transpires that we stay hand-in-arm all the way back to the villa, continuing to drop back at every opportunity until everyone is out of sight…and until reaching the courtyard of the villa…and until we exit the passage to find ourselves alone on a moonlit terrace.

The waves are breaking gently on the shore but is otherwise quiet.

With neither being ready for this ("*wonder-furll*" as she calls it) night to end, we gaze around, first generally, and then at each other. Only a few rooms have a light on; it seems only we have elected to stay up. Marie-Hélène releases my hand and walks to her room where she goes in, drops off her bag and then exits to stand outside her door. She looks at me and I smile. She returns the smile, but then strolls off at an angle to me to the other side of the terrace, and stands, looking out to sea. I join her, not too close, but close enough to take in the aroma being lifted off her neck by the sea breeze. The moonlight is bright enough to show the white of the waves as they break in running-lines along the length of the shore and Marie-Hélène invites that we take a walk. Following behind, I observe her white flower-patterned dress gently flapping around her legs – moved by the same sea air that had just lent me her scent.

On the sand, we slip off our footwear and stroll in the direction of the rock wave-breaks we had encountered the other afternoon. All is quiet as we pass the fish restaurant from last night. It already looks to have been shut up for the season. Out at sea, the silver moon flickers light off the tops of the rippling waves where we have already swum so much together. I feel content that we would already seem to have accumulated quite a bit of shared history.

Marie-Hélène moves closer and then releasing my arm, slips her hand into mine. Our hands fit together just perfectly: not one inside the other or one over the other; not one hand twisting the other or one hand lower than the other – just perfectly: one *with* the other, fingers interlinking in close comfort. Everything feels just-right when I'm with her like this. Every question understood, every perception accepted – undisputed. Every answer readily received and trusted – all *so easy*. We have expressed our wonderment at this several times now: we are just so *at ease* with one another yet, at the same time there is certain *energy* whenever we are close.

We slow and approach the sea's edge, taking in the sound of the breaking waves, but unlike the other times when we have approached the sea together, this does not seem to be an occasion for swimming. In fact, Marie-Hélène makes known she is feeling chilly and so we turn back – this being the sensible thing to do, what with the time and all…

Once adjacent to the villa our hands disengage and I follow Marie-Hélène back up the steps to the terrace where we find that all is quiet and – apart from the glow of tea-lights outside each room – all is dark. We walk to the terrace wall, and for a while, we gaze up at the stars. Then we gaze out to sea. Then we gaze at each other, back to the villa, at each other again, and then again – out to sea.

"*Somewhere-else…*" We look at each other and we know the same thought is in us both: we want to be somewhere else – alone. Marie-Hélène turns to look towards her room, and then mine. I suggest – being in the corner – that sitting outside my room is probably the quietest location and the one least exposed to the wind. Marie-Hélène walks ahead to the white cushion-strewn bench with a cosy candlelight flickering and casting shadows upon the whitewashed walls. Marie-Hélène sits down, closely followed by me – although a bit away. I feel sensitive to her situation – what with her position and the relative intimacy of our semi-seclusion, but she frowns mockingly and gesticulates, "Noh, noh, noh," she says, patting the cushions beside her.

I move close, then closer still. The knowledge that others could exit their rooms adds further to my tentativeness, and so we sit quietly and I take hold of her hands in her lap; after all, this "now" is beautiful enough just as it is.

In hushed tones we reflect on the evening; about the town and the food, the fun-under-the-table, and the dog, the long walk back…and then we kiss.

Here it is again: the *peace* – entering our space just as our lips meet. The space in which *us* exists, outside of all else. Not for long, however, for the peace dissolves quite quickly; like ice-cream in our mouths, the dense-intense flavour of our kiss now melts and the promise of greater sweetness now sweeps over our tongues and seeps deep into our very being.

My hand goes to Marie-Hélène's face, stroking her hair, her cheek, and cupping her chin. Our foreheads come together and our faces move in slow-gentle rolling movements across one-another – manoeuvring, dancing, playing softly; one upon the other. The rolling movements bring our lips once again to the point of *just* touching, and then my kisses move to her right cheek, her chin, her neck. I pause, placing a single soft kiss to her left cheek, and then our faces return to this gentle alternate undulating-rolling movement, offering first a face to the other's lips, then the other's cheek to one's own cheek, one's neck to the other's lips…

Our lips meet again and they are moist, open and the kisses fervent and filled with all the passion that our morning embraces had only quietly promised. Marie-Hélène withdraws slightly, then at once, her lips are in the nape of my neck, then on my cheek, and then close to my ear, and she whispers, "Take me to your room."

Those words, those most-perfect words, voiced with her gentle, purring South-of-France nuance. This bronzed skinned, blue-eyed, blonde-haired – for want of another word – *beauty,* whispers me to *take her to my room.* These thoughts, these very *male* thoughts, are processed in a fraction of a second, but despite the pace at which my mind is working, something *within* wants that I witness what is taking place; for this is *real –* not one of my fantasies. Moreover, I can see in her eyes that she is *feeling* something similar, and I can also see it in her smile; that smile that grounds me when I am lost, and now lifts me to aspire to an even greater *"now".*

As I rise, Marie-Hélène joins me and as I push the door open, she takes my hand. Switching on the table light I move aside to allow Marie-Hélène to find her footing, but finding the light too bright, I reposition it to the floor. Turning back, I find Marie-Hélène has stretched out diagonally on the bed: bronze on lavender. With her right arm down – hand in her lap, her other arm now bends up and arches over to tuck her hand just behind her head.

As I move closer her head tilts left towards me. Smiling through half-closed eyes, her posture, her whole being is *here –* inviting, offering…promising; and I accept. Kneeling beside her on the bed, I mean to take time in planting gentle kisses slowly around the entire periphery of her mouth, but impatience leads her to turn her head and bring our lips once more together. Our all-encompassing kisses: powered by the passion that had first been given breath in the breaking waves, then enhanced by the soft moonlight of the rooftop terrace and now heightened further by our lying together.

Her mouth opens wider; my mouth withdraws enough to allow my tongue to brush across her lower lip, then the upper. The tip of her tongue flicks out towards mine for a moment before withdrawing, inviting my return. Our mouths close upon one another's and as I move to accept in some measure the invite – her tongue continues to venture forth and back, receiving mine deeper with each reply.

Her head tilts back slightly and as my right-hand moves to the side of her neck, she releases a sigh. I withdraw from our embrace – just to double-check "where we are going", for I am not yet of the mind to assume all. However, as I look upon her beauty again – head tilted back, hair dishevelled, eyes half-closed, lips parted – this pause has done nothing but to shift my excitement up another gear. She opens her eyes and looks at me as if having sensed my previous indecision, but as she reclines her head, offering her neck I am now – *sure*.

Marie-Hélène makes to move both arms down between us, and for a moment I start to doubt the basis of my confidence, but her purpose would seem to involve grasping the hem of her dress – but, before she makes much progress I interject, "No, please – may I? I would like to undress you – to offer you the experience of being *undressed*."

Assisting Marie-Hélène to her feet, I lead her around the end of the bed. With ample room here to shed clothing, and light enough to *see* by, I move to continue what Marie-Hélène had started. Lifting the hem of her dress gently and slowly, up and up, I reveal her tanned swim-conditioned thighs, her small, fine underwear, and gentle protrusions of lightly fleshed hips. I move my position to observe behind, as next is revealed her full-bronzed cheeks. Shifting my weight, I delight in gathering the fabric into my palms, engaging with the vision of her shapely waist. Standing finally at her front, I take the stance that will enable the complete removal her dress – exposing her gently held cotton-enclosed breasts, lean shoulders, slender neck, and then…her smiling face. Her smile shows me that she has enjoyed this slow undressing, and her calmness gives me the confidence to continue – turning my attention next to her silver-grey underwear. Picked out with small pink and purple embroidered patterns – tasteful and purposeful – they replicate perfectly the same mix of strength and beauty in she who wears them…and wears them *so* well. I sink to the floor and imparting a slight twist to her body, I peel the cotton down over one hip at a time, pausing at every opportunity to kiss each new section of bare skin. Then, with the full attention of both the captive and the *captured*, I repeat the similar at her rear, taking joy in kissing each cheek. Inviting her back around to face me, I finally ease her underwear down to the floor and I steady her as she steps out of them. She makes as to move toward the bed, but emboldened and hungry for more of the same, I impart a small restraint to which she concurs, and on bended knee I plant a line of slow sensual kisses just above, then squarely upon her, taking in her delicate heady aroma.

I raise myself slowly (probably smiling like a Cheshire cat) to meet her smile and her part-open lips, but holding back from kissing, I reach around her back to purposefully…to deftly and surely…*deftly* and *surely*…arrh! Fiddling, twisting, tugging but to no avail, I guess I am not quite as experienced as it first appeared, and Marie-Hélène giggles as she reaches behind for the clasp and releases it – in a touch over a millisecond!

Marie-Hélène works along with me now in this – our delicious drama, her hands now falling to her sides, her gentle sways accentuating her recently exposed curves. What theatre: she breathing in slightly to emphasise just that bit more her already well-presented figure accented further by the triangular bikini tan lines – and me lapping it up. I do not know at this point who is the more turned on, but her sighs suggest that we are probably about even, and with me now standing up, Marie-Hélène begins to unbutton, and then hurriedly pulls my shirt over my head. At my waist, she pauses – struggles (ha-ha, *her* turn) – then deftly strips my trousers and my underwear to join my shirt on the floor.

The *theatre,* however, becomes too much for me as completely "out of role" I break into the widest grin. Marie-Hélène meanwhile, changes gear and launches toward me causing us to fall onto the bed in a tangle of arms, legs, lips and hair. We are at the same time: flustered, excited and giggling; so easy, so playful are we; so joyful, so downright sexy! Pausing the latest duelling of tongues and panting (just a little) I return to verbal discourse…

"I must just tell you something…I have had *the snip*." She stops dead.

"What, what is that you just say?"

"I have had the operation, so I cannot make babies, you know – get you pregnant."

"Oh no, it is alright – I am okay too. And anyway, would *you* stop this – now?" Then, dropping all triviality, she continues, "Do…do *you* want to use anything, protection I mean? It is okay if you do. I would understand."

"Oh no – no," I say. "No, I trust you, I trust this, and I want to feel – everything."

"Yes," she replies. "Nothing should be between us."

For a moment I ponder over making something of the double meaning – but only for a moment. Instead, quite still, we look deeply into one another's eyes, both of us recognising the simple beauty of our exchange and how it has set aside all possible further doubts.

Marie-Hélène falls upon me, yet I am still not ready to rush into *everything*. Encouraging Marie-Hélène off me and to lay back, I sit back on my knees and dedicate myself to the pleasure of offering a stream of carefully placed, joyful wet kisses from her neck – all the way down her body. To be clear, it is only through Marie-Hélène's *allowing* that I can pretend any sense of being "in control" but as one kiss moves almost instinctively to the next, it is more accurate to say that neither of us is particularly in control at this point. There is no certainty in the route I am taking, with every inroad being at first accepted, then seemingly re-directed, then willingly indulged; each twist of arm, of thigh – each wet caress, each sigh.

Taking time and pleasure with her feet, I flick my tongue around and in-between her toes. Proceeding to enjoy her legs, I sample her soft, smooth skin with gentle flicks of my tongue all the way up each thigh. My kisses become lingering, linked it would seem to her skin becoming softer and more aromatic.

My enjoyment is immense and from the way her hands are now pulling on the back of my head, I am about as close as I would like to be short of losing all control. At an increased pace I begin the journey up her undulating torso, but Marie-Hélène has it seems – waited long enough, for changing pace – she reaches down, bends forward, and takes me slowly but surely into her mouth. This lovely sensual and passionate woman seems to know instinctually just what contact is "*needed*" and where; what pressure is yearned for and how, and to that end I turn to join her in giving, receiving and sharing the most specifically dedicated pleasure and being lost to the most perfect attentions of the other.

There is *no* control now; it is our bodies leading us – conversing as if having known each other forever, and as I find myself lifted, and then lifted higher, it feels our very *souls* must know the other of some another place and time…and as souls together with bodies entwined, pleasure upon pleasure washes upon us, our minds our poor thrilled, elated minds are now all-but being towed along, in this – the most delicious and sensual exchange of our lives.

We pause; I feel Marie-Hélène disengage, and she moves to below me and I move above as together we begin a new recitation: unwritten, unchecked, yet in perfect unison – we are *together* again and anew. Moving in time across the widest spectrum of natural rhythms, we feel every slightest movement and pulse as every sense and sentiment are now united toward natures' most perfectly choreographed performance. Our rhythms lift then slow, changing and changing again until – at a point when time stands aside for what feels like an eternity of pleasure – Marie-Hélène becomes lost to her rhythm, and I become lost to mine. Yet still, the magic continues, for without and beyond our mindful intent our inner rhythms now take on a life of their own as together they ebb and fade, and then mingle and match to a point where the blending of the physical and emotional engenders a sense of oneness beyond all former comprehension. And I want more.

Reaching under, and slipping my arm around Marie-Hélène's waist, I hold her close while her arms and then her legs clamp around my torso, and in an unscripted manoeuvre, we turn first onto our sides and then – with no loss of contact – continue until she is above and upon me.

My sense of time begins to return, then at once serendipitously collapses as I sense myself simultaneously being both deep inside of her *and* deep inside of me...*and I am gone*. In the clouds, deep in space, my hands in her hair, her nails in my chest. I am lost to all physical sensation, without vision and floating now, somewhere in a mist, somewhere deep within another form and nature of *us*.

I do not feel my *release*, nor feel it receding, but instead, I first find my mind within the mist, and then I become aware of my body *around* me – hot and shaking; and another body on me – wrapped around me, vibrating together, moving together, then slowing as we gradually float back down to earth.

When at last all movement stops, there are no words. Within our stillness, it seems as if the very universe itself has vibrated with the power of our connection. Yet now, all is at peace within and without.

With something akin to normal breathing restored, Marie-Hélène is first to speak, "What is happening to us!" There is a pause, after which we spontaneously erupt with laughter. The laughter leading into gentle undulations and this then to heightened sensations, after which just one knowing look between us serves to confirm – if we were to carry on in this vein...

And we do, and as if anything could possibly be more outstanding: there is *more,* because throughout this – this new most-all-consuming sensual experience in my living memory, we have maintained almost constant eye contact. We have been present-together in this physical realm throughout the rise, the crescendo and the return, but at the end – there are as before...*no words*.

We hug, we kiss, and once more we find ourselves starting to laugh. I withdraw declaring, "Either we stop now, or I die!"

"And either way," I continue, "...I just don't care; I feel just so completely fulfilled; like never before."

There is a certain humour in what I say, but the last part is no joke. All this evening, this day and so much of what had happened yesterday, has been beyond anything I have previously experienced. Perhaps it may never end, but life has shown us both that we should not simply *assume* anything, and as we lay, we reflect on what we had said earlier: that we must "live this out": these days, this holiday, this lifetime whatever it may become, and however long it lasts. Wherever it takes us, we cannot ever imagine regretting what we have shared, and just at this moment, it feels like our whole future is bound-up in each other. There is, however, one thing we agree we can be certain of, that it is getting late – or rather, that it is getting early because in a few hours the sun will be rising again. We kiss, we laugh and we hug once again. Then we kiss, and we hug and we laugh some more…but finally we reach the last "goodnight", and I watch a vision of beauty dress hurriedly, scoop up her remaining belongings and exit my room – into the moonlight.

Now – yes surely now, I shall sleep (?)

Did that Really Happen? (Yes!)

I wake. It is dark, still dark…this is so silly. I am so fully satisfied, somewhat depleted but, beautifully, wonderfully satisfied. So why – why, am I still not sleeping?

Looking towards the clock on the bedside cabinet…I have barely slept for two hours!

The bigger picture is that I am in a lovely room, on a quiet-warm night on a Mediterranean Island – oh yes, and only a short while ago I had a most-exciting experience – no, *the* most exciting experience of my life. Perhaps at this moment, nothing else is needed.

Lying back on my bed, I find her aroma – *our* aroma – and I smile with the memories of last night and the coming-together that happened just a few hours ago. It had felt so much like we already knew each other, like a coming *back* together.

I recall the "Twin Souls" transcript that had been discussed at one of the London group meetings, and the "Twin Flames" CD given me at my local development circle, and ponder on whether I may have just ventured into some such similar territory. Also coming to mind, the retreat-weekend in Glastonbury last October, when I had witnessed my subconscious opening to express a yearning for some such deep loving-connection. Is it possible I have met my twin-soul, my twin-flame? [7]

Once again, upon finding myself amid a powerful experience and with many questions that lack answers, I resort to the same well-used reasoning, "Maybe all of this is real, or maybe I am another step closer to madness." Just for now, I am content with both the terms "mindfully spiritual" *and* "innocently deluded" for such words are only symbols, and no symbols are in themselves real. The fact that remains, however, is that just a few hours ago, the experience I was having was shared with another – which for me makes it *very* real…

Turning over, I fall into sleep once more. I awake to dim light at the window: gentle and persistent but not yet sunrise. I turn again; sleep again.

---

[7] See Appendix II: Re expressing a yearning (for change)

Waking now to a much brighter light, it feels the point in time to get up and face whatever this day may bring. Putting on some comfy clothing over swim trunks, I go to brush my teeth. It is not usual for me to brush my teeth first thing in the morning, but I seem to have an unusual taste in my… (I smile).

With freshened breath, I grab my blue mat and step out into another Grecian morning. It is later than I had thought because two of the group are already on the beach, and I have time for only a few transitions before others including Marie-Hélène, Rachel, and Henri also arrive. Then, enter Jo-Anne, bouncing along in bright white with a rich swatch of turquoise around her neck.

Marie-Hélène smiles at me sweetly – but briefly. Is she uncertain about last night? Perhaps she is wondering if the others might have heard us. Oh dear, I had not even once considered *that*. I quickly offer another smile to Marie-Hélène which she returns warmly and with no hint of the thoughts I'd just encountered.

I try a harder today to stay with the group during the sunrise salutations, but before long I am again following my own timing. Partway through, the sun which has been up for a while, finally emerges from the clouds. With final moves completed, I settle into some sun gazing. After ten minutes or so, Jo-Anne departs for the terrace and the others follow one by one; well almost, because when Henri and Marie-Hélène stand, they do not make for the steps but instead disrobe and enter the sea.

Perhaps it is time to change some of my habits, or at least vary them a little.

The water is slightly cool but very invigorating, and upon completing her exchange with Henri, Marie-Hélène approaches me. There is immediate warmth between us. There are no regrets or doubts; in fact, it seems like the conversation could continue from where we had left off last night – so to speak. Nonetheless, we maintain a respectful distance (discounting the occasional touch and stroke below the surface) before agreeing we should exit – to take another walk and swim together again after breakfast.

Breakfast feels to be a celebration in itself: a feast of sweet and savoury homemade items topped off with honey or/and yoghurt or/and fruit – or/and all! For me such joyful eating (of wholesome and natural food) celebrates our exchange of atoms with the universe. [8]

Today, in fact, I have cause for a double celebration, because the breakfast (or "petit dejorny" or something) is the first, and the second is the "something new and wonderful" that has everything to do with someone called Marie-

---

[8] See Appendix II: why does *eating* seem so important?

Hélène, and feelings of – yes, I must admit: *love*. As I sit here, across the table from Marie-Hélène, I wonder how long it will be before such words spill out of my mouth and then cannot be un-said.

Looking around, everyone seems to be very happy today. It seems I am being over-cautious in purposefully sitting away from Marie-Hélène this morning, so it would seem I am experiencing that aspect of the human condition where we so readily seek to attach our inner turmoil to our outer world, or more bluntly, we look to blame others for how we are feeling. [9]

§

Breakfast is enjoyed at a leisurely pace, this slower way of taking meals – it seems – being a normal component in the Greek way of living. In contrast, cleaning my teeth, packing my snorkelling gear and grabbing a towel on the way out to the beach takes barely ten minutes. Some (further) minutes later, Marie-Hélène walks down the steps similarly kitted out, and smiling unreservedly.

"I am a little tired," she confesses. "I think maybe we did not have enough sleep last night?"

It is, of course, a somewhat rhetorical question, and where one might have expected the conversation "on the morning after" to be a bit – well: *awkward*, we move effortlessly into a comfortable conversation as per the day before. Once we are a few villas away, we hold hands and do not let go until we get to the point we had reached two days ago; where the beach rakes steeply to a vertical rock-face. The mix of seaweed and washed-up picnic litter is not particularly inviting, but there is no one else within a few hundred metres. Accepting Marie-Hélène's initiative to lead I set out bravely – only to find that the several rocks we can see in the water, are accompanied by many others under the surface. The waves are also slightly stronger today, stirring the sand up such that if there are any fish here, we are not going to see them. For some reason, however, it does not seem to matter very much to either of us.

Twenty minutes or so later, we are back where we had entered the water, having scored null on the fish count, but counting out blessings none the less as – following the briefest of pauses necessary to push our masks up onto our

---

[9] See Appendix II: Blaming others for how we are feeling (…the human condition)

foreheads – we reach for each other. "Oh, such passion!" Marie-Hélène exclaims. "I have not known before; where does it come from?"

Finding our masks and the choppy water something of a hindrance, Marie-Hélène breaks from kissing to suggest we get out. Once again she offers her arms and her bright pink towel, and with it stretched around her back I step forward into her embrace.

"Do you remember this – from yesterday?" she enquires softly of me.

"Yes, every second," I reply, "…like I can close my eyes and, in a moment, find myself transported back; and I remember last night just the same," I continue, glancing down to adjust my trunks.

"Oh, I am sorry, does it bother you?" she asks.

"No, not at all…well, maybe a little yes, you see, I do not know what you might think: me responding like this every time we embrace."

"Oh, *no* – is it not normal?" Marie-Hélène assures me. "It is very flattering for a lady to have a man react to her in this way; a man like you," she says, drawing me close and pulling us together into an even closer embrace. Marie-Hélène has this ability to be affirming and at the same time honest and light-hearted.

"I am glad we are alone; I would not be comfortable with displaying *this* if others were about," I confess.

"It is a pity," she replies. I look at Marie-Hélène with a smirk…until she joins me in realising the other possible interpretation of her words. "I mean," she continues, "it is a pity that we are not *more* alone."

"*More* alone, really?" I query. "I mean, are you sure you are not-at-all a little – uncomfortable? I mean – last night, we were making love for – well, quite some time, and…?"

"Yes, and so passionately – oh, such a man!" (Is she teasing…slightly perhaps?) Then Marie-Hélène pulls me closer, "No, I am okay, *really*." Then, as if to make her position *very* clear, she rolls her hips slowly against me a few times, and then a few times more. "I cannot remember feeling this passion before, you have done something to me!" she says.

I withdraw to look into her eyes. "I'm having a problem," I offer. "I am finding it difficult to accept the words you say. It is not so easy for me to accept them; coming from a lady as lovely as you. Can you understand?"

"Believe it," she replies. "This is happening. I have never said such things before either. We said we would be truthful and this is my truth. It is what we are bringing for each other. Enjoy it, share it with me please."

I feel almost like crying and shouting with joy at the same time.

"Are you okay?" Marie-Hélène asks hesitantly. "I see a little sadness in your eyes."

"I am sorry – no, it is not sadness. This is something I think I have wished for...so much," I pause. "And it is happening now."

"Yes, it is – enjoy it, *with* me," Marie-Hélène whispers in my ear as she begins to pull me close again. I hear her sighs and feel her breath on my neck as we roll our bodies – one against the other.

"I think I would like to go back into the sea again," I say.

"Here, really?" She queries.

"Yes, here – really," I say ardently, looking down along the shore to see if anyone is approaching. "In the sea *now*," I say gently and yet (unusually for me) quite assertively. It seems this "talking-from-the-heart" frees me to act in full accordance with *all* my feelings.

"Okay, alright yes, let's do it! I'm not sure how but – go, you lead." Marie-Hélène is referring – I think – to the waves and the submerged rocks that had impeded us earlier, and I understand her point, but *where there's a will...*

Moving gingerly around the rocks, I turn to offer my hand to Marie-Hélène – leading her into the warm Aegean Sea, and my arms. Being baked by the sun from above and rocked back and forth by the sea from below, we squat to keep the breeze off us. Well, actually, it is not so much that we are rocked as tossed, and the challenge of staying upright and close-enough to kiss moves from being innocent to being comical. Then, all at once, we find a method that entails walking crab-like towards one-another, then with one squatting deeply, the other kneels/floats between the thighs of the other, which allows just enough time for our lips to meet. Time after time however, the waves knock us to the side or send us crashing into each another. Then more comical still, with *both* of us unwittingly opting for the kneeling stance at the same time, we embrace only to sink together into the water. (Still kissing!)

Resurfacing and laughing, we expel water from our mouths but press on nonetheless. In variation two, I am half-sitting and Marie-Hélène is opposite and astride my knees. With our bodies connected enough not to be separated by the waves, my feet can now anchor us (...ish) on the seabed. In the frame I now provide, we have a stable yet open-hold that allows Marie-Hélène to balance herself within it, such that if the waves become so strong or my balance fails me, she can float or propel herself free, or return – as she determines to be best. [10]

With successive waves lifting and lowering us together like flotsam, we begin to welcome the experience like a game. Our eyes connect us in our laughter, and then on pausing for thought – we remember why we had returned to the water. Reaching below, I pull upon my swimwear and as another wave departs, Marie-Hélène settles just that tiny bit lower, and with her ankles now locked around me, there is no chance of us floating apart.

"Are you okay," I whisper in her ear. "I don't want to hurt you?"

"Yes. Just push – *please*."

We are rocking back and forth, and as the sea turns from being our antagonist to being our facilitator, wave upon wave moves *with* us. Using the sea to full advantage, I take her weight and with my hands, I move her upon me until, with Marie-Hélène pulling herself down hard, I am at the sweetest of places deep within and, in two worlds: floating. Marie-Hélène throws her head back, and with her eyes at first clenched tightly and then wide open, she stares directly into mine – through mine – as we search one another's very being…

When the waves and wind on our faces eventually remind us just *where* we are, we hurriedly glance about; but all is safe, and after one more lingering kiss I float her gently away.

Back on the breezy beach on Skyros, Marie-Hélène brings her towel to me once more, warming and drying us together. A most beautiful perception now comes to me: of someone in my life with such strength and trustworthiness, that each time she "offers" or "accepts" I simply drop my guard and step aside from the ego that has previously feigned to protect me; moving me into a place where I feel empowered not only to give more but to truly *receive* as well. This is new to me.

Stretching out both our towels on the only section of beach that is more or less level, we sit down together. I put my arms around Marie-Hélène, holding her to my chest, but the mix of wind and waves has taxed our resources.

"Shall we walk back now?" I ask.

"Yes, I am feeling a little tired," she looks at me cheekily, "…for some reason I do not *know*." As I help her rise, we lose footing on the steep shingle bank and repeatedly fall over together, laughing. Squarely on our knees, we set about

---

[10] …and only now that I have written these words does the deeper meaning become apparent.

packing our masks and then, carrying our towels wrapped scarf-like around shoulders, we set off back towards the villa.

"So, I think you have told a little about your last relationship; that it finished – suddenly? You said she was uncomfortable with your spirituality, but she was a yoga teacher; it makes no sense to me."

Again, I am offered a straight, reasoned and very searching question, and I capitulate. The previous relationship had lasted about two years, finishing the previous September. For certain, the relationship had been founded on mutual respect, and with my girlfriend being a primary school teacher and a yoga teacher, we would discuss and partake in interests both philosophical and meditational and in activities including swimming, cycling, dancing, and even some kayaking. Living some seventy miles away from my girlfriend, involved a lot of driving and regular late nights, but the pros largely overcame the cons – apart from one inescapable hurdle: her daughters' complete and utter un-acceptance of me.

We had holidayed in Scotland, which had involved meeting up with some close friends of theirs, and we had hoped that crossing Hadrian's Wall might help the behavioural wall to crumble similarly. However, it did not and about a year later and with no congeniality as a threesome, I was quite unexpectedly given something of an ultimatum: to get married and *make* it happen, or…

I look up to find we are almost directly outside our villa. We look at each other, look down at our hands, smile and let go. "I wonder how long we will be able to keep this up," I say.

At the table this lunchtime, Marie-Hélène and I are bold and sit directly beside one another. It must seem obvious to many that we are fast becoming friends, so it is no good trying to pretend otherwise or we might come across as having something more to hide. (I mean – to think such a thing.)

The lunch itself is like all our other Greek meals have been on Skyros: long-lasting, simple and sumptuous (and of course late-starting), and I am feeling good – even with all my reflections on the not-so-happy experiences of my past – and why not? If experiences that are largely enjoyable and nurturing – involve some challenge and sadness, can they not be reflected upon lightly, and perhaps even rejoiced if the experience has led to a deeper understanding.

Marie-Hélène and I seemingly have nothing to hide but, why do I keep finding myself feeling – well, so serious about…"things"? As soon as my heart looks to soar, it feels as if another force is countering it with something like, "Just watch out: keep your eyes open; just in case," or something like that.

I look up to where she, Marie-Hélène, is sat smiling at me; and all doubts evaporate.

In the late afternoon, Marie-Hélène and I take another walk along the beach in the same direction as in the morning until we come to a point where the youngest member of our group had told us she had camped – a few nights before the rest of us had arrived. With there being some shrubs, small trees, and some grass, we have both some shelter and shade, and a nice soft slope that also offers a lovely view of the sea. We lay down and with Marie-Hélène nestled into my side, the conversation returns to where we had stopped before lunch: me having been unexpectedly manoeuvred towards wedlock…

I could not agree to marriage; it was all a bit too sudden; it would have put unnecessary pressure on my girlfriend's daughter who was coming to her final two years at senior school, and to my mind – more pressure on us all. We returned to the subject regularly over the next week or so and what had first seemed almost an ultimatum, reduced to the suggestion of engagement, but when I questioned her about her change she repeatedly refused further discussion, returning to something akin to the original ultimatum with one path leading to marriage, and the other: separation. I concluded that I wanted someone with more openness and self-awareness than was being shown me, and on that basis, we parted.

Lying on the sandy beach on Skyros under the shade of gently waving branches, I feel blessed. Marie-Hélène has listened attentively, asking just occasional questions – and those mostly concerning the few words she was not familiar with. Remaining tucked in beside me, with her head laid on my chest, there seems to be no shortage in complete and honest sharing *here*. In fact, ever since our first talk, there has seemed to be nothing *but* complete and honest sharing.

We are due to be picked up at around four-thirty to be taken to our retreat location, and checking our mobile phones we find it is already after four. I am feeling hesitant about letting go – this part of the holiday, but there is nothing I can do other than to acknowledge my feelings and put some faith in the continuance of – well, whatever it is that is happening between us right now.

Hand-in-hand, making our way slowly back, I speak to Marie-Hélène of my hesitancy and she admits to such similar feelings. "But you know, we are both grown up. We can do what we please," she asserts. "You know, if things are difficult where we are going – we have our credit cards. We can always make a booking somewhere else – yes?"

It seems I must continuously be prepared for this woman to surprise me. She grounds me with her clear thinking and re-invigorates my confidence in – *whatever* may be. Nevertheless, we are both that bit quieter as we continue back towards the villa.

Suitcases at our sides, we are stood together in the courtyard, bathed in the late afternoon sun, and exchanging goodbyes with our hosts. They seem to be genuinely sad to be seeing us depart. I enjoy hugs with the grandson and with Ya-Ya; she must have said goodbye to so many people over the years, but her expression seems as authentic as if she had just said goodbye to family-guests. Perhaps that is something else to be respected in the Greek way of being: living in the now, and with *feeling*.

The minibus departs and I turn back to look through the trails of dust at the villa and offer a silent goodbye. These first few days have filled me emotionally and mentally beyond all expectation. What more can the next days – the purposeful retreat – possibly bring? How easy will it be I wonder, to pursue this blossoming relationship? Will we be encouraged to disassociate with one another for the good of the retreat? Will I be able to hold back if I am asked? Should I *want* to?

On the other hand, could the retreat expand the joyous bubble within which we would seem to be floating? So many questions…

What if the retreat causes the bubble to burst, showing the last few days to have been just a fleeting indulgence that lacks any basis for a future together?

"A future together…" really, I am thinking of this already?

I must slow down; pause. The monkey mind is feeding on my emotions (again).

As the villa disappears into the distance and the minibus turns a corner, I receive the sunshine on my face and I make an undertaking: I shall try to remain open to the *complete* journey, to – whatever.

A short fifteen minutes later, we arrive at the next coastal village and halt outside a small complex of apartments. We are in a small gravel car park separated from a large area of grass by a low whitewashed wall. Exiting the transport, we look around for signs of Karina and Jo-Anne who had travelled ahead. Karina shortly joins us to advise that a few finishing touches are required and that all must be "just right" so that we may be received "nicely" as planned, and with that she leaves us with some soft drinks and an atmosphere of anticipation.

Looking around a bit more, there are apartments staggered in pairs over to the left going down the property, and about another thirty metres beyond is a large house where – conceivably – our new hosts live. Placing my glass down on a table I hear Karina's voice, closely followed by Jo-Anne who tells us there is a table reserved at a taverna in the village, and that we will be gathering back here at about half-seven. Prior to that, at six-thirty, we are asked to convene at the veranda of the house.

In two's and a three, the group is split up and taken to their accommodation, leaving just me. Jo-Anne comes back. "Right Wayne," she says with a hint of excitement. "You have a room of your own, and in a very special place. I hope you will like it; it is not an apartment – like these," she continues as we walk past the first group of chalets. As we proceed, I am looking for the "something other", and I start to wonder if I might end up tucked away in a corner again. Having followed Jo-Anne through a series of winding paving stones, we pass between two globe lamps marking the entrance to the garden of the main house (and what a fine place too). Shrubs are growing profusely either side, with hundreds of tiny flowers overhanging the path. The flowers all seem closed for the day, (or perhaps they are finished for the season as well). Lining the path up to the house are box hedges and some low-level pavement lights. (Well, this *is* posh). The grass here is much finer and well kept, with manicured areas containing small shrubs and hardy flowers.

"Well, this is it Wayne. This is where you are staying. I hope it will be alright for you," Jo-Anne declares. We are directly in front of the big white house. Jo-Anne continues, "The family who owns this place vacate it in summer and trust us to take care of it all – which means we also have the use of this house here…well, some of it."

"It seemed unnecessary to hire another apartment for you when we have this, and there is a lovely room in here which we've used a number of times, and in knowing you from the London meetings, we know we can trust you to look after it," Jo-Anne finishes.

The house has an integral veranda taking up the leftmost two-thirds of an extensive single-storey section, with a two-storey modest tower in the right-hand third. A tree with an old gnarled trunk and a large canopy of green leaves grows directly in front of the house and leans at quite an angle. Upon approach, with it set against the white backdrop of the house, the old tree had the look of a giant bonsai.

Jo-Anne continues, "This veranda is where we hope to be holding our sessions every day. We would be so happy if you wouldn't mind just keeping an eye on this part, tidying up the cushions and such. There shouldn't be much to do and everyone is going to be given a few tasks to keep things ticking over. We'll talk more about that tomorrow morning."

Jo-Anne pushes aside a curtain to reveal a solid dark wood front door. "And, if the weather is *not* so good, we can go inside, here…"

Inside, there is a large open plan dining/lounge area with lots of wood – oak I think – and brass ornaments and woven wall hangings. It feels somewhat like a Spanish hacienda, or perhaps this is normal for the Mediterranean; I suppose I have not travelled so very much in Europe (or in Spain either come to think of it).

"The kitchen area is just here on the right, and…" Jo-Anne points to a dark wood staircase. "Your room is up there, beyond that lace curtain." I walk up and push the veil aside to find a room with such similar wood finish on the bed bases and surrounds and the curtain poles and with lace doilies on bedside cabinets, there is a very homely feeling of – well, wood and lace. On the left is a step up to a fully tiled modern ensuite; it feels quite in contrast to the rest.

"So, make yourself at home, the lounge area and the kitchen including the fridge and cooker are for your use, oh – but please don't use the rest of the house, because it is the family's private living space. If you'd like to come back to the communal area in a little while, we'll give you your provisions."

Jo-Anne departs and I am left to unpack and settle in.

At six twenty-five, having collected and stowed my breakfast provisions in a refrigerator *already* half-full, I go down to the veranda. Karina and Jo-Anne are arranging a small display on the table at the far end and placing some cushions for themselves just in front.

"Hello Wayne," Karina greets me. "I trust you are settling in. Do you like the house? We have been here many times over the years and the room you have has been used often by one of our friends' sons – right from when he was quite young."

"Yes, I think I will be very happy," I reply. "It seems very peaceful and I quite enjoy all the wood everywhere."

"Would you like to choose somewhere to sit, I think the others will be here soon – at least I hope they will." She then turns to address Jo-Anne: "Did you mention the timing?"

"Yes," Jo-Anne assures her. "Everyone was asked to be here for half-six and then to meet again later about half-seven to walk to the taverna."

"Oh good, thank you, Jo-Anne." Madelyn and Renna shortly arrive, followed closely by Doris, and then Angelica with daughter Beryl. There are several well-padded cushions which the ladies from middle Europe quickly set about re-arranging. Rachel then arrives and sets down beside Angelica, so – perhaps I should just sit where I now stand, at the doorway to the house, completing the guardian role I have been allotted. Marie-Hélène and then Henri come next, a few minutes late and looking embarrassed. Marie-Hélène sits against the wall to my left facing the retreat leaders, and Henri then finds a place beside her. I reach to my right towards the spare cushions, and Angelica and Rachel pass them to me, and I – onward to Marie-Hélène and Henri.

Karina declares the meeting open and welcomes us all to *this* place where, it is intended we will be meeting each morning. Regarding timings: six forty-five each morning for sunrise meditation at the beach and then breakfasting at leisure. ECOS starts at nine o'clock each morning in the communal area, and we are to be seated here on the veranda each morning by ten. We are asked to bring to the workshops: our writing equipment, water bottles and anything else we might need so that there might be the minimum of disruption until the finish time – around one o'clock. At one-thirty each afternoon we will gather out on the grass and walk to lunch at the taverna, the same taverna where we will be dining this evening. There will be a little homework in the afternoons, but then the rest of the day will largely be free. For those that would like to eat out in the evenings, it is suggested that six-thirty is a good time to aim for, and if we do not want to eat out, we can use any leftovers from lunch together with breakfast items to make a light supper – supplemented by whatever we might care to get from the local shop.

Next, we hear how the owners have vacated the site completely for us and – save for the gardener who may pop around now and again to tend to the watering etc., we will be left alone. This means that there is no one to tidy up after us and therefore, we are requested to take part in the daily housekeeping.

I am specifically invited – in addition to tidying the veranda after each session – to ring the wall-mounted bell at five minutes before ten a.m. each day.

Other duties such as tidying the communal area and arranging central displays for the veranda each day are quickly taken up, with Doris volunteering to ring a small handbell around the apartments at a quarter to ten each morning.

Finally, we are advised that the following days need not be looked upon as hard work; along with having a good part of the afternoons to ourselves, there is on Sunday, an island-tour for the whole day. There will also be time next Wednesday, to visit Skyros Town again or just chill-out generally. The general plan for our departure next Thursday is for an early morning start and two ferries to get us back to Athens. Oh, and this Monday we are all invited to join Jo-Anne to celebrate her birthday at an evening meal – yet to be arranged.

"Seven-thirty," Jo-Anne reminds us, "Seven-thirty outside on the grass in front of the apartments, and then we'll all take a lovely walk down the beach together."

At seven-thirty I am on the grassed area, in front of the apartments – alone. I do not generally find myself arriving particularly early on such occasions, so I am wondering if perhaps, I have missed out on a change of plan due to being somewhat remote. Hearing voices, I turn and look at the apartments…people speaking French: Henri and Rachel. It would seem simply, that everyone has already adopted *Greek* time.

On the beach, I slip off my sandals to enjoy the feel of the cool sand in-between my toes. I talk with Jo-Anne and she enquires as to how I am settling in the house. Jo-Anne then drops back, and I step up my pace towards Marie-Hélène and Henri who are laughing together. Maybe it is not so good to keep taking Marie-Hélène s' time and attention; at least, not when she is in the middle of a conversation. Perhaps, I should instead be thinking about how I might broach the subject of our being-together with Karina – perhaps even before the retreat gets underway. Then again, might Karina in turn approach Marie-Hélène and put her on the spot?

All this thinking! Or is this *worrying*? Well, if "worry" may be considered as "thinking" that has become repetitive without giving rise to meaningful decision or action, then no – this is not yet worrying; not if I stop it *now*.

Near the end of the beach, we file off in-between the buildings, and just a few metres later we are on the main street. There is no pavement or footpath so we stay largely in single file along the roadside. The sun has nearly set and we thus rely on the occasional street lamps, but after two minutes we are brought to cross the road, and then to turn back on ourselves, for with all our chatting we have managed to walk straight past the taverna!

After scaling a short driveway, we are met and shown to a large table on a sheltered terrace. I have found myself standing not so far away from Marie-Hélène. Rachel addresses Marie-Hélène and gesticulates towards a seat on the far side, which she moves towards. As others move to stand behind their seats, I find myself with the one remaining seat, across the opposite side…ho-hum. Most fortunately, however, the seat is situated beside the lovely Beryl who immediately makes me feel very welcome. Besides, I have the bonus of an uninterrupted view of Marie-Hélène *across* the table.

(Really? Did I just think that? I must be *quite* besotted!)

Bread and olive oil (sorry – *huile d'olive*) are brought to the table and shortly after, an adjacent long table is loaded with dish upon dish of food. Buffet dining is surely *the* most congenial of group arrangements. One can peruse and sample at leisure, choose one's portion sizes, return for second helpings (or more) and, most importantly, one can talk with those persons whom one may not be sat close to.

I do not know if the Greeks just tend to eat lots of vegetables or if they are doing this especially for us, but there is such a lovely range: warm pulses, legumes and plenty of appetising leaves along with tomatoes – fresh, baked, cherry, stuffed and Italian, then more bread, oils and balsamic, *and* of course – Feta; always there is Feta (and quite rightly).

It is not that I have so-purposefully arranged it, but when I go to sample a new dish (or indeed get a refill), I come across Marie-Hélène. As we discuss the dishes we have tried, I spot something on her plate that I have not sampled: "H'mm, that looks interesting. Where did you find it?"

"Here," Marie-Hélène replies, waving her hand in small circles (*somewhere*) "oh, try some of this, I can get some more in a minute," she continues as she puts her plate next to mine and pushes over most of her portion. Then, reaching across with her fork to my plate she says, "Oh this looks good, I will just try some of it," and not waiting for any reply, she takes a scoop of an aubergine bake. "…if you don't mind," she finishes, with it already poised at her smiling mouth. I am warmed with the intimacy she shows me in this exchange. I am also warmed by the way she sidles up, leaning her body against me, giving me another waft of her scent. Then, all at once she reaches across to my plate, takes another fork-full of the same aubergine bake, and delivers it directly to her mouth; aha – so, she entertains me as a means of misdirection; I like!

"Yes, I was right to take some of this, it is *very* good!" Marie-Hélène says through her laughter. "What!" she chides at my feigned distress. "You can get some more of it; you are closer than me." Then, nodding towards it on the buffet table she continues, "and maybe you will take some more for me at the same time."

Back at my seat, and with the further smiles offered across the table, I no longer feel apart from Marie-Hélène.

Turning my attention to Beryl (sat next to me) I encourage her memories of the weekend at Karina's we had both attended the previous year. I tell her how the young French lady: Marylene – who I had serendipitously met on the way to Glastonbury and had brought to the final evenings' gathering – had travelled onward with me to do some earth-energy work at Woodhenge (near Stonehenge, but with fewer tourists and far more vibrant energies), and how she had stayed with me for the best part of a week before flying off to a new adventure at a stud farm in Germany. (So confident, so special: these "earth-children" such as Beryl and Marylene.) Beryl tells me she is currently spending a lot of time with Karina, learning more and more about the Christos energy and how to channel and work with its power towards healing and peace. (*So special.*)

Then, we are interrupted, "time for dessert…" (!)

I shall not try to pretend that Greek desserts are particularly healthy, for there are far too many calories alone, but the ingredients are at least mostly natural and wholesome. Marie-Hélène and I reason we shall simply do plenty of swimming over the next few days…as we each take *another* piece of the nut and honey-rich Baklava. I cannot help but chuckle to observe Marie-Hélène pouring on additional honey. "What!" she exclaims, as she catches my eye. "Why not, this is not my third helping – like you!"

I say nothing. I just keep smiling…as she passes me the honey.

The walk back from the taverna is blissful. The sky is almost clear and the sand refreshes our feet as we stroll along together – sandals in hand, her hand on my arm. We have decided that it must now be clear to others that we are becoming friends, so it should not raise many eyebrows. "It is simply what good friends *do* in polite company." (It just so happens that we are recollecting our earlier lovemaking, which is not quite the topic of conversation the others might suppose). Confiding that I am happy and somewhat relieved to find that the new arrangements still enable us to spend time together, Marie-Hélène replies, "Of course. No doubt we will spend plenty of time together, and if we cannot find a place to be, we will just come here to the beach."

I find her words rather evocative – the beach part particularly, and I can only guess that my face must be "revealing" because she continues, "Yes – actually, I *did* mean here." Never have I experienced anyone with this mix of elegance, intelligence, humour, sensuality, and the boldness with which to express it all (let alone to me!)

Explaining to Marie-Hélène, the access I have to the house and the layout of my accommodation she hastens, "Oh, you are all on your own…I will have to visit you."

"I am not sure how it might seem…" I start to reply, but she interrupts, "What! What does it matter? Let the others think what they want, I am just coming to *visit* you."

Before we depart the beach, we turn to each other. With faces close, hers uplifted and our lips slightly parted, we commence the almost timeless experience that is *our* slow, peaceful kiss. I experienced it first in the water at the mill, then on the rooftop terrace last evening and in the shade just this afternoon, and it is here again; now. It hardly seems possible that in just one day, I have become *accustomed* to our kiss.

Upon passing through the modest white gate to the front of the apartments, we see – in the gentle glow of the courtesy lighting – the outlines of Rachel and Henri sitting on their patio. We approach and commence chatting with them. Shortly after, and being sure to be *seen* to be noting the time, I offer to Marie-Hélène that she might come to visit me, to sit on the sun loungers in *my* garden (jokingly), adding that we can watch the stars while our food settles. Having not received a direct response, I further offer to supply blankets and a cup of Greek Mountain tea.

"Yes, you go," Marie-Hélène then quickly replies. "I just need to put something a little warmer on first. I will join you."

Back in my room, I put on something extra as well: my new blue hoodie, purchased at Gatwick airport to replace the jacket I had left in my car (the purchase of which – coming with a large paper carrier bag – had led to the handy concealment of my mini-backpack and thus the avoidance of a "second cabin-bag" charge ☺). Grabbing two blankets, I head back to the garden where I pull two loungers out from beneath the tree and arrange them side by side. Having stargazed alone for some time, I begin to wonder where Marie-Hélène might be. With it being some twenty minutes since I had left her with Rachel and Henri, I consider the possibility that she has had second thoughts. Soon enough, however, I see a backlit figure strolling towards me, and as the slim silhouette gets close enough for the pavement lights to pick out the detail of white cotton trousers and a warm smile, I relax in the knowledge of Marie-Hélène's arrival.

"Allo!" she says. "I am sorry I have been so long. I wanted to spend a minute or two to talk with Rachel and Henri, then, when I go back – got back you say – to the apartment, my roommate was there, and she wanted to talk. Oh, I could not get *away*. She has not been sleeping too well and so I give her – have given her – some lavande oil which I have with me. She is okay now, I think."

"So," she continues, "…this is *your* house? It is very nice. I *like*. Oh, and I see you have prepared the chairs for us – *thank you*," she says in her best polite-English accent.

"Yes, and here is a blanket, just for you my dear," I offer, playing along.

Remaining in English mode, she says, "I am afraid I think I will not be able to stay out here very long." Sitting on the sunbed beside me she continues, "It may be the Mediterranean but you know – it is so much warmer in the South of France at this time of the year. I am not so *used* to it." Then dropping the accent: "…You say that?"

"Yes, that's exactly what we say."

She restarts her Sunday best: "Perhaps, we can go in and have 'a nice cup of tea' in a little while, but first," she continues, now dropping her accent. "Let's do *dis*," and getting up, and pushing her sunbed close to mine, she lays down and spreads her blanket over us both.

"Ahh, now that is better; and now I look up at the stars with you."

She reaches across under her blanket, searching for my hand. I reposition my blanket to overlap hers and under such cover, I take her hand in mine.

We are silent for quite some time. My mind is also silent – well mostly…for a little while at least…then, I am wondering if she is warm enough, and if having a cup of tea might provide the occasion for some more kissing, and then – I realise I am thinking unnecessarily again. Whatever will be – will be, and – tea or no tea, kiss or no kiss – when we are beside one-another like this, all seems well and the world seems at peace. (If only my mind would behave similarly.)

"Would you like that tea now?" I propose.

"Oh yes, please. I really am starting to feel the cold now."

Taking her blanket with mine I lead her up the few steps to the veranda where we slip off our sandals. I push aside the door-veil, open the door and – oh, no light! I have not yet thought to locate the position of the light switches, but recalling a bank of switches somewhere near the bottom of the stairs, I pigeon-step towards them. I work through each one observing which light works with which switch: the veranda light, another veranda light, the lounge side lights, the lounge main lights, the light above the dining area – *doh!* Then I see some *more* switches – down the steps towards the kitchen. Continuing: the outside light, the light to my staircase (oh, should I be putting this on?) I move quickly to put it off and find the kitchen light, but… "So here is your *room*?" Marie-Hélène enquires, as she places a foot on the staircase. "You will show me please (!)"

"Yes, yes of course but, shall I put the kettle on first?"

"Yes, good edea. I had thought of using the toilet back in my apartment, but I wanted to leave – to escape – and visit you, so now I *must* – up!" she calls to herself as she zips up the stairs – white against white, tan against wood.

I work through the switches again, finding the staircase one and next – the one to the kitchen. Whilst searching for a teapot and teacups – then deciding instead to use glasses, and finding a tray, I hear from upstairs, "So, this is your room."

Leaving the kettle to boil, I go up to find her surveying my bedroom. "Yes, isn't it a nice space".

"Yes, and all to yourself!"

"So it seems. Of course, you are most welcome to visit me anytime you like," I propose – now in *my* best English.

"Oh, I like," she says moving to me and pulling me into her embrace.

We kiss – quickly. "I've put the kettle on, and chosen the Mountain Tea for us."

"Oh good, I like that very much," she says. "You would like that now – yes?"

"Well, it does seem *right"* – I having made the offer when we were with Rachel

"You do not have to tempt me with tea to see you every time you know!" "Here I am, a lady in your bedroom, and you are offering her tea?" she says teasingly. I am fast realising that I can be both a little naïve and over-cautious, but Marie-Hélène is well aware and ahead of me once again. "So, okay tea then," she says, playing along, and heading off downstairs. At the bottom, she turns to me, "Actually, I am not saying the whole truth with you; I *like* to have some tea every night at home before I go to bed. I usually like *verviene* – we call it. Do you call it the same name?"

"Yes, I think so – well pretty much the same: 'vervain' we say; it has a slightly lemony or minty edge if it is the same tea."

"Oh, I don't know, you English, you have such different teas – and you put milk in them!"

"Oh no, not me – never," I assure her. "The only time I have milk in tea is either very weakly in Chai Tea, or a builders-tea – as we call it when someone has made it so strong that you can nearly stand your spoon up in it."

"Sorry, I am not sure I am understanding you?" she queries. Marie-Hélène speaks English pretty well and generally understands it well, but I have found that when I talk too fast and use jargon – the meaning can escape her.

"It has been many years since I have chosen to put milk in tea or coffee," I re-iterate.

"Ah, yes, I understand. You know, it was a surprise for me in Glastonbury once, when Rachel and I – we – sat and ordered a cup of tea one day and when it arrived, it had milk in it! We said 'please, please take this away.' Rachel and I, we laughed – so much!" I serve our tea in my lounge – without milk, and we drink, and we chat…then we drink some more… and we chat a little more. Then we kiss.

Marie-Hélène senses there is something on my mind, "So, what are you thinking? Tell me please." I tell her that I am feeling tired and, given that I have not slept well since before I came to Greece, I am wondering if I shouldn't listen to my body now and try to get a good sleep soon. "Besides that," I continue, "what with the retreat starting properly tomorrow and…" but Marie-Hélène stops me short to tell me she is in complete agreement: that it would not be good for both of us to turn up tomorrow with tired-eyes, and she points out that she has yet to find her apartment in the dark of night. Therefore, we kiss just once more, pulling away presently to avoid over-tempting our passions.

"Ah, you are so right. You can be very lucid you know, you English man! And I am also very tired too, to-*oo* – is it? Is it a 'to' with one 'o' or a *too* with two 'o's; please?"

"Yes, the two 'o's" I advise. (I think.)

Marie-Hélène gathers her things and finishes her tea. I open the door – then close it again to steal one more kiss, and then I watch as she walks down the path, and into the night.

In my bedroom and lying back on the bed, it seems I have practically *thrown* a beautiful woman out of the house. Yet, she was completely happy with the decision. It is so easy to talk about anything, discuss anything and to review and change our minds without reproach. I suppose it again stems from being able to speak from the heart. Even better, she seems to *listen* with hers; I am *so* lucky.

Beauty *Is* in the Eye of the Beholder
(Enter the Mosquitoes)

I wake…it is…oh, something after two, perhaps half-past – I *think*.

"Oh, I need the toilet," I say out loud. (To myself.)

I should have expected this after having a cup of tea just before going to bed. Still, I am very sleepy so if I do this without putting the lights on…if I can just find the bathroom, ouch – and negotiate this step… ah – there. Oooh, *that's* better.

"*Sleep* – again then…" (Please).

Upon stirring once more, I again look to the clock: four-zero-eight (!) I guess this is just "how it is". Yes, I can *cope* with the thought of seeing Marie-Hélène again in a few hours…and talking and laughing, swimming with her again and – oh yes – making love again. I must find a way soon to tell her how I feel. I suspect she already knows, but – it might not be so.

In the past, I guess I have mostly said those "three little words" in the form of "love-you" or "loving-you" – as in everyday conversation. Just now this finds me feeling rather uncomfortable: knowing I may only have said, "I love you," directly and sincerely – relatively few times in the past. However, what can anyone ever say – other than how they feel, or what they *think* they feel, and truly, it is only through feeling this new-deeper love vibration with Marie-Hélène, that I can now reflect on my previous experiences. [11]

I guess what love means to me at this moment is that: I am *here*, and Marie-Hélène is *beside* with the energy of love vibrating between us; "I / Love / You" – yes, that is how it feels. Moreover, after only a few days knowing Marie-Hélène, I feel no reservation in declaring, "I am in love"; well to myself anyway. However, does she feel/think the same?

(I really should try and sleep some more.)

By five forty-five I'm finished with sleep and with it being the first morning in this new location, I pull aside the light cotton curtain to look across the quiet

---

[11] Perhaps "authenticity" owes its meaning as much to honesty as it does to truth.

garden and up to a nearly cloudless pale blue sky. Lifting aside the lace-curtain at the top of the wooden staircase, I go down to the kitchen for some bottled water. Having gulped a glass full, I stare for a short while at the empty glass waiting for inspiration, and then realise what I'd really like is a cup of tea. Finding, however, that I have left my breakfast tea of choice – my lemon verbena leaves – back at the last place, I reach for the Greek Mountain Tea, and as I add hot water, I watch the leaves, flowers, stalks and – twigs (!) – swirling in the pale green. The heat releases the aromas of sage and camomile and instantly I am with memories of the night before.

With the aim of doing some yoga on the beach I check the time (six-twenty) and with mat in hand, I exit the house (leaving the door slightly open!) I pause at the presumed location of Marie-Hélène's chalet, but there is no sign of anyone stirring.

Upon reaching the open sands I am quite taken with the view. The silvery-blue light of the sky reflects off the almost dead-calm sea and the shallowest of swells ripple in from the distant horizon to form the tiniest of waves that produce the soft curling, pebbles-awash tones that only seashores can do. There are hints of deep purple in the few far-distant clouds and the purple blends with pinks and then with an orange-gold before dissolving into the horizon.

When I eventually resolve to *do* some yoga, I only have the time to bend over once before hearing voices behind. With brief nods and smiles, and the unrolling of mats and blankets, all participants form a regular pattern (including me) and Jo-Anne commences to lead *us* sun-worshippers once more. As Jo-Anne begins to offer words of greeting towards the sun that now broaches the horizon, there are "noises-off" as laughter quickly becomes muffled, and turning I see Rachel, Henri and Marie-Hélène approaching. Jo-Anne resumes her morning dedications and encourages us in our well-practised Sun Salutations (and variations there-of) after which we sit for a while in silence, held by the splendour of the sunrise.

Five or so minutes later, Jo-Anne rises and invites, "Now, do as you wish" reminding us that everyone is meeting for Morning ECOS at nine o'clock in the communal area. Seconds after, Henri is down to his swimwear and is walking in a resolute fashion towards the sea, closely followed by Marie-Hélène. They continue unabashed until neck deep, and it looks such a good idea – only: I have not thought ahead enough to put on my swimwear. Shamelessly however (my choice of underwear today resembling swimwear in all but its material) I discard my outer clothing and join them.

When Henri and Marie-Hélène appear to have finished talking, I swim over to be greeted by wide smiles and friendly enquiries as to how I slept last night. Trying not to look too much at Marie-Hélène I tell them (*both*) how I had woken early but happy, even if not yet having had a full night's sleep since arriving in Greece.

When Henri departs, Marie-Hélène tells me that on getting back to her room last evening, she had found her roommate awake and still wanting to talk. Seeming that talking was needed, Marie-Hélène went with it, but it meant she had, like me, slept poorly. We exit the water together still talking, but as Marie-Hélène starts to offer her towel to surround us both, the talking turns to laughter, "Maybe, we should *not* dry ourselves this way – here!" she says. (Yes, maybe.)

Once back at the apartments Marie-Hélène goes to the outside showers and rinses the sand from her feet. "What a good idea," I offer, as I follow-suit.

"Yes, but we say 'bonne idée' in French," she advises. "For 'good idea'. You know, I have showers on the beaches at La Napoule, do you have them at home in England?"

"Not anywhere near where I live. In fact, I cannot recall seeing any on the beaches at all in the UK, but then, we do not have many people swimming all year round as you say you do." Then, saying our short-while goodbyes, we depart to shower properly, looking forward to Morning ECOS in an hour or so.

Having showered and dried, I seek out my pendant and gather my thoughts for a moment. I settle on the intention "to allow the universe to bring me what is needed and help me to let go of what is not" and placing the cross in my right palm, I "breathe" the intention as to pass it into the pendant, and fasten it around my neck.

In the kitchen, I choose some fruit and slice them over a porridge-muesli mix made with Greek yoghurt (as my first course), then turn to the refrigerator with the idea of some scrambled eggs and feta on toast to follow (one cannot let them go to waste.) Cutting two slices of wholemeal for toasting, I am just turning back to remove the eggs when I briefly catch sight of a figure dressed in white, approaching my veranda. There is a knock at the door and a voice calls out, "H'ello, may I come in?" It is (of course) Marie-Hélène. "Rachel and Henri would like you to join us – oh and me – for breakfast, if you would like?" She comes straight to me, melts into my body and offers me her lips – just briefly.

"Oh yes, that *would* be lovely," I bluster, "but I have just cooked up some eggs, though I guess I can plate them, although they won't stretch far."

"No problem. We have lots of things. We can mix it up and share or you can just eat your eggs," she offers. "M'mmm, they smell very good; I think I will just try some," she continues, taking my fork from the table and dipping it into the pan to take a sample.

"Oh yes, the Feta – it works *so* well with the eggs! You know, we do not eat eggs d'is way in South of France. I usually only eat them like that when I come to England – sorry – *go* to England. M'mmm," she takes some more, swallows and then encourages me further with, "Come, we go!" heading out through the kitchen door.

"I just have to put something on my top," I advise. "Oh yes," she giggles, regarding my naked chest. I run upstairs, put a fresh top on and return in seconds. "And err, can you take my tea out for me – it is over there in the glass; please?"

"Hah! De English man and his tea. Come, come – we go!" Following Marie-Hélène through the patio-door at Henri's and Rachel's apartment, I am greeted warmly by Rachel. "Oh Wayne, you *can* join us. I am so glad. And you have already prepared something?"

"Yes, just some scrambled eggs," I reply.

"And I have the English man's tea," adds Marie-Hélène from behind me.

"Oh, you have *tea*, here?" enquires Rachel. "Oh, I see, without milk, and in a *glass*" she observes. "And do you usually take tea that way, Wayne?"

"Herbal teas – yes, and often in a glass when I am able too." I feel flattered to have been invited, but although I am greeted warmly, I am reminded of Rachel's particular enquiring way. Henri is busy in the kitchen area but turns briefly to say, "Bonjour," before returning to his task.

"Well, I think you should go ahead and sit down," Rachel suggests. "And if you like, do please eat your eggs before they get cold."

Rachel leads me outside to a small rectangular table already quite full of sliced fruit, bread, and honey. Henri comes out with another chair. "There," he says, "now, we are four. Come, come sit."

Despite the suspicion that my eggs are cooling fast, I ignore the pre-empted experience of cold eggs and damp cheese, I wait until we are four. Just before we commence to eat, and having noticed my hands lifting towards a loose prayer position, Rachel addresses me, "Oh, so you would like to say grace – sorry…"

"No, not grace, no," I reply somewhat hurriedly.

"Well, what is it? Do tell us, Wayne?" Rachel encourages politely.

"Well, it is *'It-a-daki-masu'*. As I understand it, it is a way the Japanese briefly but reverently offer thanks for the food; in particular, expressing thanks for what the Earth has given, and respecting the contributions made by all concerned with getting it to the table." I feel somewhat under the spotlight, but I continue, "I think the simplified Japanese translation is *'I humbly receive'*."

"Oh, that is lovely Wayne, thank you for sharing that with us," Rachel says kindly – instantly relieving my slight embarrassment. "So, what is it again…eata-tikki-takki?" she says looking to Henri and Marie-Hélène and then, as if to prompt further laughter she repeats: "Eeeta-ta-tikki-takki."

As I lift the first fork of scrambled eggs-on-toast to inquisitive gazes, Marie-Hélène contributes with, "Yes, and zey taste *so* good. I know; I stole sum of zem earlier!"

A feeling of embarrassment starts to arise at not having offered to share the little I had, but for sure, I might feel just as uncomfortable if I were to have offered a measly part-portion of cold damp eggs and cheese. The smiles and the general warmness of the others, however, soon cause my discomfort to evaporate, and barely a minute later I am reflecting on how few occasions in recent years I have been part of such a cosy family type experience. Therefore, to celebrate what has been the most joyful Greek breakfast I have yet experienced, I follow Marie-Hélène in a second helping of fruit and yoghurt.

When Rachel enquires of the time, we realise we have just fifteen minutes before the Morning ECOS, and so in stark contrast to the preceding half an hour, I make a hurried grab for my dirty dishes and rush back towards my accommodation. At the entrance to the garden, however, I am confronted by a strange sound. My initial response is to look up to locate where the overhead power lines *must* be – such is the intensity of the sound, but instead, what I see around me are many-many bees, working intensively to gather the pollen. Their buzzing is not so much loud as emotionally pervasive, and upon feeling quite moved and wondering why, I then recall experiences of being in, and listening to – a choir. [12]

With the group waiting, I walk to the communal area where it is Beryl's turn to open ECOS and she leads us by the most calming of voices on a beautiful tour of a forest and into a "crystal heaven" and back.

---

[12] How precisely – how beautifully even – the mind works to bring emotions to the present, as a means of re-presenting us with experiences of the past.

The tone of ECOS is overall, more purposeful today, focussing our minds towards the work we have come to do here – on and *with* ourselves. The words of Rachel bring this ECOS to an end and we return to our rooms to ready ourselves for the first workshop at ten o'clock.

Having planned to go down to the veranda in good time to perform my first bell-ringing duty and then to stay there and greet everyone, I am frustrated by not being able to find my writing pad and pencil. With barely a minute to spare I sprint downstairs to commence the bell ringing that denotes the "fifteen-minute call". Almost immediately after, Doris walks out onto the grassed area and begins to ring her (five-minute) bell. I pop into the house to check my clock…Doris had been on time.

Jo-Anne is first to arrive and having acknowledged me, and I her, she goes to a discreetly placed music player and "The Holy Harmony" begins to float out on the air. It is a much-used recorded chant from – I think – the nineties (well used by those attending the London group that is). Karina arrives next, and because she also enjoys my silent greeting, I stay in place to welcome the rest as in twos and threes – and ones in Marie-Hélène's case – they arrive.

The volume of Holy Harmony is increased and Karina invites us all to sit and *feel* the chanting – joining in if we should like.

"*Yod-hey Shin Vav-hey,*" we – most of us – say.

The words come from the Hebrew name of /for God YHVH, with the Shin added in the middle to represent the arrival and placement of the ever-present eternal flame: the Christos light, as made manifest in human form some two thousand years ago in the form of Yeshua/Jesus/The Christ (many names apply). I may not be swayed generally towards "belief" [/belief systems – of religious origin [13]] but I have for some years enjoyed the experience that has come to me when, and after sitting with Holy Harmony, (and I do *enjoy* singing).

We sit now as the "2016 Skyros Retreat Group" come together to listen and to talk, to learn, understand and to let-go – and maybe to *find*.

"Consider that which you have brought to Skyros," Karina invites, and having been given a canvas and a pencil, we are invited to draw something to represent what first comes to mind. My immediate response is one of feeling a bit like a fish out of water, but I suppose I am accustomed to expressing things with a pen or pencil – if only through writing. So okay, I just need to hold open

---

[13] See Appendix II: Caught-up in belief systems of religious origin

a space for something to come to me in pictures, or for words I can turn into pictures…

In the bottom left quartile of the canvas, I draw a heart shape and then behind/upon it, another heart-shape. I draw some fainter broken outlines to the hearts that have a sort of ripple-like feel to them, giving a sense of vibration or harmony/synchronicity, or at least – an energetic aspect that shows some linking of, or interaction between the two. This is all very "lovey-dovey", but having just recently met Marie-Hélène, I could so easily offer myself the rhetoric: "just as expected?" However, my intuition continues, and I accordingly pursue each perception and find myself drawing what seems to be a wall (or something similar) in front of the hearts, but with a large gap in it. Enthusiastically, I try following through with what I *think* should probably be there, however, almost as soon as I try to think ahead, the ideas stop flowing, the mind-space from which they came – closing down. Accordingly, I take an eraser to where I had started over-interpreting, to the point where the "flow" had stopped. I am back to the wall I had first drawn – the gap being just enough to reveal the hearts. "Okay, that's fair enough," I say to myself. "So, the hearts are now accessible – open – to love…to…?" However, just as I begin to *think* again, the flow of inspiration stops – again. Once more I recommence – slowly – completing the walls based on the thoughts and images still in my minds-eye, but it is not going quite as I had thought, because I am sensing that the walls are of brick and that they form gateposts. Feeling somewhat deflated, I nevertheless accept the initiative and start to draw the gates closed across the hearts…and the flow stops again. Okay, so the gates are not fully closed, but now I am left wondering if these gates are on the way to opening or closing?

There feels to be the potential for the gates to be opened fully to access these two hearts and even if the gates come to close sometime, the hearts are still *there* – together, synchronised, and can still be accessed by the gates another time. (Am I getting carried away here again?)

I add some further detail to the gates – just to make them look a little more "gatey". I guess life is much like this drawing: there is always the potential for things seeming to be better or worse depending on perception, with all things subject to change. So, what would it take – I wonder – to have these gates open *really* wide?

Karina asks us to come back together as a group and I come out of my inner world. She asks that we work in pairs to share and discuss our drawings, investigating what they might reveal about what we have brought to Skyros. Oh dear, I had forgotten, the drawing was supposed to represent what we had brought with us. Doesn't mine tell more about what is just now happening? (Or maybe not.)

Rachel turns partially towards me and smiles. I turn myself right to sit opposite and so offer my complete attention, and because I do not want to entertain any more *thinking* concerning my drawing I propose to go first. I make mention of the theme coming from my meditations and development work the last year or so re: "meeting a special someone." When I begin to talk about the "longing" I have occasionally felt towards finding someone, I purposefully understate the emotional aspect. I point to the gates being partly open, but then confide my concern that they might be on their way to closing. Then, without thinking I continue, "So clearly, this retreat has the ability to show me what is needed for the gates to open." I halt, dead in my tracks. I have just said some words I had not expected to hear; words I had not *thought* of. The words are very engaging. The words yield good sense.

Rachel has been smiling patiently throughout, but, now that I have stopped talking – I see she is glancing over my shoulder towards Henri, or perhaps to Marie-Hélène. Yes, of course, the "two-hearts" might well represent me and Marie-Hélène, but I wonder, what else she may have been thinking, or what she might even have been saying to Marie-Hélène. (I am thinking unproductively – again.)

Karina had earlier asked that we not comment on each other's drawings so as not to impose our own meanings, however, we were told we could ask one or two questions concerning features that would seem to stand out. In that vein, Rachel enquires of what, indeed, it might take to have those gates open further. I just find myself repeating some of the things I had already said, finishing with, "I really don't know. Perhaps that's still what I need this retreat to show me; because I've not found the answer before."

Have I misunderstood Rachel's question; is there something deeper, perhaps, that I am not seeing? She thanks me for sharing, and feeling relieved I settle back to listen to her.

As Rachel talks me through her drawing, I note it is characterised by the straightness of its lines, going from the bottom-left towards top-right on the canvas. Rachel interprets this as meaning, "On-track, revved-up and ready to go," taking her where she has always wanted to be. She then expands: "The sky's the limit Wayne…no – the sky is not the limit!" and goes on to emote. "Whoosh – up there to the top: there is nothing now to stop me. It is time to go straight up there – whoosh!" she repeats.

My points for Rachel concern just *how* strong the "straightness" theme features within the picture, and I invite her to reflect on why there is little else but straight lines and in one general direction. Rachel simply reinforces – positively and resolutely – her previous interpretation: that the drawing tells her path now is just so clear, so simple and so unimpeded.

I am very happy to hear Karina calling "Time". I cannot help having some other interpretations of what Rachel has drawn, and if given the time I might have found it difficult *not* to offer such a question as, "Are you sure you have not simply drawn what you want as your future?" [14] However, what I know of Rachel suggests she is such a nice person that I would not want to challenge her unnecessarily. Even if there is some good worth in such a question, the truth will, in any case come-out at some point in time, either to challenge or indeed to confirm Rachel's perceptions; after all – isn't that what time is for? Alternatively however, am I being crass: one might also have asked the same question about my picture? Perhaps she has granted me the same grace in allowing me – my perceptions. Therefore, what else can I do: I smile and thank her similarly – for her sharing. Accordingly, we hug. The hug is meaningful; it truly is…I just *love* retreats.

Being the time for a toilet-break, we are asked to turn our drawings so they cannot be seen, and not to talk any further about them.

Once back on the veranda, we are told our next task will be to choose an object to refer *to*; but – first, we are invited to be still and open ourselves to a guided meditation…

---

[14] When someone presents an opinion with (too) much confidence and assertion, it could indicate there is a nagging doubt that is being pushed aside. The expression of truth on any matter does not usually need vigorous assertion; the truth, simply and peacefully – just *is*.

Karina asks us to visualise a host of colourful images, finding ourselves on a path through wonderful and nurturing scenery that brings us to a place where we are invited to access: our Life Angel. When I sit still to access that place/space within, I can often perceive words arising that hold great meaning.

Whether there is an angel or any other manifested intelligence waiting at my shoulder – I know not, but today and right now, I definitely sense a "presence". There is not a voice with this presence but I perceive a feminine – loving wisdom.

Without further thought, I reach for my pencil and pad…

My Angel Guide talks and I feel the impression of two hearts.

Two hearts that share purpose, that have shared purpose before but in this life being positioned so as to come together in joyous + productive union.

Both experiences of being in this world has involved much learning already that will help in healing past-life karmic residues & position both so as to give practical advice to others based on this-life experiences & the deeper spiritual understanding that is in both.

Until this time, both hearts have been bound by past life & spiritual purpose so as to open to one another at the right time in this life.

I put down my pencil and hold my writing pad in my hands to read again what I have just written. "Healing past-life karmic residues," is not a phrase I recall *ever* having read or heard mentioned, and the idea that experiencing so many aspects and forms of healing have had the purpose of enabling me to advise others based on practical experience – seems entirely sensible, but this is also new to me. Moreover, the words say something similar about the other "heart". This could all simply be from my subconscious – my conditioned mind – wherein the monkey-mind plays. Fortunately, I have been on enough retreats and development workshops to be neither alarmed nor elated off-hand; however, the tone and the choice of words here are either not mine or, they come from a very new and well-constructed alter ego unknown to me. *If, however,* these words are from another place, a place of wisdom; *if* they are not a mischievous ego giving me what it wants me to hear then – okay, and – wow, these words would seem to leave so very-little margin for doubt. [15]

(Moving onward – to the task as previously mentioned…) Karina invites us to stroll through the garden (the real garden of this house) and take time to look for one particular feature or object that attracts our attention. If possible, we should gather it and bring it back with us and if – after the bell is rung in about fifteen minutes – we have not chosen anything, we should return to the first thing that captured our attention and bring that back. Henri is having some difficulty understanding what Karina is saying. He talks and understands *some* English, but mostly the sort of words that one might use at work or in a restaurant. However, Marie-Hélène is at hand and soon he is nodding and smiling.

I take my time to rise, allowing the rest of the group to file out into the garden ahead of me. Once down the steps, and looking down along the garden path, I take in the sunshine, the aromas, the shapes and colours and within a few seconds I feel attracted to some small yellow flowers on long stems arching out over the path that runs the perimeter of the house. They have the shape of a champagne flute that opens into separate petals of a golden cup approximately two centimetres across. Observing most of the group busily sampling a number of things, and not wanting to succumb simply to the first thing that attracts me, I decide to indulge the opportunity further. After all, if this flower is to be my object, I will be coming back for it.

I walk the inner circumference of the garden, and then head out onto the grass pausing to find the sound of the bees, but finding there are now only a few. Finding nothing further to interest me, I return to the path around the house. On the way round, I come across some fragrant wallflowers in shades of dark-red,

---

[15] Re: "a mischievous ego giving me what I want to hear": it is often useful – and occasionally very productive – to observe ones' thoughts from various perspectives; particularly when one wants to make some sense of what they mean or where they have originated. *

* I must admit, there have been occasions when, subsequent to an experience of most-interesting thoughts/perceptions arising without/within, the only resolution I could find was through accepting that one of two possible states may be relevant – either: i) something within this experience is so *real*, or: ii) I am going mad. **

** This only stopped when – after being so fatigued with repeated "real vs. mad" events, I chose no-longer to differentiate/label the two: if such experiences influence my decisions as to take me away from suffering – towards more joy and/or understanding, and if they appear to bring others towards the same – why worry! (But at some point, of course, all the '*' just must stop so that normal life can be resumed!) ***

*** "*normal*"?

deep orange and rusty browns. As I bend and take in their scent, memories of my childhood home flood back, and with them, I recall little pink and orange flowers that had grown near them; "bunny-rabbits" my mother would call them, which when squeezed gently near their base, caused the flowers to open like a rabbit's mouth. Should I take one of these perhaps? No, whilst they give rise to pleasant memories, they are of the past; I feel more inclined to seek something of the future…

The bell rings the end of fifteen minutes, and so I go back to the first yellow flowers, plucking a full-bloom (and a significant piece of its stem) as I pass. Back on the veranda, it seems that a few others have also chosen a flower. Rachel, however, has a long blade of grass, while another has a twig, and another – a small branch. Henri, meanwhile, holds in his hands a small silver plastic spoon.

Karina asks that we now write down a few words to summarise what we experienced while looking for our objects, and then write down what we think our object might have thought if it could communicate with us about *its* experience. I write…

Object Referral – flower

- *finding something of beauty easy to be attracted to then thinking it is /may not be the right one*
- *looking for something else that might be better (to someone else's understanding)*
- *finding such detail in the flower – stem, cup, leaves, centre*
- *finding inconsistencies, defects/deformities, variations,*
- *feeling movement around me, time passing, sometimes feeling a connection, being appreciated, being nurtured by watering, empowered by sun*
- *life taking place around me, within me.*

When asked, I readily volunteer to read what I have just written. In the process of reading, I notice that the tense of my words changes gradually from me *describing* the flower, to – *being* the flower. I am not sure what may have happened in this exercise, but I guess I will find something deeper in the words some-other time.

139

The rest of the group follow on: showing their objects and sharing the words they have written. Rachel presents her long leaf and says it shows her how to grow and where to grow – up; and it reminds her of her drawing – indicating "straight-up" with her hand as she speaks.

Beryl presents a dainty shapely leaf and says that a butterfly had landed on it when she was watching it in the garden; that she had wanted to bring in the butterfly, but that of course, it had flown away. She says that if the leaf was good enough for the butterfly, then it is certainly good enough for her, and that it offers her the memory of being touched by the grace and beauty of the butterfly that had, for a while, entered her life.

The last to speak is Henri. Expecting that he will not be understood, he starts by offering an apology: "I will try and speak English, but if I am stuck…" he offers, lifting his hands in an "I don't know what" gesture. Having not attended such a workshop before Henri is probably feeling very-much "in at the deep end" as he tries to do what men usually feel un-crafted to do: get in touch with feelings and share them with others – and additionally in this case: in a different language!

Karina invites, "Just have a go, and if you do get stuck Henri, well – I am sure Marie-Hélène will help you out. Just try."

Henri lifts the small silver plastic spoon. He says that he realises everyone has chosen mostly flowers and natural things, but we were told we should choose something we are attracted to and this is it (turning it over within his fingers). He says he enjoyed the way the light reflected off the surface like a curved mirror and that as he lifted it from the ground, he saw in it the reflections of colours around him, including the colour of his clothing and colours in his face and things. He repeats he is not sure he has found the right thing, but that he hopes we understand him okay. We do understand him. Through his mannerisms, it is evident he is experiencing a lot of emotion. We do not need to know why; we are just humbled by his courage at taking part in what to him must feel a strange and revealing exercise. Karina thanks and congratulates him for his efforts and his success which just serves to move Henri even more, and he speaks to say how he cannot see the beauty in the spoon itself but that he sees the other beauty reflected in it.

I cannot hold back from offering some words of support that now come to me: "Henri, if you would care to just lift the spoon to see your face in it, you will be looking at the beauty that we can all see in you."

Henri appears quite moved by all the appreciation being offered, and as tears well in his eyes – I feel blessed by his participation.

Karina asks that we sit still for a while and invite our Life Angels to come close and whisper in our ears something extra: something special – something just for us. It sounds almost far-fetched to hear "angels" mentioned again, but making an allowance for the human need of imagery to service belief, I try to discount my *dis*-belief. In seconds my endeavour is unexpectedly rewarded by the opening of another *space*, and the shapes of words fill my senses. I write:

*Believe you can be loved for **all** that you now are and all you are becoming.*
-M.

Before I can get the last few letters written, I find that tears have now come to *my* eyes. I know not what the tears mean. It is not sadness; it is more alike to…loving support. I feel…released, and there seems an invitation to receive and understand another word: *acceptance*.

Still looking at what I had written, I see at the end – the initial "M". So – who/what is "M"?

I close my eyes and try to seek out a flow of understanding – but there is none. Being emotional, I feel unable to *reconnect*, so I resort to re-reading what I had written. In years gone by, an "M" has often come with the name "Michael" associated with it, but there has not usually been much by way of emotional content – just a sense of wisdom and connection. One other "M" I recall is from "Mary" in more recent years, but I cannot say that I sensed the Mary presence just now…although – yes, the feeling now – of *loving support*, and the *softness* – yes, actually, I *can* associate these with the Mary presence.[16]

The morning has brought me much more than I might have expected; perhaps the last few days have been something more of a preparation for this retreat than I had thought.

Before we prepare for our walk to lunch, we are told that for our homework, we should go to the communal area with our drawings where there will be some

---

[16] It can become a distraction to actively seek identities/characters when I experience inspired/random words. Nowadays, I am more inclined to allow the words/thoughts to flow until they stop, and then allow the meaning to be taken directly – without being coloured by the perceptions/misperceptions that can arise when one actively tries to attach an identity to the origin. However, in this case, the "M" simply came; it was not sought.

acrylic paints, brushes, and pots of water. We are to take our drawings, decide on a colour, and wash the entire canvas in that one colour – obliterating the pencil. (Well, that sounds easy enough.)

Everyone is subdued – perhaps with thoughts of what is yet to come. A retreat often involves sharing – even though the general aim is to plunge the depths of ones' self, alone. Although one never knows what might be found when the doors to the inner-mind are opened, a group retreat means – at least – we will be together in *going alone*.

§

At one o'clock (or thereabouts), I arrive at the grassed area outside of the apartments to find some have already left. After a minute I realise I am waiting for Marie-Hélène without knowing if she has already gone, so I decide to investigate. Popping my head into the apartment that (I think) is Marie-Hélène's, I am greeted by her roommate who tells me Marie-Hélène has just left with Rachel and Henri. I offer that I might instead wait for *her*, but she declines saying she is finding it a difficult to rush anything at the moment and would rather go at her own pace.

Therefore, I start off in a trot, and as I pass the bushes at the edge of the beach I am greeted by a lovely view of golden sand and blue sea and the warming sight of the group in ones and twos – walking, talking, stumbling and laughing as dresses and shawls and hair are blown by the wind. Marie-Hélène and Rachel are walking arm in arm, but appearing they are in deep conversation I opt for remaining behind and enjoying the view.

It strikes me, just how empty the beach is. Jo-Anne told us only Greeks generally visit the island and only locals tend to come here, but still – it seems *so* empty. I guess the locals are mostly back at work and that summer has already passed for them.

We exit the beach before the point we had reached last evening, and many begin removing their sandals to release sand, stones, and such. The route appears to be an alley between two large properties, and both are as quiet and empty as the beach. As I walk, I become aware of something soft being compressed beneath my feet. On looking ahead, I see large fig leaves overhanging the path, and then I see the squashed fallen-figs beneath – and behind where I have just walked. Some of the fruit are still whole but they are all rather mushy and accordingly, there is a sweet figgy (!) smell – and a sort of toffee aroma along with it. I am saddened to observe the fruit that I enjoy so much in the UK – being left to fall and rot away. How often it is, that we perceive an object's "worth" by the measure of its availability, instead of by any unique/intrinsic characteristic.

Crossing the road and turning at the entrance to the taverna, I find Marie-Hélène stood aside and looking my way. *"Allo."* she says, smiling, "So, where shall we sit?"

Lunch evolves to be both relaxing and filling – entailing light conversation and (several) visits to the buffet table. After the first helping of bread and oil and the (first) helping of "mains", I return for *"just a little bit more of something"* before dessert. Marie-Hélène appears at my side and looks somewhat mischievous as she scans the buffet table.

"Ooh that was nice," she says gesticulating rather generally. "Yes – oh, and that…" she says, addressing a dish close to me. "Yes that – please, could you get some more of that for me?"

I reach to the dish and scoop out a "sharing" portion, but when I turn, she has gone-off in search of something else. I put the entire helping onto my plate, and then skirt around the table to join her. She is now looking at some freshly cooked chips.

"Mmm, they look *good*!" she declares. "Look, my plate is almost full again already," she says nodding to it. "Can you take some chips onto your plate for me, and I will share some of my tomatoes and salad with you."

Marie-Hélène's plate appears not so full; it has some leaves and tomatoes on it but it would appear to have plenty enough space for chips. "Yes, sure," I reply.

"Okay – good, we are done, we go!" she concludes.

As we sidle towards our seats, I notice that Marie-Hélène's plate looks to be nicely full of very healthy leaves, tomatoes and Feta, whereas, anyone looking at my plate would see it stacked with baked stuffed peppers swimming in olive oil, pasta and bean bake topped with cheese and a sizable pile of chips. (A-ha!)

As soon as we are sat, Marie-Hélène reaches over, transfers a stuffed pepper onto her plate and then proceeds to give me a few leaves and tomatoes. As she eats, she helps herself to the chips from my plate. I offer to put some chips onto her plate but she declines, assuring me that she doesn't want very many at all. Never the less, she continues to help herself to the chips from my plate, and until they are all gone.

We walk back to the accommodation slowly, Marie-Hélène linking her arm into mine without a mind to whom-else might see (though to be fair everyone else is some way ahead). We cannot wait to get into the sea to find out what is under the surface here, but all the same, we agree not to hurry to give our food the time to settle.

At three-thirty I am on the grass outside her apartment, feigning nonchalance. Marie-Hélène has advised me several times that she is not particularly good at timekeeping, so I am not concerned with waiting. When she emerges, she is already in her orange bikini and with her towel hung over her shoulder. Walking to the beach Marie-Hélène recounts something of the morning with me. "That was so good you know – Henri has not been to anything quite like this before. I am sure Rachel is very happy. I think he makes very good progress. Don't you?"

"Yes, I can understand why Rachel and you might be very happy for him."

"You know, most of my friends are not all into this: courses, meditations, retreats and things. They must think I am quite mad. You know, one of my friends 'as said he is quite concerned I may be part of a "sect" you know, like some crazy religious group. He thinks I might be giving all my money away to it." She laughs. "I have some friends with who I have done yoga – with – for some time. I have been on some yoga retreats – in fact, I have a friend who *is* a yoga teacher – *was,* a yoga teacher. I would see him once or twice a week, but now he is older and he does not do the teaching. He is writing a book about yoga. He thinks that most of the yoga done nowadays is not *real* yoga – just exercise. He spent much time with a Yogi Master and he wants to try and pass what he was taught onto others. But you know, it is strange, I do not find him very spiritual. I thought he would talk about and be interested in such things, but no."

"That's interesting," I add. "It seems to me that one of the main purposes of yoga is to help one towards meditation, towards stillness – sort of, using the connection with the body to focus within, and that the connection to the spiritual might naturally follow."

"Yes, me also – but no, that side does not seem to interest him so much."

"You remember me saying, the lady I was with had been a yoga teacher, well she only finished her teacher-training the summer I met her, and she had even been on a Vipassana retreat and such…"

"And yet I think you said she was not happy with what you were doing with spiritual developments?"

"Exactly! No, it was strange; it was like she also had some fear of me being taken over or controlled I guess."

"Ah, so it is like my friend and his *sect!*"

"Yes. Isn't it strange how people can fear something they do not understand," I reflect.

"Ah, or maybe we are both mad!" she says, prompting our laughter. With no one but ourselves in the entire bay, we drop our towels, put on our masks and get straight into the sea. Immediately we put our heads underwater, we find the water is clearer than at the last place. There are no signs of fish, but we are in the part which has no rocks or stones for the fish to shelter under or feed on, so we agree to head over to the rocks and cliff face to the right.

At last, a fish! Then another…or was it the same one again…well, things are at least starting to shape up. The rocks appear to be bare: without shellfish, urchins and suchlike, and not much of seaweed either, but it is nice just looking and floating. Nearing the cliff face, we get closer, lift our masks, kiss, and then we talk. It seems Marie-Hélène has not spotted a single fish yet. She usually wears glasses of course, so I guess looking for sandy-coloured fish against the seabed was always going to be a bit of a challenge, but I tell her she is not missing so much. We decide to try the bay a bit further down; it looks only to be about another hundred metres away.

Ten minutes or so later we find ourselves in a small rocky cove with the seabed a mix of rocks and sand. It looks all quite lovely and natural above, but under the surface to one side of the bay, there is an assortment of sea-debris including a significant amount of waste such as plastic bags – floating just under the surface. The clear plastic bags look like ghostly emaciated jellyfish; the black and grey plastic bags are simply an eyesore – just plain sad and ugly. Just to top it off, I start to see occasional beer bottles and cans on the seabed. Not a pretty sight.

We lift our masks: "No fish!" we say simultaneously, breaking into smiles at our synchronicity. I can only gather that Marie-Hélène had been hoping for a deserted sandy bay as well, because she now wraps her arms around me, pulling me into another kiss. Only seconds later however, our kiss is countered by a wave which pulls us apart. We try again: a few more seconds of kissing, but then we are parted once more.

"Perhaps," I say spitting out water. "Perhaps, if we get really-close we can float together, like the other day."

"Ah, the thinking man," she retorts. "And, what are you thinking about!"

She knows full well of course: the rocking of our bodies against one another, the hugging, the brushing of skin on skin *and* the kissing. It has excited us both. I can see it in her eyes.

"Okay, let's try – you crazy Englishman."

She moves close and with her legs around my waist, I pull her closer still, until we are one floating love-bundle. The water still splashes up into our faces but with our noses held clear of the waves, and our lips sealed around one another's, the water does not interfere.

Marie-Hélène settles herself deep into my lap and wiggles. "What even here!" she says jovially.

"I think I am always ready for you my darling," I (try to) say romantically. "M'mmm, I like – my lover…" she whispers as her passion begins to rise. We are already finding each other's bodies to be – *familiar*. Yet, at the same time, there is nothing customary about it, for every touch feels new and exciting.

Her hand wrestles for some seconds to release me, and then she settles herself back down. I reach under her, and as per yesterday, I pull aside the thin material that is the only thing now separating our pleasure. We meet, and we *meet*, and her head tips forward to rest on my shoulder as she murmurs in my ear.

Once again, the ocean is no obstacle to our love. It does admittedly, put us off balance rather, but as we move in keeping with the sea's rhythm the bobbing up and down feels more like an encouragement than a disadvantage. In just a few minutes, our lungs and our voices reveal above the surface – those pleasures that are accumulating below. Marie-Hélène's fingers dig into my back and her arms and legs begin a series of clenching and releasing movements. As I start to feel my own wave rising, it is all I can do to support us and hold our balance. All at once, both our heads tip back to voice our joy and to permit our gasping lungs to fill with air.

It is so tempting to stay just like this, but we are both practical – "lucid" as Marie-Hélène puts it, and accordingly we let-go our arms. Marie-Hélène's legs, meanwhile, are showing some reluctance, and for a few seconds we bob and drift together connected at the thighs. After gazing at one another's sea-soaked smiling faces for a few more seconds of *forever*, we disconnect and drift apart. However, with neither of us *entirely* satisfied yet, we come back together into another embrace. We connect in a kiss – but only for a moment, then the water parts us once more.

The breeze feels that bit cooler, the sun has virtually set, and as I glance around – the cove that had first looked so inviting now feels grey and slightly foreboding. "If we start back, we should get a little warmer from swimming, and perhaps we'll find the sun when we are nearer to the beach," I offer, still rather hopeful. "Ooo…bbbrrr – yes, we go!" she replies and mask down, snorkel in, she takes off at speed.

Perhaps my body really is remembering how to swim again, or maybe she really *is* feeling the cold because I am not so far behind her today, but dodging the plastic bags (and worse) now takes away much of the pleasure. It is strange just how much waste has been washed up here; it is like the bay's trashcan.

As we turn towards the main beach the sun is restored to us, and feeling warmer we swim side by side for a while – simply observing each other. Before we exit, I dip my head down just once more – but no: no fish. Once out of the water, the warmth of the sun surprises us both and after drying my hair I am tempted to let the breeze finish-off my body. However, when Marie-Hélène approaches with her soft pink towel I offer no resistance – because this is now "what we do". She shivers and tucks her head in towards my neck – nuzzling my ear. For a moment my thoughts lend towards passion again, but her need for warmth together with the lack of privacy prevents such inclinations from taking root.

On the walk back, Marie-Hélène finds her towel is large enough to wrap around her entirely and seal out the breeze. My towel, however, is doing all it can to wrap around my waist and hide the most of my legs; but then again, I am the mad Englishman who yet appreciates this as being "nice warm weather".

We are rinsing our feet and legs of sand at the showers when, Marie-Hélène reminds us both, "Oh, we are supposed to be painting over our drawings."

It takes little more than twenty minutes to find me showered, dressed, and at the covered-in communal area between the apartments with my canvas from the morning. I clear a workspace amongst the baskets of acrylic paints, mixing-pallets and water-pots and wait for inspiration. Looking at the walls of brick on my sketch (not wood or trellis), and at what seem to be heavy gates, I cannot help but feel a little deflated. Then again, at least there are gates, it is not a solid wall – and the gates are not locked shut. Moreover, behind them are two vibrant interconnected hearts.

I think Karina had said we should paint completely over our drawings in a single colour – any colour of our choosing. "Okay, it sounds simple enough," I say to myself, "but which colour?"

Marie-Hélène joins me and with uncharacteristically few words, she takes a pallet, chooses paint and a brush, and sets to work. "Well, at least this is easy enough; I am painting every week at home. How are you doing?" she enquires.

"Err, I'm not sure which brush is best and I haven't quite decided on my colour," I reply.

"Ah, you need a brush like this – look," she says holding up a stubby handled, short-haired, wide-headed brush. "The colour for me is easy; I shall choose my favourite colour."

Now that I have stopped *trying* to think of a particular colour, one comes to mind: the colour I have often sensed around me at the end of my development circle meetings when we are invited to have our spiritual gate-keeper hand us our "cloak of protection" – the colour of the lining being purple. [17]

The colour ends up being a little more lavender/lilac than purple, but it *feels* right. Using the brush (as advised) I wash over the entire canvas with (lavender/lilac) – well, sort of, because I have not considered the extent to which the paint would soak-in and the result is *pleasing*, but not altogether the complete wash-over I had intended. It looks coloured enough, however, and the pencil drawing seems obliterated so…that will have to do.

Having worked on the table behind me, Marie-Hélène whisks her canvas away before I have even glimpsed the colour she had chosen – let alone caught any detail of the drawing, but then, Karina had said that our painting should be a private endeavour (…but all the same).

As I walk along the beach to the taverna, I foresee – without a doubt – another veritable feast, yet I am not hungry at all. The evening meals were not included

---

[17] In the western esoteric spiritual tradition (yes, really – there is one) we each have a spiritual entity that assists us at the interface with the spirit realms to guide, interpret and protect. *

* Some say "protect" – because of the darker forces that reside "there". I have not encountered "dark" forces myself. I have experienced presence that felt as being lost, lonely, confused, dumbfounded – almost characterless entities, but never any that seemed to be set mindfully on causing distress. Maybe it is because I have not developed or adopted a belief that would support such a fear and so have not attracted such, or maybe it is because from my early Reiki training I have always and only – intended to connect within the light and to channel energies "for the higher good of all".

in the retreat price, but I have had quite a busy day and do not feel to be preparing food; and as it happens, Marie-Hélène is going as well, so…

The last shades of the sunset are still perceptible inland, but all detail is lost to shadow as we head for the alley that will lead to the main street. We are down by two in number this evening because Jo-Anne and Karina are taking the car.

This time I am *expecting* the figs; it is therefore not a surprise to see them in such quantity: withered, squashed, and eaten by insects, birds and lizards. *This* time I am not suffering the perceptions of the figs as before, and so there is perhaps a further lesson to be taken from all this: yes – good things may come along in such abundance that the lack of them need no-longer be a source of concern, yet when presented with such treasure, we can always *find* a cause for worry, if we so lend our attention. [18]

I have often thought that walking can be part of a meditative exercise, but it does not usually become quite as productive as this walk in "fig-alley". (I do *so* love retreats.)

The meal at the taverna is in many ways a continuation of my experience of fig-alley re everything good being in abundance. Tonight, I do not find myself thinking unnecessarily about where I might sit; Marie-Hélène and I simply look for where we can sit together. For a moment I contemplate whether others may have purposefully held a space for us, but perhaps, it is the universe's response to the two of us no longer having any reason to be separate.

Some hour-and-a-half later, as we near the end of eating, and as we complete the final "*Baklava*" chorus to proclaim once again, the supremacy of the honey-sweetness that is our favourite Greek dessert, we all dip into our pockets to share the bill. I am relieved that there is enough in the kitty for a good tip, because several customers have departed in the time we have been here; I fear we have flavoured the ambience somewhat with our loud conversation and laughter.

The amount of food left over is – well, almost embarrassing, but then, one of the family attends carrying some large food containers. With many baked items still being in their foil trays, the pasta and salads are the only items that need much attention. I can now comprehend another reason why Karina recommends this taverna (and, perhaps why she and Jo-Anne had come by car.)

The sea breeze feels just that little bit cooler than the previous evening as we walk back along the shore. It might just be that I am more acclimatised to the

---

[18] See Appendix II: We can always find cause to worry – if we so lend our attention.

heat of the day, or indeed that I am a little tired from the exercise I am having – the swimming, and such. We agree that in having had such a lovely full day, it would be wise to catch up on our sleep. Marie-Hélène hopes besides, that any talk with her roommate will still leave enough time to get a good nights' sleep.

"Just a nightcap then," we agree (meaning a tea at my place). It will be a nice way of winding down together and we can share some of our photos of the homes, family and friends we keep referring to.

On the big red sofa, we sit with our Greek Mountain Tea and Marie-Hélène leans her back on me as she swipes her phone to show me: her mother and her two sons, some friends down on the beach, her apartment, the view from her balcony to the big outdoor pool, the nearby mountains where she walks with her friends, and the castle at the beach where she loves to swim. With quite some glee, she says again how she can walk in the Esterel Mountains in the morning and swim in the sea in the afternoon – all in one day, and that in the colder months she can be in the sea while looking at snow-capped distant mountains. I tell her I am impressed. (Moreover, I am.)

"Good – I hope so!" she jests, and then more directly she says, "I hope that you will come and visit me sometime and I will show you – yes?" Until now, we have spoken only in general terms about the future, so this speculative invite is quite something to my ears. "Oh, that would be so good – yes, thank you. And of course, you must visit me as well," I insist.

"Yes, of *course.*" she beams.

"I expect it will not be long after this retreat before we will want to see each other again – but…"

"No problem," she cuts in. "There are planes. It is just a matter of organisation. Remember at the Mill, remember I said it: *No doubts*". She says it lightly and at the same time, so assuredly. No insistence, no rebound from complaint just "this is how it is". Once again, just as on that day, the minor doubts that have started to niggle me have simply evaporated in the light of her confidence, and I sense a future "us".

"Yes, I am sure you are right," I say meekly, offering my mouth to hers but she holds back. Then in almost a whisper, she says, "Yes, we will *do* it – I know it," she concludes, just before our mouths meet once more…

Remembering we are having an *early night*, it is time for my photos, and thus upon the screen of my mobile comes: a shot of my garden – from the dining room, one view of the front of my house, and one of my mother with my daughters and their husband/partner at a birthday gathering earlier in the year. Following this, we each show a quick selection of places we have visited and sights we have seen – both of us eager to share more of our personal history. (Alternatively, perhaps we just do not want to say goodnight.)

It comes to me that some of the inspired writing I have mentioned previously, is right here on my phone. There is a project I have worked on for over a year, a story of sorts – that has been given the title: *nucreationstory.* The way I am thinking, if our relationship is to evolve, Marie-Hélène will come across the manuscript sooner or later – so why not get it over with. It is not a shocking story, but with it being about creation itself, and beginning *before* the "big-bang" – I have already witnessed how it can lead to a few eyebrows being raised… but, where do I start?

"Marie-Hélène, you know this "nucreationstory" I've said I had written – from ideas and words that would seem to have been given me?" I venture.

"Yes…?" she says sweetly, inquisitively.

"Well, here on my phone, I have a copy of *nucreationstory* – as far as it is currently written, and also some of the other things I have written, and some of the recordings of what I have spoken."

"Oh, maybe I can see. Would you like to show them to me now?" she asks.

"I would like to show you *sometime,*" I offer. "But it does not need to be now because it is late. I just realised they are here on my phone, and thought it might be good to share them with you – or at least not to hide them from you, but I do not know if, or what, you might think, or if you'd like to do it tonight, or do some of them tonight…I know it is getting late…" I waffle, over-thinking.

"Yes, it is and I am starting to feel a little tired," she admits. "But I would *love* to see them. Is there something you can show me – or *read* to me now, so that I do not have to do anything?" she asks lightly. "I think I would like to listen to your voice and hear you speaking what you have wrote – 'written,' is it?"

"Yes, what you have *written* or that you *wrote* – I think."

She smiles. "Ah, it is like in French, using "have" in the past-tense. So okay, you choose."

(It is always so easy with her, yet I seem to keep finding things to be concerned over – even *before* anything happens; I wonder why this is?)

"Well, some of the stuff here," I say picking up my phone again, "…some of it might be a bit heavy for this evening. How about if I read just the start of *nucreationstory*?"[19]

Receiving no response, I continue, "This part is written quite lightly, poetically even. In fact, in Part Three, the words evolved into an almost all-rhyming four-line pentameter – if I am using the right term. Anyway, may I read Part One to you? It is only a few pages long, like most of the sections."

"Yes, yes please do. Wait…" she turns around on the sofa and stretches out to the side of me – resting her head back on my lap.

"Part One: In the Beginning. Oh, this was written in March 2015 by the way, and it is just two pages long," I say, to re-reassure her.

"Okay," she says. "Now, please start."

"Nucreationstory: A Creation Story," I recite…
"Intelligence and the void."
"Consciousness that has knowing, yet is isolated, inactive,
Aware of self, and of more.
Consciousness – as crystals suspended in the dark of night…" [20]

(After a while…)

"…And in that space – within those patterns that now exist without their presence – is something of the Light, the Good-force,"
"The Oneness giving something of its very matter,
In an act of Creation."

"Well, that is the first part," I end, excited at having given breath to the words for the first time, but then hesitating – waiting to see how they have been received.

"Wow…" she says. Nothing else follows… for a while. "And you wrote – that?" she asks.

---

[19] The title was something I had pondered over at length before finally resorting to further meditation to seek a resolution. Surely it should be: *"New Creation Story?"* I had ventured, (to myself) but no, it stayed as *"nucreationstory"*.

[20] See Appendix III for the complete extract.

"Yes, well that's just part one, there are eleven parts so far. I do not know how much will come to me, or how far the story will go – perhaps it will in time reach up to the present…"

"But, where does it come from – you are a poet?" She interrupts. "You say you just sit and write, and the words – they are coming to you?" she queries.

"Well, yes basically – yes." Marie-Hélène says nothing.

"It can be quite exciting for me – writing like this." I offer, wondering if I have been speaking *at* her instead of *to* her.

(No response.)

"But you know at the end of the day, it is only what one might call inspiration. I guess all people like writers and artists tap into the same sort of inspirational source. It is not *so* strange…is it?"

Marie-Hélène lifts her head off of my lap then sits up beside me. "You know," she says. "That was wonderful – really!"

I feel awash with relief, and my face shows it.

"Oh, no it has been good for me – really," she assures me. "And you know, to have strange experiences is not so unusual, so don't feel uncomfortable. Do you remember, I told you I was regressed to experience a past life in Scotland? Well, it was as a *man, a* Scottish lord. I felt myself at first a young man returning from the crusades to find my parents had died and the castle being disrespected by the local people, and then I was old and very lonely on my deathbed, with my books all around me and then came many bright lights… Perhaps you may know something about that? Anyway – maybe another time; now I think I am tired. There is something about hearing your voice…"

"Oh – my voice makes you fall asleep!" I cut in jokingly, and we both laugh.

"No," she corrects. "I listen to your voice and I feel so relaxed. It is lovely, I do not normally relax so easily. I think perhaps you are tired too – no?"

She is right: I *am* tired. Marie-Hélène carries on, "So, in the morning I will see you on the beach for the sunrise and meditations, and then you will come and have breakfast with Henri and Rachel and me?"

"Oh yes – that would be lovely. I shall look forward to all of that." We both stand, and we kiss – soft, gentle, but not for so long.

Walking to the door hand in hand, we turn to face one-another, foreheads touching. One more kiss, short this time, almost playful, lips touching and then – almost bouncing off each other with joyful anticipation of the morrow – we part.

"Good night," we say in unison.

"I hope you may sleep better tonight," Marie-Hélène says to me.

"That would be good," I reply, watching her walk down the steps, onto the garden path and (again) into the night.

"Yes, that would be good," I repeat to myself, looking at my reflection in the bathroom mirror as I clean my teeth. I am so tired, so happy, so relaxed; surely, I must sleep easily tonight?

"Maybe tonight," I say to myself as I climb into bed, pulling the loose cotton sheet over myself, but before I have had the time even to start to sleep at all, I am stirred by a noise: a buzzing/whirring in my ear. "What the…?"

There it is again – coming slowly, getting louder and then receding – and there again. Oh, and something just touched my ear! Sitting up semi-startled, I stretch over to the bedside light. Mosquitoes: two, no three, four – oh!

Taking the flannel from the bathroom to use as a fly swat, I walk from bed to bed, and to the chair and back, stalking the insects where wall meets ceiling. After about five minutes I have culled three, but having shortly observed the "taking of life" I begin to regret such vicious action. When *another* one then buzzes close to my ear, however, the threat of continued tiredness dulls my guilt. Ten minutes later, with the "them or me" attitude having triumphed, there are seven ex-mosquitoes floating in the toilet pan.

Back in bed, with lights out and with sheet closed tightly around my neck, it seems there may yet be some time for some serious shut-eye…and before dawn (*yawn*)…but – what was that she had said about having remembered a past-life in Scotland…and if I might know something about that…?

The Truth Will "Out"
And So Will the Stars ("I Love You")

Waking up…to renewed buzzing around my ears, "What, again…!" With barely two hours passed, another strategy is needed.

This time I set one bedside lamp on as a trap – a decoy, and I sit and…reaching for the flannel – *slap!* A predator is eliminated, but the lamp goes with it, rolling and falling onto the adjacent bed.

Slap – another kill, but again the lamp goes over. I observe it – expecting that it will roll as before, but this time it turns towards the hard-tiled floor, where…I catch it, just in time.

Taking the glass shade off of the lamp (!) I decide to scout the room as before. *Snap…snap* – two more gone, and then with the flannel skilfully skimming over the naked lightbulb – *snap*, another. *Slap* – the flannel meets the bulb this time, but the lamp just rocks as the insect is taken out of the air and so I smugly return to the hunt. Snap…snap…slap – BANG! All goes dark.

Switching the other bedside lamp on, I see the silver metal screw fitting of the lightbulb is still in place, but the glass part is on the adjacent bed, still intact – but perhaps it is time to stop. (I sleep.)

At four-thirty I wake – roll away from the light of the window, and then I sleep some more. When I next stir, the room is light. Being that it is six-twenty I go downstairs with thoughts turning towards the beach. At six twenty-two I head up the stairs to swap my underwear for swimwear. At six twenty-five I head back down.

I am attracted to the idea of doing yoga in the glow of the early morning sun, however, it feels decidedly damp as I walk the garden path – no: it *is* damp, and there is dew on the grass. Upon looking closer (because there is *a lot* of dew) I notice that there are watering points – several, and all around the garden. Of course, however else could this grass have stayed so green with *this* climate…is it this that woke me?

Alone on the beach and with blue mat and towel laid aside, I find myself walking around and feeling-out the earth energy lines with the palms of my hands – not so unlike like the way people do with metal detectors. Walking slowly until I sense I have crossed a line, I then move my arm side to side to feel out the point of maximum sensation and mark a cross in the sand with my toes. Next, I walk in the direction of the line until I can sense another, and then do the same again twice more until there are four crosses spaced some four metres apart. Finally, I form a line between the crosses to form a parallelogram.[21]

Ah yes…yoga, so – where to sit?

Deciding to sit on the corner of the marked-lines closest to the sea I place myself on my mat and am just starting to feel the band of energy around the crown of my head that usually (only) comes along with meditation – when I sense someone else is present. Looking around I see Marie-Hélène, who smiles and says gently, "H'ello, may I join you?"

"Yes, yes please do," I encourage.

She is dressed in white linen trousers and a pink T-shirt with her pink towel about her shoulders. She continues, "Have you been here very long?"

"No, I had meant to do some yoga but got a little caught up with feeling out the earth energies here, and I have only just now sat down."

"So, maybe we sit together then? You can tell me another time perhaps, what these markings are in the sand. May I share your mat, the sand is still quite cool."

Soon after, we are joined by "ones" and "twos" until, with the normal crowd gathered, we greet the sunrise with a visualisation from Jo-Anne. This is followed by the yoga; the normal routine – but taking place in virtual-unison today (yes – me included).

---

[21] The term "ley" or "ley-line" is often used, but I do not find there to be a tangible *line* of energy, but instead – points of fluctuating resonance that when plotted, form a line; akin to a contour line on a map. On open stretches of land, I have found these lines (/leys) to be of varying strengths and at spacings that seem to be closer as energy levels increase and more spaced out as the energies decrease. I find the bunching together of leys can often reflect the actual contours of the ground. There are places however where this principle is broken – as if some ley positions are in sympathy with something deeper; predestined to join places of similar resonance rather than similar altitude. These leys would seem to be across all the land and beneath (/in?) the sea, and on a macro scale are routed in pairs – masculine and feminine, some would sense – forming wave-like grids that connect/align to many noteworthy places, including virtually all old churches, and traverse the entire world, joining up at a number of *very* noteworthy places.

Afterwards, some of us venture into the water: Henri, Marie-Hélène and I being the first in *and* the last out. Having discovered yesterday that the sea is not quite so *natural* as it should be, it does not feel the same. Therefore, I focus less on swimming and more on the sunrise and what this day may bring. I find myself moved to reciting a short dedication, a favourite first made known to me by someone from a former relationship: "As the sun rises this new day, it brings all that is needed." [22]

These days on Skyros have brought me so much more than I could ever have expected. Would it not be good if we all could wake up and walk into each new day without expecting what it would bring? To live – just trusting that it would be – as is *needed.*

After a while, Henri swims off and Marie-Hélène comes over. "So, how did you sleep last night? Did you sleep well – tell me?" she asks.

I hesitate – not wanting to talk about "not sleeping" again, however, upon recalling the mosquitoes, I describe my night's petty destructions.

After we exit the water, Marie-Hélène turns to me, "You know, I did not sleep so well – either," Marie-Hélène confesses. "When I get back to my room – *got* back, my roommate was not sleeping yet and needed to talk again. So, we talked for some time. I think she was very happy with that, but when we had stopped the talking – you know, I could not get to sleep at all!"

There is a pause as Marie-Hélène starts to dry herself, and I become lost to watching the towel move across her skin, soaking up the droplets of glinting water clinging to her body, each one containing tiny reflections of the sun.

"What?" she says, noticing me observing me. "What is it?"

"Oh, I am just enjoying watching you dry yourself; watching you move. You have such a beautiful body," then, realising my confession. "Oh – sorry, not the right time of the day for that."

"You are so *special,*" she says. "You know, I am not sure I have heard anyone tell me that before – not straight at me."

"Really?" I query. "Oh, you know – I think the men in my life have not been so direct. I think they want to control; do you know what I mean? They tell me

---

[22] In fact, by someone named Helen who – now I come to think of it – had introduced me to another Helen, who had, in turn, introduced me to the London based group I now meet with…which of course has in turn led me here to Skyros and thus to Marie-Hélène (…*Helene* – by coincidence) (?)

what they think they *should* say. They have not been so straightforward as to tell me what they really think – as you do," she concludes, opening her towel and moving in close.

"I find it so easy to say what is true, whatever you ask," I have to admit.

Marie-Hélène glances around briefly then, moving closer, she kisses me gently.

"Do you think," she stalls… "Do you think we might sometime get to have the beach to ourselves? Wouldn't that be *sooo* good?"

As I reach down to adjust myself, Marie-Hélène chides, "What…what are you doing – *here*?"

"Sorry, the thought of that has moved me somewhat – and my body as much as my mind."

Marie-Hélène throws her head back and chuckles, then kisses me again. "Okay, then we should stop this," she says, withdrawing, looking at me quite furtively nonetheless. Then she carries on, "So, last night, I left my lavande with my roommate, so I am hoping she finds it useful to relax to…*with*. I shall try to talk with her – not *so* much tonight."

"Last night was so good – *lovely* I think you English say; '*so lovely*' I think you are saying too. And I enjoyed you reading to me so much. You know, it was very hard to leave you last night, I am so comfortable in your arms."

Her words are like music to my ears. "Well, perhaps we can do something like it again this evening – though perhaps not so late?"

"Yes, we must," she replies. "But let's not be worried about the time. Not having so much time together in the day, I would like that we spend as much time together in the evenings as we can. We are both grown-up, I think we can manage it – yes?" she says humorously.

I enjoy her gentle assertiveness. I have become so used to having to do everything for myself in life; making all the decisions; it is so refreshing to feel a different balance with Marie-Hélène.

"Marie-Hélène…"

"Yes?"

"I am still feeling a little concerned about – well, with what we are experiencing here together, or rather, about what others may know, or not know, or what they perhaps are misinterpreting," I confess.

"Ah, I understand, but there is nothing to be afraid of – you know. This is so powerful – so important. No one can prevent us, I know it." She pauses. *"No – Doubts.* Do you remember – at the mill? *No doubts."*

"Actually, I was thinking particularly about Rachel and also about Karina and Jo-Anne who might all be looking out for you."

"But Rachel knows me very well, and remember – I told you the other day she said, 'This man has something to teach you'. Do you remember? You know, perhaps I will tell her everything soon – well, not *everything*…you know!" she finishes, deliberately bumping into me. "But Karina and Jo-Anne – ah yes, but what can we do about that?"

"Well, I guess we could let them know that you and I are happy with the situation," I suggest.

"But I do not know if I can do that. I am perhaps not quite as confident as you may think." Marie-Hélène replies.

"That's okay, I will do that. I'm sure the words will come to me if I chose the right time," I speculate.

"Oh good, rather you than me, and – are there other concerns that you have?"

"Not really but…well, okay – so we are here for this retreat, yes? I mean, we have both come here for more than just a holiday. So, I am a little concerned that it might affect the retreat process for one or both of us; that we might not learn something important for us."

"But we can talk about everything," she assures. "I cannot see that there is anything that we would not say in the group just because both of us are together and if there is, then I will tell you afterwards and you can do the same. Yes?" she points out so, so clearly.

"Okay, yes – you are right. Of course, you are right." I concede. "So, when will you tell Karina?"

"As soon as I can," I propose.

"Okay, good luck. Like I say, rather you than me. You can say that: rather you than me?"

"You know more English than you think. Yes, that is the correct usage. But I would say *'rather'* with more *'thhr'* and less *'zzzr'*," I tease, returning a nudge.

Back at the apartments Marie-Hélène opens the gate wide for us both and we walk across the crisp grass towards the showers. "We must get ready for breakfast. Oh, oh will you prepare for me some eggs this morning – please?"

"Yes, it will be my pleasure."

"Okay, we go! We meet at Henri and Rachel's about eight-fifteen, yes?"

"Yes," I reply joyfully.

"And remember, you are cooking for me – the eggs," she says as we part company. I desperately try *not* to look back, not to watch her every step and sway as she strides towards her apartment. I fail miserably.

I walk towards the garden entrance at a pace, wanting to be back in the company of Marie-Hélène as soon as possible. However, I am brought to a sudden halt by the wall of sound and activity. The flowers have opened to the sunshine and I am mesmerised by the activity of the many, many bees working to gather nectar. The bees are flying above, around, and close by me, and I wonder if I should be more concerned, but it feels almost like I sense their joy in their work and feel no threat. Maybe I am simply feeling *my* joy at what I am doing, or perhaps, the bees and I are *exchanging* our joy – *buzzing* for different reasons.

Showered, changed, and with the largest tray I could find loaded with my glass of tea, my bowl of fruit and muesli, and a covered-pan of my best scrambled eggs, I am greeted warmly by Rachel who tells me Henri is just coming. Marie-Hélène floats a "Hel-lo" from behind and places some items onto the table beside me; the table that today has a place set for *me*. Henri joins us and as we all sit Rachel leans towards me and says, "Wayne, would you like to say that 'eatta-ka-kitti' again?" (…to our laughter).

"Ita-daki-masu," I intend.

"Thank you, Wayne. Okay, shall we eat…"

"So, Wayne, how are you finding life alone there in the – oh what is it, a *chateau?* Yes, it is Wayne's chateau!" Rachel enthuses.

I reply I am very comfortable there, that I have a full ensuite and a complete kitchen at my disposal, and that I am not alone for long because Marie-Hélène is so kind as to visit me quite often.

"Yes, and in the evening too," Rachel chips-in, smiling at me and then at Marie-Hélène. Henri notices that I have started dishing out eggs to Marie-Hélène. "Oh, that looks *good*," he says. "M'mmm, Wayne – is there some for us as well?" Rachel asks.

Upon comprehending I have not thought ahead enough to prepare *four* portions, I feel somewhat deflated. Apologetically I reply, "I had not thought to cook enough – but yes, please do have some."

"Yes, and if you like them, Rachel…" Marie-Hélène chirps in, then looking at me carries on, "…*you* will cook eggs for us *all* tomorrow."

ECOS flows nicely (again) today and I think somewhat quicker, with only a few notes and reminders afterwards. Consequently, I find enough time to be on the veranda back at the *chateau* with the kitchen tidied, and with all my things – with time to spare.

At nine forty-five I ring the bell – quite expertly, I might add – three times loud and clear.

Remembering how the reception I gave yesterday was so welcomed, I repeat it, with many looking up to match my smile even as they approach. Today, I bring my hands together and offer a slight "Oriental" bow, to which virtually everybody – similarly and happily responds.

When Marie-Hélène arrives, she seems slightly demure. Perhaps she is simply trying to show herself to be more "the retreat-participant" and less "the lover" to any suspicious eyes. (Oh yes, I *must* address that later.)

The delightful Holy Harmony musical-chant is now playing, so to honour the retreat I must try to relax my mind and forget my hosting role – letting go of all wishes, fears, and uncertainties regarding what the morning may bring. If we can each do this, then with perception not pre-conditioned, skewed or filtered by expectation, presumption, conjecture or inference, our experiences will be all the richer.

Yet, and despite my knowing-better, with my eyes closed, other senses are heightened and my attention is drawn to a certain scent: probably citrus. With eyes still closed and focussing (trying to) on the chanting, *we* sit just around the corner from one-another with backs against the wall. Marie-Hélène's crossed-legs are not touching mine, yet I *feel* her. How can I manage to let go and enter retreat mode today with such thoughts and sensations: such attachments to her very presence?

"Journey to Childhood," is the title given for our work this morning. We will be seeking our life angels' involvement again, asking that they assist with memories from our childhood. We are told there is always something to learn from such memories. Similar to yesterday, Karina talks us through a meditation that helps clear the mind of our immediate environment and opens it to our higher presence. Soon enough I have a multi-sensory experience incorporating memories of much meaning; things I had forgotten but which now provoke such feeling as if they are of the *Now*.

They come as separate scenes to my minds-eye – almost as dreams in the way they meld together, flowing and fading in and out…

When we have finished our "journeys" we are asked immediately to make a few notes with the idea that this will make the memories more accessible again later. I therefore, pick up my note pad, but before opening it to the next blank page, I read the subtitle on its front cover: "…*the last great adventure is the journey back to yourself*." (Poignant.)

I take my pencil and in between short periods of closing my eyes to roll through the memories recently projected, I write…

Memories of sitting on a brown semi-textile/plastic mat in the sun, and with the smell of the mat & colours of its fading and its degradation on the side.

Playing with a castle built by my father.

Sounds of disrespect, disagreement & disapproval from my home, from between father and mother.

I'm sensing that it's focussed on my father having built the castle for me but not having done any such thing for my brother – who he has displayed much distaste of, and anger towards.

Mother is saying untruths & I pull back from my connection with her slightly because she is not expressing truth, so I wonder how much else she says is not true & I find much.

As I sit with the echoes of these memories bouncing around in my mind. I feel restless. Something is missing…perhaps a question is needed — one that will lead me to understand how the suffering of this experience has affected me. "What else was like this?"

I close my eyes once more, and bid the story to roll on…

In my mind's eye, I sense I am of relatively young years – around six perhaps. I am with my mother at a neighbours' home, and it feels like it is summer, and it is an afternoon gathering of neighbours – mostly mothers with their children. I am playing, not far from my mother and her voice is relaxed and happy. I listen as she shares one or two home truths that leave me feeling a little uncomfortable, facts concerning my brothers' behaviour, and then my father's. Then my mother mentions me, and there are appreciative and warming words telling of how I am never any trouble and able to keep myself amused. She mentions how I was born with so-much dark hair and then comes, "Of course, I

162

had been waiting for seven years…//…I wanted a little girl, but…//…and he's never any trouble." However, the words had been heard: "I wanted a little girl," and I recall the doubt that then arose: "What does my mother really think of me." Following this, I had stood up and stepped back into a cup of freshly poured hot tea that caused a bad scold.

As I start to recall the several visits made to the local clinic to have dressings painfully changed – the "movie" stops, and I am back, but with such powerful emotions that I am stunned and cannot write all of it down. I write simply…

(I recall she may have wanted a little girl)

I sit for some time – not knowing what more to do. However, with a returning sense that there is more to come, I once again ask…

"So, what else was like this?"

This time I have flashbacks to events previously remembered, but nothing contains anything new. Nevertheless, I write a few words to help focus my concentration on these re-remembered experiences: *1) illness, shops, school; 2) mothers' breakdown.*

I have gathered thoughts from around these keywords before, but I feel I should respect the fact that they have returned. Therefore, I decide to "go there" once more:

"Why are these memories back again?"

Surprised by the clarity of what follows, I am instantly transported to a time when I had been refusing to go to (junior) school due to severe stomachaches that would tend to clear as the day went on. I recall how unsettled this made my mother, and how often she had expressed fears of the school board man coming to see her and how we would get into trouble. One morning, my mother had said we were just going to the shops, and that this would be good for me – giving me some fresh air – but after visiting a few shops and buying me something to eat, she held my hand and led me…past the shops. When I queried what was happening her grip had increased, and I recall being *pulled* along – crying. I also recall hearing numerous fears expressed and threats and bargaining ploys launched at me as she sought to get me to school. However, I had become so distressed that she eventually gave up /gave in, and we came home. I had learnt not to trust my mother.

Remembering my place in Skyros, I open my eyes. The amalgamated memories of the behaviours I had been subjected to as a child, now – as an adult – feel akin to abuse. Observing that I have yet to cover one of the two things I had written down: "mothers' breakdown", I find myself wondering what else there can be to learn; I have never really forgotten about my mothers' nervous breakdown – *breakdowns* – nevertheless, I close my eyes again.

"What else – was like this?" This time, however, nothing comes.

On opening my eyes, I find myself asking, "So what was that about?", and immediately, in the space in my mind previously held clear for imagery – arrives the understanding…

"Not everything needs to be re-experienced. It is for the purpose of learning and not for suffering, that such as thoughts, memories and images are available."

It is true, I had had a number of experiences prompting me to feel un-worthy as a little boy, and these had clearly led to a certain distrust of my mother. Furthermore, I now understand that the witnessing of my mothers' breakdown had in turn led to the perception that I could never again be sure of the support of my mother.

I do not need to write anything further only…it is interesting that my father does not seem to have appeared in my imagery or thoughts this morning. He had been somewhat absent throughout my earlier years and when I was a teenager he had been diagnosed as having tuberculosis, and then terminal lung cancer, so I guess I had never *looked* to him for much support.

Also absent from the imagery had been my brother, seven years my senior, and who had been in the army for a number of my teenage years, but had always been an antagonist. He had come out of the army around the time my father went into the hospice, which was around the time my mother had experienced another breakdown, and which all happened round the time of my sixteenth birthday (…)

I guess I have experienced quite some shit in my life, but I have never before reflected on how the heaviest years may have affected me collectively. I think…I have done all right for myself – I mean *really* quite well. However, there still feels to be something that is still resonating within me from all of this past stuff, something resonating now – today, and it is again linked to my mother.

I close my eyes once more and ask, "What is it; what still needs to be understood?" I wrote just one further line…

Did I ever receive her full affection?

After a short break, we return to our places and invited to share something of our experiences – if we would care to. As usual, I readily volunteer, but I only cover the first part of what I had written – the rest still needing some processing, and in particular, the main underlying perception: the assumed unworthiness of the little boy.

Others also shared – Marie-Hélène included, with her memories of severe discomfort in response to her fathers' behaviour. In fact, nearly everyone stepped forward to recount some childhood trauma or other. There is a poem, by Philip Larkin I believe, from which come the lines:

"They fuck you up, your mum and dad. They may not mean to, but they do."

Today is a *powerful* day. I would like to say, sitting here in the shade of the veranda on this Grecian Isle, that today is a good day, but just now, that particular sentiment escapes me. However, we are not finished, for we have another guided meditation; inviting our life-angels to help us consider…

"What yet is to be gained from all this? From suffering there is always the opportunity of learning, and with learning there is healing, and through healing our power is restored, by which we may live more in a state of Grace."

Coming up from said-meditation – short as it was – I must admit to feeling quite different compared to just before. I still feel slightly "numb", but not as deficient as I had been feeling. In addition, I now feel more purposeful, like there is more than simply knowledge/understanding to be gained – like there really is *power* that can be restored. Karina invites us to make some notes of the changes we feel and any new understandings we might have gained. In my notebook, not wanting to go past the current page (…?) I write the following in the only space left (in the top margin):

Gratitude:

- *towards the return of my energy, for learning and how knowledge will help me teach others;*
- *for the freedom to have more open-heart relationships.*

Homework: the homework for today – we are told, is also going to be the same for each remaining day of the retreat:

"Following each morning's work put into the picture – that which represents the experiences of the morning."

Finishing later than yesterday, it is twenty-past one as I walk from the veranda towards the group congregating on the grass, and I am feeling lighter in both my emotional and physical states, but my head, however, seems to be rather "slow". I seem to have recounted/re-experienced events that had significantly shaped my perceptions of "self" and the world around me, and I keep returning to emotional glimpses of the "unworthy little boy". Is this why I have so often tried *so* hard to do the best that I can: in the hope that it might be *enough*…in the hope that I might then be *good* enough…that I might then be seen as being worthy?

Mid-way along the beach I see Karina ahead, talking with Doris. Remembering my undertaking to inform Karina about Marie-Hélène and I, and feeling in some way "inoculated" by my morning's experiences, I step forward. "Karina, can you spare me a minute…"

I find Karina open, receptive, and non-judgemental, and – as earlier speculated I seem to find the right words. I tell her we are experiencing a strong mutual attraction; that we do not wish to make our relationship a feature within the group but that we also do not wish to repress our emotions unnecessarily. Karina thanks me kindly for informing her, and as we part, in a moment of clarity, I comprehend that I have made my first public declaration regarding "us". (It really is happening then.)

Walking the rest of the way to the taverna at my own pace and in my own space, I look between the sand and the sea. Looking at the sea, I recall what I had seen under the surface and particularly in the bay the other afternoon. The surface looks quite normal, but the man-made debris that has been deposited without thought for so long has now accumulated to such a degree that it has started spilling out at the edges. It is washing up on the shore with the waves and being exposed by the ebb and flow of the daily tide. The surface appears normal, but underneath it is lacking vitality and unable to support the flourishing of life. It is interesting, how nature – the outer world – may just sometimes reflect so clearly, one's inner world.

§

At lunch, sitting beside Marie-Hélène, as now feels quite normal, I impart that I have spoken with Karina. She responds quickly with, "Oh, when…what did she say? She has said nothing to me." Still feeling some of the relief of earlier I reply, "Just now – back on the beach, on the way here. It was much easier than I expected."

"And, did she say anything?" Marie-Hélène quiet-reasonably asks.

"Err, no…actually, she didn't – other than thanking me for telling her and appreciating how responsible we have been in the group activities so far."

"Do you think she will want to speak with *me*? Oh, what do I say?" asks Marie-Hélène.

While eating, I respond, "I suspect she will want to talk with you a little – just to know how you are with it all." Then, in between further mouthfuls: "You know Karina, she will be kind, just tell her your truth. I think you'll find it a relief as well."

Lunch is most-welcomed by all and not the least because it has been quite-some hours since breakfast. No doubt, many are like me: pondering over the process of the morning to seek a perspective on "what it all means now". It would seem clearer than ever now, that the experience of an emotionally powerful/painful situation can give rise to behavioural responses that would seem to repeat/regenerate the pain (as "suffering"). Perhaps this is all very purposeful, so that at some time we can look afresh at the original events with wiser eyes, to find the truth that seemed hidden from us at the time of the original trauma.

§

Lunch takes significantly more time than usual, and it is close to three o'clock before we start to make our way back. Marie-Hélène is ahead of me, talking with Madelyn, and I have the company of Renna as we together digest (in both ways) "another big lunch." Having seen me doing some yoga independently in the mornings, she enquires as to my experience. I tell her how I came across yoga through attending various retreats, and how simply "feeling good" from it had then brought me to its daily practice and its use as a precursor to meditation…and so on. During this time, I watch-on as Karina catches up to Marie-Hélène and their pace slows…and then they take a different route – over to the side of the beach. Madelyn then walks up alongside Renna and for a short while the three of us are talking about the weather (as we English seem fated to do) but as the subject changes to one that loses my interest, I withdraw to find a slower pace.

Looking at Karina and Marie-Hélène, they seem quite deep in conversation. Perhaps Karina is attempting to persuade Marie-Hélène to reconsider. Perhaps, after all, Marie-Hélène is being carried along with the joy of it all and is just smitten with my attentiveness. Alternatively, Karina could be enquiring as to the deeper issues she senses within Marie-Hélène or me, and pointing out the need for space so that these may be dealt with during the retreat, or… (!) Alternatively, of course, they *could* just be talking about the weather.

Standing and feeling the sun and breeze and listening to the gentle breaking waves, I can still sense something of an after-shock following the mornings' experience. I wonder if perhaps the un-worthy little boy identity I had unwittingly agreed to adopt as a child may yet be influencing me at times when there are "unknowns" – like now. I suppose it is the emotional/behavioural memories of "my" little boy that influence my subconscious – looking for what he might be doing incorrectly, or might not be doing well enough. *Surely* it is time to let go of that mentality, that conditioned-mind response, and to become more aware. I must try not to feed this mentality any further and instead, apply myself to establishing the belief that I do not need *that* part of me any longer. The little boy has fulfilled the task of taking me back to a past untruth, so to have it corrected in my understanding. It is time to trust: that all which is good and true about the core "me" will never be lost, and that all other goodness is built upon that base. Yes, today I desire to step-around those monkey-mind thoughts and instead – in the space that "worry" might otherwise fill – I will choose "hope". Today I will use my perception of the greater-good to empower me in *holding* that space, that it can be filled with all the goodness that comes as the balance to my hope. (I guess this is "faith".)

Back at the apartments, I am trying to maintain this most-positive mind state while walking to the communal area to do my homework – only to realise I do not have my picture. (So much for being mindful.)

Returning from the *chateau* with my picture in hand, I stroll along the garden path and from the vantage point where the bees like to *be* in the morning, I see the enticingly familiar outline of Marie-Hélène already busy. "*Hel-oo,*" she says to me as I arrive, (always smiling). "So, I am finished here. I think we have not to – must not – look at other's paintings; so now – I go!"

I find myself considering her words for a second, and within that second I can sense the *little boy* looking to enquire, "are things are alright – or not?" "Has the conversation with Karina changed anything?" (…and all of this in just a split second.)

"Ah, you have your painting. Do not show it me!" she stresses, seeming otherwise happy.

"No worries," I say. "It is just a wash of purple at the moment, nothing to show."

"Ah, of course, you have not done it yet. Well, you must not look at mine," she says half-heartedly. "You know, I really do not know what I should be doing here – with this painting. So, I take some colours and I made some lines and, *phurph* – I don't know!" she emotes, with hands offered up in 'that way' "So okay, now it is done, so perhaps when you are finished, we can have a walk down to the beach together?"

I am close to entertaining further queries from the little boy when Marie-Hélène continues, "I have spoken with Karina; she was very nice. Everything is good," she says lightly, glancing over my shoulder. "Perhaps we will talk later?" she entreaties.

Of course, everything is good; why should anything about Marie-Hélène and me, and anything we might say or do – *not* be good? Therefore, *why* does doubt keep creeping into my mind and infecting my perception? Perhaps there has always been this doubt: the "little boy feeling unworthy". Perhaps I am only now beginning to observe it.

We agree: after I have done with my painting, I will call by her apartment and we shall take a walk along the beach. As she goes, I *watch* her go: every inch… (Oops, every centimetre I should say!).

Turning back to my painting: the drawing part had been easier than expected, and the use of the purple wash had come well, so – what is to be lost. Looking at my picture, I had remembered it as being largely purple, but actually, it has quite a lot of the white canvas showing through. However, that was yesterdays' painting; I am supposed to leave yesterdays' as it is and today: "Put into the picture, something to represent my experience of this morning," or something like that. So, I ask myself, "What do I feel? What can I remember from this morning? What can I 'see' on the canvas? Before long, I begin to sense thoughts/ideas – something…ah – the incomplete lilac/lavender wash-over no longer seems to be an error, because I can see a trace of the original two hearts, and it feels meaningful. Something about them being *faint*…like a reminder that they still exist…and I am trying to hold open a space within from which some inspiration can flow…to find some meaning there…but nothing seems to arise, until – oh…"

"I must paint what I can see, bringing forth from the past – that which is to be in my future."

I need ask no further. I choose a blue-green for one heart (for me) and then find myself attracted to a bright signal-red for (her). Great! Therefore, I'm done then…but, *"No"* – there feels to be a space being *held* open in my mind, and so I try to find my way in again. What I sense, is that there should be something at the core – a bright colour; one that should be behind, or perhaps within both hearts, but – which colour…?

"It starts with yellow and moves through all colours of the spectrum."

I am neither hearing or seeing the words; the thought simply appears. It comes more like an empty-space *shaped* so that only those words can fit in. It is a bit tricky and somewhat time-consuming, but after several minutes and much brush washing, it is done. Therefore, what do we have here: concentric hearts – one red, the other a blue-green, perhaps representing the desires or intentions unwittingly brought to the island – but rekindled in the now, and with a certain power at their core. However, there is more, and without any asking comes…

"There is another yellow – a key to opening the gates that once were closed."

170

Instantly recalling the yellow flower, I attempt to include a meaningful representation alongside the concentric hearts. Due to my haste to get back with Marie-Hélène however, it all becomes rather messy and I find myself painting flowers – one over the top of the other, making each one bigger to hide the former, and at the same time trying to make each new one look more *flower-like*. The final flower – well, flower *shape* – appears larger than I had first imagined it, but now at least I am...but "oh" – I have still yet to add something from this *morning's* work! How can I represent something about those painful memories and the learning process that then followed, and without them spoiling the feel of it all?

A spiral comes to mind; that image of circulating-moving energy that to me represents change. Therefore, if the spiral is to depict "change", it has to represent "coming before" or "leading to" – all else, so...it shall go above the hearts. As for colour, I suppose the memories are of my past, of my roots – ah, the colour of the root chakra: red. However, it must not be too evident and it is a hidden force bringing change, so because change is continual, it must also appear to be going into the future. Seeing that the colour-wash is largely in brushstrokes that go diagonally, I can use this sense of momentum to make this spiral show "where things are going". Subsequently, I show how the hearts are subject to change – by incorporating a similar sensation of movement into them as well.

With almost half an hour gone since Marie-Hélène had left, I hastily clean the pallet and the brush, tidy the paints, and then speed my way to deposit the picture – correction, the *painting* – on the table in my room. In the process, I deposit my phone on the bed to free my hands to take my sunglasses, then I rush down into the kitchen, knock-back one...two glasses of water, then upstairs again I go...to recover the phone I had just discarded. Finally, I am outside and in the warm late afternoon sun.

Virtually skipping down the path from the *chateau* and across the grass, I bring myself to a halt just outside her apartment. Here, a short trail of stepping-stones leads to the patio doors of her bedroom. At the entrance, I see a figure laid on the bed, phone by her side – sleeping? Not sure what to do, but confident in knowing Marie-Hélène will be pleased to see me, I step into the comparative gloom of the bedroom...to find myself looking down upon her roommate(!) From the *other* bed, Marie-Hélène says in a near-whisper, "Ah, okay – you are here. Just a minute, she is sleeping. I think I might have just been sleeping as well, but hold on – I will meet you outside. Just a few minutes..."

"*Just a few minutes.*" I am sure she uses that phrase quite often – as if to celebrate when we are about to spend time together; paradoxically of course, because *nothing* we do ever takes *just* a few minutes.

"So, you have finished your painting? You took a long time, much longer than me. Humm, I do not know what I am doing with my painting. I am not sure it has any meaning to me," she declares.

"I guess we have just got to wait and see," I propose. "Perhaps *all will be revealed* in the end. It is certainly taking me much more time than I thought."

"Yes, *time* when we could be together!" she interjects, to my appreciation. "But I must say that mine is starting to feel quite meaningful."

"Really, oh – you will tell me about it sometime?"

"Yes, when we are *told* we can of course" I offer humorously. "Sorry if you have been waiting for me."

"No, not really; I have taken – taken/took – *taken* the time to check my emails. I do not want to do it so much, but I have some business I must attend to, so I was able to do all that I could," she says, taking my hand and moving us towards the gate. I look down at our hands and then at Marie-Hélène's face.

"What? What is up? Is something wrong?" She quizzes me, jokingly.

I think she knows why I am looking, so I quite purposefully say nothing. Almost instantly, she lets go and laughs. "What? It is wrong that we do this – I think not! It is a problem for you?" she taunts. "No, it is lovely. I was just a little surprised because we have not held hands openly yet."

"So, Karina has spoken to you perhaps, about us?" I venture.

"Yes, she was lov-e-ly. Knowing a little about my past, she was really just concerned for me. She told me a little about what you had said to her, and she just wanted to know how I was. I told her that I am very happy, and that was it, really. We spoke about a few other things as well – not just about us. So, no problem! She said that we are two consenting adults, so it is all up to us – or something like that. So, we can both relax a little now, yes?"

"Yes," I agree, "I guess we can."

I stretch out my arm, offering to reconnect with Marie-Hélène's hand. She looks at me, then looks back at the apartments, then says, "*Okay*, maybe not here."

On reaching the beach, we both confide that the main reason for coming here had been to talk about what Karina had said to us, but with that having been covered we decide to simply enjoy a stroll together. Partway around the bay, we remove our footwear and taking one another's hand, continue our stroll with the water around our ankles.

We pass a small family group – locals we surmise, making something of the late summer sun: a couple sat on a rug and their children running around and playing in the sand. As we approach the end of the bay, I notice a dirty tidemark I had not seen earlier. The tides are not very perceptible in this part of the Mediterranean, so I figure that what *is* washed up, is all deposited in this one area, and I walk on. Walking out of the water to avoid the debris, we stand still for a moment, and then – realising that we are quite alone – we kiss. (Just for a few minutes.)

From about mid-way along the bay, the size of the beach had been gradually reducing until at this point, where some buildings start, it extends only a few metres beyond the tide-line. The buildings are like most of the others here: whitewashed and in good visual order. This closest building looks as if it is a small hotel, but it looks closed just now, shut for the season perhaps. There is a large open-plan room that might serve as a dining area, and a small terrace enclosed by a low wall – exiting to the beach. There is the sound of contemporary music from a distant radio, so we venture that someone – perhaps the owner or a maintenance man – is cleaning up after the summer, or perhaps making repairs.

Something else then *drifts* into our attentions. It had started further down the beach, and I had taken it to be an aroma from the tidemark weeds and other debris, but now it is an obvious "smell". I offer the opinion that it is most likely to be from a blocked drain or a sewer, and having resolved to depart presently – we then spot a semi-buried duct coming from the building and disappearing under the sand. A little further down, a darkened stain emerges in the same line of direction, finishing only at the waters' edge. Saddened by what we have just witnessed, we now walk at a faster pace and avoid the sea. If it had been stale or stagnant drain water – or worse – that was being released, it could be the reason why we have not seen much sea life. We talk, trying to find a good reason to dismiss such concerns, but we are conscious that such a similar scenario might be the cause of there being so few fish at the last resort. We decide not to think about it any further, but we are most of the way back before we rekindle our appreciation for the sea enough to walk in it again.

Ahead, we see Madelyn and Renna standing in the surf and gazing towards the horizon. We have not seen them spending much time in the water here, and we reflect on whether it has anything to do with what we just found – if they might know something that we do not. Marie-Hélène lets-go my hand as we get nearer, but instead takes a gentle hold on my upper-arm and walks with her head almost on my shoulder. I am about to enquire on why she should choose now to let-go my hand, when a warm emotion washes all concern away, encouraged by the image of such a couple as we, walking together bathed in the orange glow of the early evening summer sun. (Additionally, I think I may be feeling *proud*.)

On the subject of food this evening we decide to join with those who we have heard talking about re-heating the leftovers from lunch. We also talk about what we might do *after*. Reflecting on how lovely it had been to look up at the stars outside the chateau the other evening, we agree it would probably be better-still to bring some blankets out to the beach and lay back to do some star gazing here. Yes, that would be nice – just for a few minutes (!)

Skirting around Renna and Madelyn to leave them with their obvious contentment, we pick up the path at the rear of the beach and arrive soon enough at the small car park ahead of the accommodation. We resolve to freshen up – well certainly our feet at least, then to dress up and meet back at the ECOS around seven o'clock to partake in whatsoever supper arrangement may evolve.

As I walk the short winding path from behind the apartments towards the chateau, I find myself thinking upon whether Marie-Hélène is as serene inside as she appears outwardly, because I know I am entertaining "doubting" thoughts on a daily basis. Perhaps this "suffering" is not – as I have often thought – simply *my* share of society's social burden; perhaps all these doubts have their roots in that same "unworthy child" identity. Having walked between the bee-bushes, the flowers all closed up for the evening, I stop to look along the box-hedge lined path towards the house. Staring through the house in deep thought, I ask myself, how much of my worry comes out of this one deep-set conditioning from my childhood? Is it possible – normal even – just to *be* and not to have such thoughts as "how I ought to behave" – arise so regularly? Why do I always need to try my hardest and do my best before I can feel content with myself?

Except, here I now am on Skyros, engaging with these thoughts and memories in what seems to be a process of growth. So, how much blame should go to my parents, or society in general, for setting up the environment that gave rise to my conditioning, and how much responsibility should I take for holding onto it all this time? On looking back at the years of what is now revealed to be repeated-suffering from my childhood conditioning, I can see how the suffering itself has contained a silver lining; it has initiated the reflections that have in turn led to the revelations of "my truth" in my earlier years.

It is somewhat like the whole situation with the sea around Skyros: we have been "suffering" the experience of there being few fish and poor water quality, but we have simply taken it as being "an experience" and have not found the motivation to establish the real cause until the stench of a related encounter came upon us. Conversely, however, why is it only *now* that I have come to face this particular "unworthy-child"? Why have I not worked with it before; moreover, what historical "stench" has been the trigger here? [23]

Perhaps what may have brought me here, to work with these issues from the past, is one of two things: either, i) I have simply suffered enough; or ii) I have sensed the proximity of a higher truth or a "truer-connection" and the personal-curse I have carried now presents as a veil (/a gate?) that would seem to be separating me from a fuller, richer and more beautiful experience of life.

Perhaps, there is always a point of balance when one returns to such repeated suffering, when one is able to go one way or another; to just live out and accept the suffering or to decide, "Enough is enough." I suppose however, there is then yet *another* choice to be made – at the point where one chooses either to blame others /the world in general, or take responsibility for one's own experience.

We can certainly find reasons for avoiding responsibility: "I CANNOT do it, it is beyond my capability," is a common one. Or perhaps we may decide we risk losing something important we already have – something we really need. However, if we are honest, can we not hear within us – that voice: the voice of the inner-child acting out their fear again? Is that not the memory of the innocent-one believing that goodness and love can only come from/through others? Is it right that the fear of losing the love of others – back then, provides the reasoning for living with suffering – now?

Something tells me that nothing *true* can ever be lost; [24] that the experiences entailing hope and faith – giving rise to others such as peace and love – are in abundance, but *not* when we constantly look outwardly for them. Such experiences are witnessed with others, shared to some degree; but we truly cannot *give* love or *receive* faith. We can only think or act *out* of love – our own

---

[23] See Appendix II: Why have I not worked with [my unworthy child] before?

[24] About Truth and Love {no expansion, see above}

175

love, and think or act *out* of faith; allowing love, faith and ultimately the higher truth – to empower our thoughts and our actions.

§

Having made my way to my bedroom, I am sitting on the bed, I am…well – just sitting on the bed and wondering, *wow,* where did *that* all come from? One moment I am content with the world, looking at nature and toward a lovely night of sharing, and the next I have found myself considering a new form of understanding regarding *"suffering".* I know I have ventured into components of this understanding before, but I have never-before put them all together in such a complete form. Such thoughts/ideas – such conclusions – have surely been formed before, and probably in many contexts, but only now do *I know* it.

It seems that the process of learning – really *learning* – is never any more effective than when we have found our own way to it. It is not simply a case of digesting the information and taking on the understanding of others by way of "belief". I recall how, as a father, I had repeatedly advised one of my young daughters, that "a candle flame is hot", and that she would burn herself if she kept putting her fingers near it. I told her many times, and many times she returned to continue to play with the flame. Then, one day she touched the flame and received a burn. She did not do it again.

I do not think that we (human beings) are inherently ignorant – just innocent, and curious, and wisdom in the physical world is not gained through mere belief; it comes through experience. We can choose what concepts and understandings to apply in our lives because we have the free will; therefore, we can choose to learn, and then choose to apply i.e., extend our learning – or we can choose…*not* to.

Right now, I choose to sit on the bed and let my new understanding settle within me a bit more. Perhaps it will then reside enough in my knowing that it does not need learning again, and maybe I will be able to call upon its wisdom to help someone else. Just now, however, I prefer to look out through the window and… Oh, it is seven-fifteen; I am already late.

There I go again – judging myself; I have taken time to work honestly through some important thoughts here and yet I have presumed *myself* as "being late", but on the whole, this has been *good* stuff. Maybe I should now try to forgive myself – let it slide. How fortunate I have been that my inner-judge has not held me so steadfastly to the purpose of this retreat, because I may have missed the blessing that has been Marie-Hélène coming into my life.

In addition, I have not been wrong to use my time this way; if I were to tell Marie-Hélène of the thoughts and the concepts I have been forming, she would understand completely, so – why the self-judgement? Is it the unworthiness of the little boy "looking out" for me – looking out for himself: the little boy. I think it might be. (I think I may need to talk with my inner-judge sometime.) [25]

Marie-Hélène arrives at the ECOS area the same time as I, but we simply smile and say hello. Only a few others are present. If no one else turns up, then judging by the number of food-containers and foil-wrapped parcels recovered from lunchtime – we will *not* go hungry. Marie-Hélène busies herself investigating the containers and as she peels back the top off one, the aroma of lunch greets me: one that promises pasta, olives and mushrooms.

"I have a very large pan in my kitchen, it will probably take all of this," I offer.

Rachel steps forward. "Perfect. That would be lovely Wayne – thank-you, and can you heat it up at the chateau?" she asks.

"Yes, my pleasure," I reply – feeling happy that I can contribute (and additionally, that I am *not* late.)

Having repaired to the chateau, and used the biggest (cast-iron) pan with some olive oil, salt and pepper to re-heat the food, and having dribbled some hot water into it to keep everything moist…and then more oil, I grab some bread with one hand, balance the pan in the other, and head back to the group where I find the number to have swelled.

Just before my wrist threatens to give-out from the weight, I manage to drop the bread on a nearby chair and use the hand thereby freed to take the balance – just as Marie-Hélène positions a placemat on the table beneath.

"Ah – *perfect*." she says, and lifting the lid, "oh, and you can cook…!"

I just *love* the way she has of humouring, flattering, and teasing me, all at the same time.

Supper is lovely (as well) and not so busy and so full as the taverna evenings have been. There is also not so much food, but it is all the better for this. A fresh

---

[25] See Appendix II: There I go again, judging myself (simply for being) (/stuff happens)

bottle of wine and then olive oil are opened, and tasty bread is on hand to make it "just perfect for us Latin types" as Marie-Hélène puts it. After eating we stay around the table sharing jokes, talking about wider life situations (yes, including "Brexit"). We start talking about interests that are outside of the ones we have in common: like our hobbies etc., and it leads to Rachel telling the group about my exploits concerning acting, dancing and singing, and after saying I had been in musicals she adds, "Oh, and did you know, he knows Opera – perhaps you could do some for us, Wayne?"

My theatrical pursuits are not something I usually talk about. I have many fond memories of rehearsals and of being on stage, but they are of the past, and when most people hear that someone is an actor or a singer, the real and total content of such endeavours – i.e., hours and hours of learning words – is distorted by misperceptions concerning fame and celebrity.

However, the subject is not dropped. "Isn't it right Wayne – you can sing some opera for us?" Rachel continues. "Perhaps you can do one from Puccini; one that you were telling Marie-Hélène, Henri and I about earlier?"

"Well…yes, okay – why not," I reply, knowing that the song I had mentioned was one I had used as an auditions piece only a few years back, (not to mention in the shower a few times). "I will just need a moment to find the right pitch…" I say reassuringly, singing the first few words repeatedly to myself until I find the pitch low-enough to enable the "big-ending" when it comes. "Okay then," I say confidently, standing up and walking to the end of the table…

"E lucevan le stelle…ed olezzava la terra…stridea l'uscio dell'orto…e un passo sfiorava la rena."

Feeling content that all seems to be going so well, I continue…

"Entrava ella, tragrante…mi cadea fra le braccia. Oh! Dolce baci, O languide carezze. Mentr'io fremente… le belle… forme… (…) (!)"

Coming to a complete halt, I am lost for words (literally!)

"Oh, sorry about that," I say. However, and even though I quickly rehearse all the words up to and past the point at which I had stopped, when I start again, the same thing happens. Feeling embarrassed, I offer my apologies and sit back down. It is all quite light-hearted, and everyone is appreciative for what I had managed to produce, but all have seen my expressions of confusion, and are no doubt wondering why I am so concerned over such a *little* thing. However, it is quite a big thing for me: I just *do not* forget words from songs this way – especially those I have performed before. For some minutes after I feel quite a stranger to myself.

With normal conversation returned, I eventually "let go the bone" and resign myself to the fact that things may have changed: I may have changed, and "forgetting my words" may now be a thing that can happen.

At the end of the meal, we agree to do the same tomorrow, and to give some thought to what food we might choose *not* to eat during lunch – so that we can bring back a wider range for the evening. I join Marie-Hélène at Rachel and Henri's place to wash-up; some of mine, some of theirs, and some of others – it doesn't really matter, we simply take the cleaned items back to the tables and everybody just reunites themselves with the dishes and utensils they had brought earlier…or something close to them.

Back at the chateau, and with my thoughts firmly set on the beach, I go to the bedroom and fetch out a big tartan wool blanket. With a blanket over one shoulder and a towel over the other (you never know) and my yoga mat under my arm, I go to wait for Marie-Hélène outside her apartment in the rapidly darkening night.

It is something after nine by the time we are on the sand together. The silver moon shows the pale forms of the occasional clouds and there is a light offshore breeze. Whilst walking, all we would seem to be talking about are the lovely stars, the backlit clouds and the sea, but throughout the afternoon we have each referred to the beach, to how nice it would be to spend some time – as in alone; as in – being wrapped in one another's arms. (Similar to the sea, we display calmness above, but are vibrant with the knowledge of treasures below.)

Having positioned the yoga mat, then floated the blanket off-centre upon it, Marie-Hélène queries, "Oh, don't we need it in the middle?" Upon pointing out that when we lay on the mat, the blanket can then wrap over us to keep us warm, I receive a lingering kiss.

"But if you like…" I say – feigning to reconsider.

"No, that is a good edea, I *like*. Oh – yes; you know, I go to the beach so many times and I *never* do that," she says, gesticulating towards the sand pillow I had formed. We sit side by side, arms clasped around bent knees, chins virtually resting on our kneecaps, gazing out to sea. The gentle break of waves is quite mesmerising and the white tips of the running waves highlighted by the moon produces hushed whoops of joy when a long one comes.

"It is a pity about the water. They should take better care of it," says Marie-Hélène.

"Yes, it is strange. You would think that with money not being so easy to come by, they would want to get as much out of tourism as they can," I advance. "Maybe, reliance on tourism has led to them to losing the greater connection with nature through such as farming and fishing etc. I do wonder if it would not help energise the whole island if they respected their environment more."

"But we did not come to look at the sea, we come to look at stars," asserts Marie-Hélène, and with that, she lays back onto the blanket. With arms behind her head, she turns from looking down the bay to looking deeply into my eyes. Then she looks away again, straight up into the sky. Does she know what she appears to be communicating to me: well to my ego anyway?

"Come, lay with me. You said you wanted to watch the stars, so let's do it together," invites Marie-Hélène. Upon joining her, she wriggles until her head is under my chin, and then she rolls into me – her whole body close; and her scent – ahh…

I look up at the stars. "They say that shooting stars are actually not a rare thing at all; that we can see them about every twenty-minutes or something – if we keep looking up at the same piece of sky." In the space of only five minutes, I am pleasantly surprised to see two, but each time I mention it to Marie-Hélène, she replies simply with "A-ha", without making any effort to look up – just nestling into me that bit more.

"Oh, and there's another!" I confirm with purposeful glee.

"What, have you really come to watch the stars? Okay. I shall to it too!" and with that, Marie-Hélène rolls onto her back, feigning indignation and smiling broadly.

After less than a minute Marie-Hélène concedes, "Oh, you know I see nothing without my glasses. You will just have to keep a watch for me, and I will just have to lie back here," she teases, turning her head away from me, and again laying back with her arms above her head.

"M'mmm, I think there *is* possibly something else I would rather do, than watch stars," I confide.

"Oh, and what is it?" Marie-Hélène says softly, her grey-blue eyes looking deeply into mine, and as I turn to her, she reaches up and takes my face in her hands, and we kiss.

With my left hand planted firmly on the sand to support my weight, I hover over her to plant kisses on her lips, and then her cheeks, her chin and her neck. Wriggling her lower torso ever closer, she pulls her head back, "What, you are already, ready – for me?"

"Sorry, I really cannot help it," I confess, with some pretence.

"Don't be sorry. I like," reaching down between us where she gently squeezes me and murmurs her appreciation.

"So, you are okay with the idea of making love here?" I enquire, quite honestly.

"Do you think I came out here just to look at the stars with you?" she retorts. Then, pulling away and returning once more to lay back with her hands above her head, she carries on, "Actually no, no – you are right, this is *actually* what I want to do."

Then, dropping the act, Marie-Hélène enquires quite genuinely, "And you? It is not a problem, you are okay with this?"

It just so happens, that being here together in nature seems to be something of a turn-on for me, and thus I reply, "No – no, I mean Yes! Yes, I am okay with it – thank you."

I move back over her. "I am *good* with this. I am very, (kiss) very, (kiss) good with – this…"

No more words; none are needed – our bodies now doing all the talking, our minds connecting with what the other wants, needs or is excited by. Marie-Hélène reaches down to expose me and I lift myself to assist, feeling the night air on my nakedness. She wriggles beneath me and begins tugging and then pushing on her white linen trousers. Then, releasing the belt-tie she pushes the fabric down to her thighs in one swift move. She takes some time in caressing me but having encouraged me closer, further progress is impeded by her trousers. Unperturbed, she moves me directly to the place she desires, but there I stay – close, but not close enough.

"We are alone. Can you come further in me?"

Having realised that I cannot, her hands move quickly to release my belt-tie and push my waistband down as far as her arms can reach, returning to lift my shirt and expose my chest. I feel the refreshing night air on my legs, replaced presently by the touch of her soft warm thighs. Having momentarily felt her breath on my neck, the mood is disrupted somewhat by further movements of a more general and vigorous nature, but all becomes clear when her wiggling and straining ends with a sigh and the removal of *all* her clothing. Accordingly, and soon enough, we are back in place; *I* – am back in place.

This is all beginning to feel *so* very naughty now, but it is not as if it is illegal or anything – is it! (Is it? Let's not go there.) Despite us both now being *ready*, I redirect my attentions to do some wriggling of my own, moving down until my face is close to the bare skin of her mid-torso. There, I commence to kiss her belly button and then her hipbones, holding my lips there and then clenching my teeth – *softly* – upon her pliant flesh. Urged on by the scent that reminds me of our first coming-together, I realise that the rushes of pleasure that my lips and tongue have played upon her softness – have led to my arousal as well. Nevertheless, my need for reassurance leads me to pause, and with simulated humour I venture, "I take it, you are okay with everything of course…?"

The movement of her hips assuredly towards me is answer-enough. There is little control now other than restraining our voices, for the rest of the night is set apart from our passion. I lift and lower with a pace that I try to hold with, but as her fingers dig into my rear and my thighs, I am not so sure of my holding. When her hands move up to grab my head and my hair, my movements become all at once small and subtle, and – just as on our first night, Marie-Hélène becomes lost to a series of tender tremors affecting her whole body.

There is such physical sensation within me and around me: something emotional, something super-sensual, and at the balance between the physical, and the "beyond". The sensation builds, and as I near the point of becoming lost to it, a sound wells up from my throat and as it finds release – so do I; and again, and again until my stomach threatens to cramp.

Remaining deep within, un-wanting and unable to instigate any other action, I am now taken by a hypersensitivity which causes each continuing tremor of Marie-Hélène's to be followed by one of my own, as from deep within – a new duet is played to the fundamental rhythm that has served the species so well.

After a few minutes (…) we return to a more settled state, but with the continuing exchange of smiles and kisses we remain very much connected. Looking to each other as if to ask, "What *was* that?" It feels almost as if we had just met-up after some distant trip, but before either of us can comment, there is a bright light from the far end of the beach. "Oh, what is that?" Marie-Hélène asks, alarmed. I hastily pull back onto my knees.

"It's okay," I assure her. "It is just the headlamps of a car. There must be a road further down. But, are *you* okay?" I ask.

"Yes – oh yes, I am. I am – *good,*" she says, then stares back intently towards the distant road. "Oh, I see nothing, are you sure? I thought maybe that someone was coming…?"

When her words first hit the brick wall of our consciousness, we are both still and silent, for just a second – before rolling about in raucous laughter. Following the commotion, we find ourselves close again; she lies on top of me, I pull the blanket over us and, "No, you cannot be…*really*!" Marie-Hélène declares, gently grinding herself against me. "Oh, you *are.*"

"Oh yes, that would be me," I say lightly as if I have no specific inclination at all. However, as I now regard her totality, knelt over me and with her eyes shining, I know I would certainly *like* to – again.

Marie-Hélène reaches down obligingly, and with her hands on my chest, she intersperses deep lifting/lowering movements with short enticing rocking movements to bring us both to feel *that connection* once again. With head tilted back, she moves to balance some of her weight by planting her feet firmly either side of me. I move my hands between us and taking some of her weight, I lend her movements some additional impetus, such that she now rises and lowers to greater length and a slightly slower rhythm – the overall result being a response of some abandon.

She is in the same sweet sensual place as before, and as her eyes screw up and her hips shake, I join her. This time however I am resolved to keep my eyes open, taking pleasure from her take-off and landing, watching her gradual descent as she slows her pace, opens her eyes and smiles…then swiftly looks around – just in case.

She drops onto my chest, I pull the blanket over us both and – deep in one another's embrace – we are again for *a few minutes,* without words.

"What is this?" she says into my ear, head still tucked into me. "I have never known this before – have you?"

"No, not like this," I agree. "I have experienced what I thought was very good love-making before, and certainly with some abandonment too, but no – nothing has been quite like this."

I could say more, but it does not feel the right time – not yet. However, we have said we should be free to share everything and at *any* time – just as our hearts and minds may dictate…therefore, "Marie-Hélène, you know, something about what I was feeling just now had its origin in "the animal". There was something seeking satisfaction that was deep, earthy, and powerful: a part of me I am not so familiar with," I try to explain. "I also had sensations of flying, soaring, of being blissful and full of love and feeling so complete – and that didn't quite feel like *me* either. I cannot find any other words that can fully describe it just now. There are just…no words."

We lay together, on the beach, under the stars, wrapped in the blanket, half-dressed and fully satisfied. I know I am in a *most*-special place, but not because of the place *here* as such, but more because of where *I am* – within myself. [26] For sure, I am lying in the arms of a most wonderful person but what is making it so extraordinary is that this "here and now" finds me in contact with my "space within" at the *same time*. Sensing this inner space just now – after…*with* lovemaking, and not as part of meditation or such: this has never happened before.

I feel so complete, powerful and yet sensitive – soaring high and yet fully grounded. I have read of the theory: that time exists merely as a side effect to the experience of having intention separated from action, but at this moment, it feels I have *lived* it. In this moment, my truth is that I am with my true love, my soulmate *and* twin-flame.

In this moment, I know that what I perceive as *me* is but an aspect of a higher self: the spiritual whole that is the origin of my awareness. Yet here, in this physical manifestation we know as life, governed by the fundamental law that finds action and reaction always in equilibrium, I can resonate only as one part of my higher-energy balance: the "masculine". However, with me here right now is the feminine energy balance of my higher self. *She* is truly my other-half that in a higher sphere of being has resonated together with me as one, and it is thus that our presence together brings me to sensing that same "balance in all" – here and now.

My truth is that the balance to all that is *me*, is laying here – in my arms: *her*.

I suspect Marie-Hélène may not be contemplating such words just now. I am full of respect for her current state – her who lies with such peaceful countenance, but such is our balance, I suspect that in this moment whilst I am preoccupied by

---

[26] More on "Truth and Love" {no expansion, see above, and next page}

much internal dialogue, she is almost certainly *feeling* something of the same. Yet, I must render something out of this moment; some words to honour the truth – shared but not yet spoken… "I love you."

"Moi aussi – je t'aime," Marie-Hélène replies.

I – Love – You. In this moment I know these three words – set-apart like the points of a triangle, or perhaps a pyramid, with "Love" – above, extending down to co-join the "I" and "You" – or rather, the *she* and *me*. Moreover, in this moment I *know* that Love is the perception of the connection between all souls – felt in different depths and countenances only because of the differences in *knowing* that abides within each of us.

The energetic exchange between Marie-Hélène and I may have proceeded without the rest of the world having noticed, but here on the beach the deeper meaning of those three little words has been received in our hearts, and the heat and sound of the physical has been absorbed into the cool night air, such that our energies are already mixing with "all-else" that is in Being this evening.

"I am getting cold," Marie-Hélène says. "Yes, me too," I agree.

Maybe the energy of our complete exchange will in some way be absorbed by this place and in time help to lift it from the sullen-sadness evident beneath the surface, but for now: enough said, enough felt, enough experienced; it is in the time that we move on.

Folding back the blanket, the cool air greets our naked bodies as we move on our hands and knees, sorting and gathering our clothes. In my mind's eye, I visualise headlamps sweeping across the beach to pick out our two stark figures pulling on trousers and T-shirts, and I smile.

Walking back up the beach towards the apartments, I am feeling complete yet unready to say good night. Nevertheless, I am tired – *still tired,* and I am sure Marie-Hélène would benefit from a good nights' sleep as well.

"I am not sure what to do now," I confess. "I know we could both do with sleeping, but…"

"No, no I am not for sleeping yet. Perhaps you will make for me – we can have another tea; in the chateau?" she enquires.

"Yes, good idea." I say, relieved that there is no need for any excuses from me. "Bon idée…in French," Marie-Hélène reminds me.

"Ah, I must confess, I have caught you saying that: 'edea' a number of times, but I thought you were just mispronouncing our word *idea.*"

"No – it is idée, a French word. *Another* French word you have stolen from us!" she exclaims.

I feel light – lighter than light – as we stroll the garden path, and when Marie-Hélène slips a hand into mine a sense of warmth flows through me. "I could not find enough words for everything I was feeling on the beach, there was so much 'swirling' around my mind," I declare.

"Okay…and?" she replies.

"Well, you remember I mentioned I have been writing down insights that come to me in morning meditations, and that sometimes I have not known what it says until I have read it?"

"Yes, go on – please."

"Well, at a development group meeting in London some months back, I spoke intuitively on the subject of synchronicity. I transcribed the recording of what I had said, and I think a lot of it was similar to what was swirling around in me earlier. I think I have the words on my phone."

"Perfect," Marie-Hélène interrupts, "you will make the tea then I will lie down again and you will read them to me – yes?" she declares (perfectly). Settled side-by-side with (tonight) camomile tea steaming in front of us, and the wall-lights adjusted to a comfortable level, I extract my mobile phone and swipe through the saved documents.

"Okay, here it is: from 7th May this year. I hope it doesn't end up with me feeling embarrassed. It's just, I can't remember quite what it says. I know I have to simply trust in what I have written; trust that it will be good for us."

"So okay, so – you read, and I will listen," she says, taking a swig from her tea and swivelling round to lay her head back on my lap. "Okay, go."

"Oh, it seems that I have the original voice-recording on here too. Maybe I should just *play* it?"

"No, perhaps – another time, I would like to listen to your voice now. Please read, I am getting a little tired," she says, nuzzling into me as she settles her head back into my lap.

"Okay – here goes…" I commence…

"Synchronicity"

"Does everything happen for a reason? Yes, of course, everything does happen for a reason."

(…and a while later…) [27]

"… So, synchronicity is the way in which our thoughts, our actions, our experiences fit in with the Greater Plan and the thoughts actions and experiences of others – guided also by the same Plan.

Thank you for this space. Shalom (…)"

"Oh, you have finished? It was not so long. The words are easier to understand than the ones you read yesterday; was it just yesterday? I think so."

"Yes, last night, but it does seem longer."

"The words, they were deep. I am not sure that I understand them all, but I am tired. So, what do you think; you were feeling a little bit concerned with what you might say?"

"I feel good, thank you. The words are as they are, but they do seem relevant to what I am experiencing with you. I have more recordings and words on my phone…"

"Yes, but another time," she says reassuringly. "Not tonight *please*," she concludes with a hint of humour.

Tea is taken, kisses are shared with 'goodnights' and with that done, I watch her walk down the path, through the garden and (once again) out into the darkness.

I take a shower; a long warm shower. I stay there for quite some while. It is not normal for me to spend so much time in the shower like this. Perhaps having the water wash over head-to-toe will help prepare me for sleep…or something. I guess it is possible that all these wonderful experiences – not just with Marie-Hélène, but here generally – have been destabilising; leaving me feeling I have less /a lack of, control over my life.

Perhaps being away from home, work, and the normal routines of daily life have denuded my frame of reference such that I am struggling to take all of this in – all the information, memories and feelings-past; and all these feelings arising in connection with Marie-Hélène.

Perhaps this is as it should be.

Perhaps it is sometimes not so good for us: being in control. [28]

---

[27] See Appendix III for the complete transcript.

[28] See Appendix II: A lack of control over my life /… /not being in control

Eventually, I feel wet – wetter than wet: drenched, devoid of emotion and in truth – somewhat cool. Sometime after midnight, I climb into bed pulling the sheets tightly around my body, and close-around my neck to leave only my face exposed…yes, a little bit cool still, but – oh yes, I feel *tired*.

The Past Remains Present –
Even After Breakfast
(More Work to Do...)

It is morning when I first wake – but only just. The sheets are still tucked around me the way I had fallen asleep. There is a dim light at the window and the sound of water sprinklers. I close my eyes and drift again. I am reluctant to start another day, but I do not know why this should be. Unless…this is what remains of those distant childhood memories, when I wanted *not* to get up, to avoid my parent's arguments in the kitchen below. What with the joys of last evening pulling my emotions one way and now the memories of unhappy childhood pulling me another, I cannot sleep further. Laying the blanket used last night on the floor in between the two beds, I unroll the yoga mat hoping that a bit of yoga and meditation will bring me a better balance.

Sometime later, with a more relaxed mind, and with dawn now well underway, the alarm clock rings to remind me it is time to go down on the beach.

The fresh air feels particularly good this morning and as I pass between the flowering bushes that feed the bees, I chuckle to myself: I am off to the beach to do *more* yoga, and perhaps some meditation as well. Of course, the group-visualisation will be quite different. [29]

Once again I am first on the beach. With the sun yet to rise, the light is soft and indirect, producing silvery-blue colours in the sky and sea differentiated only by the contrasting ripples of the latter. To my right are the remnants of the lines I had marked out in the sand yesterday. Being that energy lines change their position day to day somewhat, I smooth them away with my foot before repeating the process anew – letting go of yesterdays' and engaging with what is "now".

Just as I finish setting out the new line-arrangements, the others arrive. "Good morning Wayne," Jo-Anne says, with quite some gusto.

"Good morning Jo-Anne," I reply, quite taken by the energy of her positively joyful expression. "Good morning…good morning…good morning…" the

---

[29] See Appendix III for an introduction to Group Meditation/Visualisation

exchanges continue. "I gathered from yesterday," Jo-Anne says to me, "that you had been working with something here?" she enquires, looking at the markings in the sand. "So, how does it happen for you; would you care to share with us what you've marked out here?"

I proceed to give a brief description of what I sense, and what I know of the energy-lines and the grid they would seem to form across the entire planet; how they resonate with different natures and intensities such that one might be drawn to recognise them as masculine or feminine. I explain how there seems to be two lines of particular intensity that weave a sinusoidal path around the planet, and how the masculine "Michael" lines often may be found to track the mountains and higher places of the land, whilst the feminine "Mary" lines are often found in the valleys and with rivers and streams

"Just for now Wayne, can you suggest how we might sit so as to best experience the lines this morning?" Jo-Anne requests.

Pointing out which lines I sense as being masculine and feminine, I advise that most intensity is often felt where lines cross, that being on just one line or another is sometimes accompanied by a sense of movement/change and that a gentler experience is often associated with being in-between as opposed to *on* the lines.

Just as the sun appears, so do Marie-Hélène, Rachel and Henri – and it lights up their faces. Proceeding then into our sun-salutations and a short meditation guided by Jo-Anne, there follows a general departure to the apartments by most, and a short dip in the sea by a few. Having sat still with the golden-orange reflections off the sea a while longer, I hurry towards the light and the wetness to join those "few": Marie-Hélène and Henri.

Tolerating the water only to the extent necessary to dissolve all remaining inclinations towards slumber, we dry and are together making our way back to the apartments when we realise that we are…half-way through the holiday. It is sobering to think I have only five more days with Marie-Hélène, but the mood does not last for long, because the subject turns to breakfast and as we separate, both jovially remind me to, "Bring the eggs!"

Passing close by the hedges on the way from my kitchen with six eggs worth of scrambled yellow delight in a covered pan, the bees are in full song.

Fruit and oats make up the first course and so by the time we are ready for the eggs, they look to have shrunk somewhat. From the speed at which they are consumed, I gather that the eggs have gone down well; that and the fact that shortly afterwards, everyone goes to their rooms to return with all their remaining eggs for the morrows' petit-dejeuner.

"So, should I assume that I am invited for breakfast again?" I enquire.

"But of course," Marie-Hélène replies, smiling. "Who else will do us the eggs so *well?*"

At the morning ECOS, we are led smoothly and timely through the group meditation and are then informed about three key matters. The first is a reminder about tomorrow (Sunday) when the Island tour takes place, and secondly: it is Jo-Anne's birthday on Monday and there will be a meal to celebrate it in the evening that everyone is welcome to take part in. Thirdly, it is time to restock the general provisions, and we are invited to offer items for the shopping list, the response being, "olive oil and Feta – oh, and more eggs!"

Before we close, there is just one further matter: "Who is going to lead the ECOS meditation on Monday morning?" Karina enquires. I volunteer, and the meeting ends.

I am first on the Veranda and having arranged the cushions neatly in general keeping with individual preferences, I hear a faint bell, and I look to see Doris walking adjacent to the main accommodation. After a few minutes, I reach to the bell on the sidewall and ring it: once, twice, three times: clearly, resolutely and – punctually as well.

It has become a joyful habit to greet everyone at the head of the steps, and upon receiving the last two – Henri and Marie-Hélène (looking a touch contrite) Karina welcomes us to this – our third retreat day. With very little introduction, we sit to Holy Harmony and with quite some satisfaction I realise an even deeper sense of peace than yesterday; a peace within which my pre-conditioned thoughts have been resigned to second place (maybe even third).

"Today our spiritual quest is 'Journey to Our Past'," says Karina.

Before we get going, however, we are first invited to share anything that comes to mind from the previous two days. Upon seeing that everyone is attempting to offer something, I feel obliged to capitulate: "Yes, I also have found that a number of things arising out of these last two days has been clarified by interactions with others." From around the group, I note several knowing smiles directed towards me and Marie-Hélène.

Asking that we set yesterday aside, Karina bids we close our eyes, and via certain combinations of stillness, invitation and attention we are led into our next journey – joined once again by our life angels. Light-being, spirit-guide, inspirer, aspect of higher-self or whatever – something (and yet no 'thing') comes again as *my* blessed representative from that place within. Whilst knowingly sat with eyes closed on a cool veranda, I am yet aware of images within my minds' eye that would put me somewhere very different…rocks and mountains, a region where dryness generally prevails but just here – in this sheltered place – there are small waterfalls and rocky streams. There then comes further detail by way of small outcrops of luscious green vegetation, including some with long, delicate flower-stems. In this place, everything seems to be thriving from being in a certain balance with its surroundings. *I* would seem to be sitting in front of a small group of young people (/older children?) with a deep orange shawl or something similar wrapped around me. There are flat cushions scattered around in colours of red and gold and there are bolsters of mint green and royal blue. I sense I have very short hair, deeply tanned skin, a roundish face and kind brown eyes. The others are attentive and respectful towards me. They are students, and I am teaching them.

Karina brings us back to remembering we are on the veranda, and tells us we have been communing with our life angels for about half an hour (!)

Before we share with the group, we are requested to ask one specific question of our guides: while sitting here, and without *going back* to any distant place. Karina advises we should simply remember a feature of where we had just been and then ask, "*What guidance can you give me that will enable me to take that which was important from my past – into my present.*"

I find it easy to remember the imagery for I can yet almost *feel* it, and as I close my eyes, words come immediately…

"*Walk forth and do what you can do.*" 'Walk forth and do what you can do?'

The term "walk forth" is not one of my own, and the over-simplistic "*do what you can do*" is – well, far simpler wording than I would normally use. I have been doing some healing and teaching in recent years, and now it is clear: I should now *do* it – not approach it as if it were a rehearsal.

Working in pairs once again I describe to Rachel the scenarios and surroundings of my journey. When I have finished Rachel asks, "Well, where was this; where did you do this Wayne?" Immediately, I respond with, "In the East – somewhere in the mountains north and east of India." (!?)

When Karina invites us to share with the whole group, I volunteer. With everything still being so clear in my mind, the task is easy. When I stop talking, there is quiet – almost as if my continuation is expected; but I have nothing further to share.

Everybody's journeys are *so* different. One person is happy to share but struggles to recall what were only quite vague perceptions. Another describes in beautiful pictures, a past in something akin to the fabled Atlantis. Another shares their reflections, but being largely a scenario that had represented gloom and despondency, it casts greyness over us all. Karina moves to offer a different interpretation, and following her insight, the clouds seem to part…at least for most of us. Perhaps the participants' effort to broach such difficult matters will at least make for easier progress another time. Due to the time, and the onset of lunch (and I would guess – so as not to trample over what may be "sensitive ground" for some) we are asked to come back to the veranda this evening before dinner, to recap, and to confirm the arrangements for the island tour tomorrow.

Lunch is, as lunch has been previously – both filling and *fulfilling*.

On the walk back, the sun is warm, and the sand warmer, and the beach remains quite deserted; *as bare above as the sea is barren below*. Marie-Hélène and I agree that we should give some greater priority to our paintings this afternoon, more than in the previous two days at least. Therefore, the half-hour later finds us standing at opposite ends of a long table staring down at our paintings. I am looking "through" mine, reflecting rather than planning. Having gotten to know Marie-Hélène here on Skyros, I crave to know what it all means and what I can do to make it continue. Over the past five days, I have been living life both intensely *and* lightly at the same time – letting it come and go, ebb and flow…and maybe that is the key: allowing life to flow – in all its content. I have found several ways to achieve a sense of balance in life, through rest and activity, stillness and action, but just now, as I look at/through my painting, I am sensing a new way. When Marie-Hélène is present, it is almost as if I am in the process of meditation; even while life is proceeding at a relatively fast pace it is all so wonderful – so enjoyable, so deep, so productive; life moves and flows so easily. When we talk, I feel compelled to answer every question fully and truthfully, and I find answers to questions I have never before thought of.

At some point during my rumination, I have begun to employ the paints and brushes, and as I now stop thinking, I find myself looking down at the rendition of this morning's journey. I seem to have found colours and shapes with little effort: arrangements of red, gold, blue, and green in the lower right part of the picture, with the left half containing the hearts and the red spiral. Compared to the distant faded spiral, these latest depictions are relatively bold and present, but interestingly, they appear to be influenced similarly to the other features: leaning towards the right.

"I really don't know what I am doing – look!" Marie-Hélène exclaims aloud continuing, "No! I don't mean look – sorry; we are not supposed to see each other's. Where I paint at home, the people do not understand how I start with nothing and just paint what comes to me, but this: this is less easy," she concludes.

"I cannot see what you are doing of course, but perhaps these pictures will become more meaningful as we work through the week," I offer reassuringly. "But I am finished, and I guess we should take some of *this* back with us today," I say, waving my arm in the general direction of the provisions stacked on the table and chairs to my side.

"Yes, yes – you are right. Okay, I am finished too. 'Too' – is that right, or *also* and t-o or t-o-o please, tell me if you can?" Marie-Hélène enquires.

"Yes, the *too* there makes sense and I think the t-o-o."

"Oh sorry, I know; it is me. I want to get it – *everything* – right, and language is very important to me," she replies, following with a "urr'm" of dissatisfaction. That sound, that very French nasal sound, is almost a part of her normal grammar and really quite sweet.

We agree to meet back here shortly with our swimming things. As we part, juggling with loose and bagged items, *and* our paintings, Marie-Hélène says, "Oh, and today *I* will clean the paintbrushes and things. It is closer to me – for me, yes – *for* me," she concludes.

"Thank you, Marie-Hélène," I say over my shoulder. "And yes: *for* me."

Before heading back down to meet Marie-Hélène, I think to take my mobile phone. Finding it still switched on, and remembering having had it on the last two nights as well, I check the battery level. It is at sixty per cent; that will do. Actually, now I think of it, I have not given a single thought to going online, on Facebook or anything. Then again, what would I say; where would I start? To say simply something like: "*Yes the weather's hot, I'm getting to swim a lot – and the people are nice too,*" would be a gross diminution of the overall experience, but I'm not ready say: "*Oh, and by the way, I think I have fallen in love.*" I could well expect to receive a few follow-up questions with the smileys; and I'd rather be more certain where things are going first. So okay, the phone is just for photos.

Seeing that the glazed double-doors into Marie-Hélène's apartment are wide open – I venture into the comparative gloom. I am about to voice my entry when I see something: someone – asleep on the bed to the right. As I begin to retrace my steps, Marie-Hélène comes out from the bathroom to my left with fingers to her lips. Once clear of the apartment Marie-Hélène tells me she had found her roommate asleep when she returned after the painting. "I really do not want to disturb her but you know – it means she will probably be keeping me up to talk again. I think I should stay with you tonight." It was said lightly, but as I am fast learning, a simple phrase from Marie-Hélène can pave the way to outcomes of quite some significance.

"Of *course*, you are most welcome to join me in the chateau this evening. I am sure we can find a place for you if you cannot sleep well in your apartment," I offer, and not with just a little humour.

"Well thank you," she courteously responds. "An evening *and* a night in the chateau – how *kind* of you!" Laughing ensues. "And, do you think we shall sleep at-all; I am not so sure, but I know it will be easier than talking for a long time *again.* I am sorry to say that, but it is true. In fact, it might be better for her as well. Therefore – yes, I will accept your offer; for me *and* my roommate.*"

What fun. Play-acting I know, but not hiding anything, and in fact – bringing about a decision on a sensitive topic very easily. How wonderful life can *be* when two people are on the same wavelength.

At the beach, we are not alone. There are only about a dozen people scattered across the two-hundred metres of sand, but we have been spoilt by having the place virtually to ourselves until now. This surprises us for a while – until we take account of this being the weekend, and that the people are probably having *their* weekend on *their* beach (whereas we are simply tourists). It is another unexpected change, but I guess overall I am rather beginning to enjoy the regular exposure to new and unexpected experiences (…as Marie-Hélène drops her towel and runs into the sea).

Although it was not arranged such, neither of us has brought our mask and snorkel. It would seem the swimming today is only for refreshment purposes and – let's face it – another excuse to be somewhere else – together. After about fifty metres of quite purposeful head-down swimming, I find I have gotten some way ahead. I note, however, that Marie-Hélène is not putting her face into the water at all (which probably accounts for it). "I see you are not swimming with your head under."

"No, I do not feel so well here now."

We both know why, and it warrants no more talk. Instead, we come together for a brief kiss – ending with each of us looking up and down the bay…before laughing.

"There is some progress; now we kiss first and *then* check to see who may be about!" I chance.

"Oh, there is no problem really. They all see it when we are together. We sit together, walk together, and eat together; everyone knows."

She is close now, and her lips are at my mouth again as she repeats, "There is *no* problem," and with that particular French accent that serves so well in the transfer of words from her lips…to mine. This time, I make a conscious effort *not* to look elsewhere. (It is not so hard to do.)

Out on the shore, I reach for my towel and – feeling my phone – I remember why I'd brought it. So, right, what should be the subject (a certain pink towel and orange bikini perhaps)? I lift my phone but before shooting I catch the time. "Oh, it is nearly five-thirty. Was it at six o'clock that we were asked to meet again at the chateau?"

"Oh, yes… no! No, it was six-thirty, we have time; no rushing me – please," she implores – as if challenging me to kiss her in front of *anyone*; and as I catch her *again* looking out over my shoulder my mouth breaks into a smirk. "What?" she says pulling away yet continuing to shoot glances. "What is it?"

"Oh, it is *nothing*," I reply, attempting to imitate her. "It's just that I can see you looking towards the apartments…*no problème* – is it?" I taunt.

She laughs. "Okay, yes, it is a little different kissing *here,*" giving in and dropping her head onto my shoulder in her mirth. "Okay – we go then?" she suggests. (We go.)

At six twenty-nine I am on the veranda with most of the others, watching as Karina lights the candle in the middle. "It's always nice to do this when we meet here," she says. "Spirit is here whenever we are and it just seems right to honour their presence with a flame, don't you think?"

It transpires there will be eight of us tomorrow on the island tour – travelling in two cars. No ECOS tomorrow, and moving out just after breakfast "at nine *sharp",* Karina tells us. She continues that we have a long day ahead with lots of lovely places to visit, and that now she is sure of our number she can confirm the booking for lunch at a beachside restaurant. "I know you'll just love it," she says warmly. Karina goes on to say how the family there are very friendly, with a son who has learning difficulties and whom we might find roaming around. "He is quite harmless, but he cannot make his wishes and intentions known in the normal way, so just say hello if you see him," she assures us. Before we part, there are further discussions to discern who is going to the taverna this evening and who is eating here. It seems most of us want another night in – this admittedly being encouraged by Doris, Angel and daughter Beryl – who discloses they had been shopping and are planning to share a "little something special" later.

On opening my refrigerator door, I see there is plenty of pasta still left, but being that it is somewhat dry I set about re-hydrating it in the wok, finishing it off with a splash of "huile d'olive". Finally, I cut up the remaining tomatoes and then slice in – *of course* – the remaining Feta, followed by a sprinkle of black pepper and basil.

At the communal area, there is quite some activity. As each person arrives, the existing dishes are moved around to make space for the new offerings. The process is repeated until what had first appeared as a range of tasty sharing platters, now looks like a generously over-ordered group takeaway. Candles are lit and placed around the table, most of the electric lights are switched off, and peace descends as we behold our good fortune. I find myself minded to place my hands together and say quietly to myself the *"Ita-daki-masu"* – but no chance of that, for Rachel spots me and launches her own rendition "Itti-tikka-takka". Then, with the attention of everybody, "Wayne, can you tell me again please, what it is, how to say it and what it means?" With all other action having ceased, I (obligingly) try to respond on all points – quickly, for there follows a chummy feeding frenzy as everyone ploughs into salads, hummus, Tzatziki, Feta, bread and oils; then pasta, potatoes in jackets, stuffed peppers, baked courgettes…then a *little* more bread and Feta and salad. New this evening: some red wine. I suspect the wine is a local one, for most are sipping rather cautiously. Subsequently, quite a splurge of it goes into the freshly re-heated courgette-bake – taking the edge off the heat and adding a certain fruity zing.

Marie-Hélène meanwhile, enjoys a *full* glass.

Reclining with a somewhat full stomach, I observe Doris, Angel and Beryl, depart for their apartment, to return with trays of… something. The trays are set down to reveal – amongst other things – that brown, sticky-sweet Greek delicacy that has become our most celebrated holiday dessert: "Baklava" (we call out together). The "other things" are further cakes of undetermined content but offering comparable honey sweetness. After the (second) Baklava, I manage to persuade myself that I really should try some of the others – bringing me flavours of almond and…apple (?) and perhaps – cinnamon (?) For sure, whatever their aromatic origin, they will most-certainly contain plenty of calories.

After helping with the washing up at Rachel and Henri's place, I am gathering the items that appear to be mine, when I spot the large pan I had brought set aside on a chair. The lid of the pan appears unwashed, and then on closer inspection, I see why: it still has some contents. Lifting the lid, I find there is…well – only a *few* mouthfuls remaining…

"Wayne!"

It is Marie-Hélène, addressing me from Rachel and Henri's doorway. "Is it that you are still *hungry*!" she exclaims – fortunately to an audience of one. "I have *seen* you tonight; it is just as if you cannot stop eating."

"It will save me some washing up and it would be a shame to waste it," I retort looking for some measure of excuse for my gluttony. Then, as she emerges into better light, she sees me, as I observe her – *chewing!* "It is true, it is all *sooo* good!" she agrees, wiping her mouth.

Back at the chateau, I am yet wrist-deep in soapy water when Marie-Hélène knocks on the door and enters. "Only me!" she sings. "So, what can I do to help?"

"You can get the tea," I suggest.

"Yes, bonne idée – good idea, but please not the *camomile*, it is not for me, I think. I will bring mine to you. You can use it – but, do you perhaps 'ave any *montagne thé*?"

My guess is that she has been speaking with Henri and Rachel, and that she has helped finished the wine because her accent is quite a bit more pronounced. (I love it!)

"There, next to the water," I advise, turning and nodding. "No, the other side of the toaster."

"So, you have said you would like to have me 'ear something; something that you have spoken? Like the one you spoke me – to me, did read me – last night, yes?" (I love that characteristic of her as well, the part that seeks to "get it right"; I do it too.)

"Yes, I found quite a few things on my phone earlier this afternoon. *Actually*, I think I should offer you the chance to listen to a live one – so to speak."

"Live – why, what do you mean? What does it say? If it is spoken by you, I should like to listen to it in any case. Ah, you are too polite – you English-Man," she politely mocks.

As the sage-aroma of our Greek Mountain Tea drifts across the room, Marie-Hélène observes her preferred relaxed posture, laid out to my side with head on my lap. When she has settled, I pick up my phone; right then – what might be an interesting recording…perhaps one about relationships, or even better: the one in which I talk *about* myself and a relationship yet to come.

"So, this is an interesting one. I am speaking about the natural laws relating to love, oh – and a special thing happened when I made this particular recording; to do with the music playing in the background. It's from the CD I mentioned was given to me about 'Twin Flames' – like Twin Souls or Soul-twins, if I've got it right."

"Oh, you mean – perhaps like us?" Marie-Hélène interjects. (Pause…) "I don't know. I am always wary about labels; I find they restrict understanding as much as they serve to communicate – but yes, I think I could apply it to what I am experiencing."

"What *we* are experiencing – both of us, I know it," she confirms. I pause, trying to contain my heartbeat. "So anyway, here it is – here I am – with the music of the CD in the background."

With my right hand on the crown of Marie-Hélène's head and my left hand held within both of hers against her chest, I set the phone to 'play'…

"Today I talk of Love."

"Love ultimately extends to and originates in Spirit. It is that connection which binds all souls together and acts through the Law of Duality that finds divine intention separated – in this physical plane – into two sides of the same coin: the Ying, the Yang, the woman, the man…"

(…sometime later…) [30]

"…And, if by chance we find our lives entwined again with that person, then in truth we have a Love divine.

Thank you for this space."

---

[30] See Appendix III for the complete recording.

Just as yesterday, Marie-Hélène remains still and quiet.

"What can I say?" she eventually says. And yes, the music seems almost made to fit it; "you did not plan for this?"

"No, nothing was planned other than that I had put the music on first; oh, and actually – it was the first and only time I had put some music on whilst planning to speak like that."

"Well, it makes much sense. I cannot say more," she finishes. However, she does say one thing more. "So, I can stay *with you* – tonight? And, maybe I will sleep better, and maybe you will too?"

"Yes, and maybe," I reply. "*Maybe.*"

"What *maybe*: '*maybe* I can stay with you' or 'maybe we will sleep better' – what are you saying?" she teases.

"Yes, yes of course – do *please* stay with me tonight; *maybe* we will sleep… eventually," I add. We stand up and kiss for a moment and while I take our teas back to the kitchen, Marie-Hélène goes directly upstairs to the spare bed – the one still tidily arranged – and pushing the cushions aside, lies back. "Well?" she says, as I arrive with water for the night.

Everything in her manner delivers a clear invitation, but with it being the first opportunity since our first night to really appreciate one-another, I find myself a little adverse to speed. Marie-Hélène however, has other thoughts, and lifting herself from the bed she drops to her knees and pulls my clothing deftly to the floor. After this (brief) and mutual pleasure, I leave the luxury of her semi-nakedness to switch off the main light. With the bathroom door ajar, the bathroom light produces a bright stripe that runs across the floor and folds up onto the bedcovers, to pass snake-like across the contours of her body…her body…

Marie-Hélène picks up all the cushions apart from two and I deposit them on the other bed. I un-tuck the tightly fitted sheet and she lays the two cushions side by side at the head of the bed. Turning to face me, she reaches up behind herself and removes her bra. Her exposed skin invites my lips and tongue – my hands travelling slowly down to her waist, to the thin band of her Brazilian lingerie. It is then my turn to drop to the floor, where I am met by the slight roughness of finely trimmed hair. Planting a brief kiss on her bare skin, I take in her aroma as I nuzzle with lips and tongue. She shivers, pulls away, and pulling back the sheet, climbs into bed – holding it open for me to join her. I join her.

If I had any doubts remaining after that first night (…etc.) as to what manner of consistency there could *possibly* be regarding such heady passion, they were now to be entirely relieved. We have made love every day since then, but the excitement of the location and the risk of being caught have always contributed to the intensity of the experience. Now, there is just her and me.

We kiss, caress, stroke, touch, taste, tease…turn, turn, kiss and after *a few minutes*…we consummate. I have experienced *new love* a few times in life, but I do not ever recall lovemaking feeling both so exciting and – at the same time – so comfortable; as if we have been making love this way for years. [31]

Knowing there is no one likely to shine a light on us tonight (metaphorically and otherwise) we now discover even more freedom in our expression; giving and receiving, asking and encouraging, calling/singing-out – however it comes. Having the patience to refrain: just for a moment, and to hold on: at the deepest point of longing. Waiting just at the edge, sensing the calm before the next wave, and then when it threatens to be all-consuming – riding to its peak where time itself seems to be held in abeyance; where the slightest further movement will surely mean submitting to the depths of a crashing, turbulent – out of this world – crescendo…

It is all and it is now, and it is all only in this now.

A few more hours later, we find ourselves in the early hours of the next day before we recall the part of our original plan that had included getting more sleep. Surveying the room – bed covers, sheets, and cushions now scattered around on the floor with our clothing – we look at one another and laugh. We decide to tidy up and then *try* to sleep together – something we have not done yet.

Showering slows our minds and cools our temperaments (sort of) and upon lights-out, we pull the sheets in tightly. It is lovely and cuddly, but there is not much room in this (single) bed for two spooned' warm bodies on a warm night. With my ardour still somewhat apparent, Marie-Hélène wiggles against me and I return the favour. Unsurprisingly (you might well understand), my ardour remains. Plan 1 is not working so well.

The second plan of action is to arrange ourselves on separate beds. Being just able to make each other out in the darkened room, we exchange a few short observations of kind and complementary nature.

---

[31] When one's general health has been maintained along with a good measure of fitness and vitality, their combination with the confidence and patience that comes with maturity and the heady excitement of "new love" has the effect of elevating everything to a whole new level.

These are followed by a few comments of a humorous nature, and then the sharing of such jokes and giggling that moves swiftly on to all-out laughing – the overall effect being as if we are on some kind of childhood sleepover. It seems the second plan is not meeting the original aim either.

"If I am going to be awake all night talking to a beautiful woman in my bedroom, I really think I should be at least trying to share the same bed with her," I say as my final offering towards humour for the night. Fortunately, the beautiful woman agrees, and thus we submit to a revised Plan One which entails little (i.e., no) sleeping, and concludes in the (not so) early hours with showers and an extended search through the pile of clothing to find Marie-Hélène's.

Subsequently, I follow Marie-Hélène down the stairs where we exchange "Bonne nuit" and "Good morning" and following one last brief kiss at the open door I watch her walking the garden path under the light of the moon.

As I begin to drift off to sleep – tucked up, alone – I have just one more experience: the rather unexpected and totally unwanted sound of the water sprinklers…

The Island Tour
(Two Hearts of Stone Find Their Place)

The morning appears still as I look through the window in the general direction of the sea. There is a semblance of stillness within me also, but I cannot say I feel rested. I switch on my phone and when the wispy purple wave motions have finished, I select a gentle chant to play – with a half-thought that bringing some small measure of routine into my life might help balance my (returned) disquiet with "not-sleeping". It has now been over a week since I have had anything like a good nights' sleep, yet all said and done, my body is not showing signs of fatigue. Perhaps, I should try to accept this as normal now.

Following a refreshing drink of water, I prepare for the sunrise and head off, down the veranda steps, and along the path, taking in the invigorating morning air. At the end of the garden path, I come across only a few bees, but my spirit rises as I observe Marie-Hélène ahead. Dressed in her white linen trousers and pink vest, and with her pink towel around her shoulders, (ah the mill…) today – she awaits *me*.

"How did you sleep? Did you sleep well?" I enquire.

"Yes, good thank you, I think I fell asleep almost as soon as I got into bed, but it did not feel like it was for so very long. And you, how did you sleep? I know you have not been sleeping so well." she ventures.

"I think I fell asleep quite quickly as well, but I was woken early by the garden sprinklers and I am not sure I slept properly afterwards."

"Oh, what time was that? I did not hear anything?"

"I don't know exactly. I didn't want to see the time in case it made me feel worse."

As we set off for the beach, we discuss ways we might be able to spend the whole night together *and* get some sleep. "Perhaps tonight we can find a place to move the mattresses," I venture, "so that we can be close enough, but not so close that we keep getting aroused."

"What do you mean? I would rather we do not sleep at all than to be apart again. We do not have so many nights left – you know," she concludes.

"I do not mean different rooms, just – oh, I don't know. We'll see. Anyway, we will have the entire day together today," I offer as compensation for any precise plan.

At the beach, we find Renna and Madelyn already seated. We exchange "hello" but stop short of any conversation that risks disturbing the general ambience. Spreading out my mat on the cool – almost damp – sand, we sit facing the horizon and await the sun. Another day in paradise; what more could I want, and another day of great potential because after breakfast, we set off on a tour of Skyros Island. Despite a full schedule for the day, I take a few minutes to do some yoga poses – stretches really – to free-up my lower back. Marie-Hélène watches on. We agree to a short dip in the sea (always enough time for a short dip in the sea). Today, however, there is only us two, and today my head (also) stays above the surface.

While seated at breakfast with Marie-Hélène Rachel and Henri, I comprehend this *breakfasting with friends* routine will become a dear memory to me. Today, however, it will be a short one, because there is a need for all breakfast niceties to be condensed. Accordingly, only half an hour later, we are waiting beside two cars for further instructions. Jo-Anne informs us that she will be driving *us,* and then encourages us to check we have swimming gear, water, some money, and some footwear suitable for walking…and we are off.

Having travelled over dry and largely unpopulated land for some thirty or so minutes, our first stop of the day is Palamari. We depart the metalled road to take a dusty track that winds for about half a kilometre before we catch sight of the sea and a small deserted bay. We stop affront a pair of rusting metal gates. Behind, there appears to be some paving, and low stone ruins, a small modern shed, and what looks like some archaeological excavations.

Karina and Jo-Anne look at the fading notices on the gate and together they reach the understanding that – it is closed on Sundays! I am not so worried: the ruins do not look particularly exciting, but I am interested to learn how – as legend would have it – Achilles had stayed here as a young man for quite some time (before – that is – being moved away and disguised to protect him from being taken to fight in the wars).

We return to the cars and after doubling back a short distance, we divert over towards the opposite coast – the plan being to find a particular chapel that sits directly beside the sea. Upon reaching the coast road and turning due south, we soon find ourselves in a much more vibrant area, with several well-maintained residences, some shops and small industrial units, and a few boats onshore and offshore. A little further, we pull off to the right into a dust and shingle car park – beside Kalogrias bay.

Once out of the car, Jo-Anne informs us there is time for a short swim, and she points out a natural rock pool before asking that we first hold back so that she and Karina can discuss the arrangements for the chapel. Jo-Anne and Karina walk only some thirty metres to an all-but inconspicuous, small, whitewashed square building built on the rocky shoreline. It has two flags flying from the roadside elevation and a small cross that from where I am standing appears to be – well, "fluffy." A minute later, Jo-Anne returns to confirm that *this* place is open, and we should re-assemble in about thirty minutes to enter the chapel.

I approach Marie-Hélène and enquire whether she is interested in swimming and exploring underwater here. With repeated glances towards Rachel nearby, Marie-Hélène seems reluctant to participate and offers that she will join me in a short while.

Figuring I might use the car as shelter while I change, I hastily return there, but upon ducking to retrieve my things from the car, I spy Jo-Anne already bent-double at the open door on the other side. Consequently, having grabbed my things I step away to give her some privacy. Having turned to see Renna and Madelyn a way over beside the rock pool, I press ahead with changing – relying predominantly on my towel for coverage. Well-before I am ready, Jo-Anne makes her way down the small incline into the rock pool and proceeds to float in the water whilst Renna and Madelyn watch on.

Supposing she might have some personal connection with the place, I leave Jo-Anne to the rock-pool and head further up towards the chapel where the rocks slope more gradually into the sea. Donning mask and snorkel, I step gingerly on and around sharp and slippery rocks until I am about knee-deep, at which point I squat down and then stretch out into the water. Just before my head goes under, I glance back to see if Marie-Hélène may yet be ready to swim; but she is not – she is now talking with Renna and Madelyn. Perhaps, therefore, I shall now give the water my complete attention.

Within seconds, I see vibrant sea-plants, shellfish, urchins, and several fish. I am at the same time happy to be here and slightly sad, because this confirms my suspicions about the poor state of the sea where we are staying on the other coast. Heading left in the direction of the rock pool, I swim for quite a distance before lifting my head to find I have swum – indeed – *quite* a distance and in fact, past the rock pool. Upon returning, I find that the rock pool when viewed from seaward is more of a mini rock lagoon forming something of a bath, with underwater openings – somewhere; I decide to explore.

There appears to be two very small caverns through which the water enters, and I choose to enter the largest one. The first indication of entering comes when the sun is shaded, and the second comes when – still floating – I feel my snorkel catching on the roof overhead.

I am excited by the idea of getting on with this exploration, but although it is hardly a Jacques Cousteau expedition, I find myself pondering over the fact that no one else knows I am about to do this. With the excitement winning out, I take a few deep slow breaths and on the last one, I release some air so as not to be too buoyant – and go under. With the first metre accomplished, I am taken by the many pretty colours on the rocks below and to the side, with more on the rock pool floor ahead. Completely underwater now, the cavern roof starts to lower – necessitating the use of my hands to keep me moving. With some surprise, I notice there is less space either side of me than I had estimated, and with much-reduced light here, it *feels* closed-in now. I know I have plenty of air and if needed I can push myself out backwards and so, accordingly, I push on, adopting a porpoise like movement. After little more than a metre, I find myself able to stretch forward to jagged rocks that provide a handhold. With increased light, it seems I am nearly through, but it is taking considerably more time than anticipated; instead of being engaged with the beauty of it all, I am finding it more an exercise in self-control. It is only a few more seconds – making about fifteen to twenty seconds in total – before my snorkel finds air again, but the last few are *enough*. My exit has not been made with quite the flare I had expected either – needing to double myself to the right to get around a corner before pulling myself completely through and into the sunlight. I do, however, manage to hold onto *some* self-esteem as – staying in the water – I roll over and execute a decidedly "nonchalant" mask removal. As it happens, no one witnesses my exit, but having felt both elated and anxious in equal proportions, I seek no further accolade. With the sun hot on my face, but with the shine taken off my appreciation of the rock pool, I am ready to get out.

Having scrabbled directly up the slope to find my towel, Marie-Hélène walks (!) down the other side to make a speedy entry. She is only some metres away but it seems almost as if she has not noticed me, or is inclined to be showing some space between us. Alternatively, I suppose she may simply have been so-delayed by conversation that she now craves the water. Seconds later, with worry let-go, I observe Marie-Hélène floating on her back – smiling up at me. Such fickle creatures as we are, I drop my towel and re-enter the pool to commence talking as if we had only just stopped. I start to mention how I had entered the pool via the rock cavern, but there is no time to continue; the others have started to gather in front of the chapel.

After hurriedly drying and dressing, and confirming my mobile phone is still in my shorts-pocket, we make our way to the chapel. As we approach, I note that the fluffy cross I had seen earlier is in fact, made from wood and straw, with ears of grain and dried flowers wrapped and threaded around it; very pretty. (I really should not have forgotten my glasses.)

Having gone down the few steps into the chapel, I pause to allow my eyes the time to adjust to the relative darkness. Everyone else has found a place on the built-in white-painted concrete benches that line the walls. Marie-Hélène takes up a sole position on the left, and I am in a similar position on the right.

The overall design is much the same as the other chapels: there are the same two internal doorways at the back separated by a central pillar and with a space beyond, but there are no doors in them and whereas one opening has a squared-off top, the other one has an arch and is wider. There seems to be a wooden bench beyond the arched side and – although I cannot see very much, it does look like the 'chapel within a chapel' or maybe it is the confessional (but what do I know). The ceiling is of wooden slats laid across poles – branches even – supported by heavy oak-looking beams. Dried flowers decorate the ceiling, the beams and frames, and the iconic pictures and doorways. There are fresh flowers in vases on the floor, and – I realise I have slipped into *intellectualising* my experience, instead of *being* in it…

Karina invites us to close our eyes, breathe deeply in through the nose, and out through the mouth – several times in a controlled manner – before allowing the breath to return to normal. After a short pause, she leads us in a visualisation and the sense of peace becomes deeper, and then – deeper still. I am not aware of anything other than that someone is still speaking. The words seem gentle and meaningful, but I am not registering them; they flow through me and around me, and the sensation of light on the other side of my eyelids is replaced by near-darkness, with an impression/shadow of a fuzzy circular shape (not unlike my iris) that pulses with a gentle rhythm (not unlike my heart). The sensation then changes to one where I am slowly entering the centre of the darkness, and as I accept this route to that space-within, I remain aware only of the *sound* of Karina's voice.

Karina stops talking, and I open my eyes. Although I am aware of everything around me, I am also aware of that *same* still-space being available to me; and I am aware of a "presence". Then, from within that space, I sense the invite – almost a compulsion – to get up and go outside into the sunshine and to the waters-edge. Being engaged by the sensations without/within and at the same time inquisitive, I stand, take a photo (– *well!*) and head outside. Once on the beach, I walk directly to the waters' edge and squat there to find myself looking down at crystal-clear water and a pebble-strewn bed. There are shells of varying shapes, sizes, and colours and the sunlight is acting on the gentle undulations of the waters' surface to cast patterns of light that – in each second – come into focus then instantly diffuse in all directions. I find myself perusing the stones for a minute, before once-more becoming aware of a presence. I sense the invite to *'Look for the heart'* and I proceed to look for a heart-shaped pattern within the arrangements of shape and colour, but I see none. Then, even as the thoughts of a query are still forming, I sense that the heart is a single stone. As my eyes sweep across the small section of water directly in front of me, I sense an impulse at a certain point, and my sight falls upon a small pale-coloured stone: *'Yes,'* I sense, but what I am looking at is simply a pale stone roughly oval in shape. Then I sense, *'No – turn it over'.* As I commence to turn the stone in my fingers, I see significant contours – particularly at one end, but nothing of much clarity. With the stone still in the water, I rub my thumb across the contours and I sense *'Yes'.* Taking the stone out of the water, I note one end of the stone having contours that come together to look something like a point. As the water runs off, the other end of the stone reveals such colours and contours that do – I must accept – depict a certain double-crest, much like the top of a heart shape. The intellectual observer now fails me, and unable to proceed, I feel overcome. As tears form in my eyes, I find myself asking "How – why?", and I sense in return *'This is Love, **the** connection'.*

My left-hand goes down into the water to steady myself, and I remain, squatting. I look again at the stone in my palm. It is not quite the conventional heart, but it is most certainly *of* a heart shape, and besides, the manner in which I have been led to find it is astounding on its own. Moreover, with my hand yet in the water, I retain the sense of that *connection*; that intense love feeling bringing tears of joy; tears that – like the words I had sensed, did not feel as if they were all-alone – mine.

The sounds and reflections from the water together with voices behind me interrupt my thoughts, and as I focus on the physicality of where I am, and what I am doing, the brilliance of the stones and shells in the water noticeably reduces. I feel peaceful, but in some way, I also feel different. I no longer feel the presence of earlier, but I do feel – accompanied.

I also feel – no, I *know* – I must take this stone with me.

Placing the stone securely in my pocket, I stand up and go over to where the others are talking on the chapel terrace. Marie-Hélène is there, but she is engaged in talking. I want to tell her about the stone, but it is not the right time.

Riding along in the car, I have some internal conflict regarding the stone. Despite having only just found it, it feels right – a good thing, necessary even – that I give it away. Yet, I am also reluctant to let it go. I know the feeling that came was not from the stone, it just accompanied the stone, yet I cannot easily separate the two. I have felt something akin to that "love connection" before, the first memory being during my Reiki training, and subsequently, when witnessing a moment of realisation/self-revelation; but on those occasions, the feeling came with less depth/purity. Whilst I am open to the idea of letting-go the stone, I feel reluctant because I do not yet know where or how, although – as I think of it, I have had another similar sense of *connection* and stillness with it: when my lips first met Marie-Hélène's. Oh, of *course*, I must give it to her.

Coastal images change to valleys and then forests as Jo-Anne drives us inland and across small valleys until after about twenty minutes, the road narrows and weaves down between tree-lined slopes and occasional rock outcrops. As the road begins to level out, we pass a few outbuildings, then some houses and then – we are at the sea once again.

We arrive at Atsitsa, a small village that Jo-Anne tells us she has visited before and fondly remembers. The size of the roads and the number and positions of junctions and driveways at the village centre present some challenge to parking, but in that time-honoured tradition, we drive around for some while, only to return to the same slightly off-road place. Surely, this dusty drive being so wide; is it not part of the public road system (?)

The occupants of the other car are already investigating a covered terrace that just might be a café. I arrive to find chairs, tables, and attractive-homely displays of large pots, glassware, and some orange and yellow webbing – a bit like fishing nets. In point of fact, there is a lot of that webbing…a-ha – they *are* fishing nets, and elsewhere they are laid across tables and chairs as if being repaired.

Seeing there are no waiting staff, I go over to investigate the beach. The coastline to either side is mostly rock, whilst here at the centre the beach is many large flat stones. There is a long jetty adjacent to the terrace – part rock, part concrete – some fifteen metres or so long. There are also the remains of other such similar stone structures, one being to the right where the bay starts to turn back on itself – where the now crumbling tower was once perhaps, a crane that would load the tall-ships directly from carts.

I take a few photographs and then having turned to capture a few of the bright nets stretched out over tables and chairs, I go back to seeking a drink.

A few of the tables now have the earlier arrivals relaxing on chairs around them. I take one of two unoccupied chairs on the covered terrace, set back from the beach. Marie-Hélène is perched on the low sidewall directly beside the beach, in the sun, and reading the screen of her phone. Her hair, tied tightly back, is still wet from the earlier swim. She is wearing a brightly coloured large-patterned dress sporting Aztec/semi-psychedelic patterns. She lifts her phone, pointing it out across the bay: a beautiful sight (the bay as well).

Jo-Anne takes our orders for coffees and refreshing fizzy drinks and passes them on to a man hidden in the shadow; the man who perhaps runs the café and mends the nets and goes out fishing – just to make ends meet.

Receiving my glass of lemonade, I take occasional sips and partake in the occasional conversation, and meanwhile – shoot occasional glances over towards Marie-Hélène. I have still to tell her about – to give her – the heart-stone, but that aside, I would prefer to be over there talking with her than – well, anything really.

After reaching the end of a (very pleasant) discourse with Karina, I stand and take out my phone – for more photographs of the bay (mostly). Starting to frame firstly the more distant objects, I then zoom out to include (various) features in the semi-shadowed foreground. Expanding the frame more, I bring in from the right, the profile of a large earthenware pot set with small blooms. The blooms (almost) capture my full attention, but then – my attention moves to the other pots further to the right and then – oh, perhaps the lady in the bright-patterned dress wouldn't mind me taking one or two photos…

The next drive takes somewhat longer than the previous ones, and at a point where I am no longer entertained by the views, I reach into my pocket. Now seems as good a time as any: "Marie-Hélène, I was in the chapel earlier this morning and felt I should go to the sea and look for something there. You may have noticed; I went straight out at the end of the meditation and over to the waters' edge?"

"No – I don't think so. Why did you go there?" she asks.

"Well, I found this," I say, taking the stone out of my pocket and placing it into her open palm, facedown.

"I say 'found it', but it felt more like I was guided to it. I was almost ready to give up when I felt given to this stone, and that I should turn it over and – well…" I turn it over in her palm. "Look, a heart; I would like to give to you."

"Thank you but, do you think that you should?" she queries. "You found it. You should keep it (?)"

"No, I know it is for you. I *give* it…to you," I say, solemnly.

"Thank you. I…I don't know quite what to say," she says quietly, kissing my cheek.

Marie-Hélène is silent. I do not wish to be overly dramatic, but – the significance of the Love I have found on Skyros sits profound within me. Marie-Hélène continues to be quiet, but moves to take my hand and places the stone securely in-between our palms. I think she might know what I'm feeling.

The next part of the journey seems to go much quicker, and as we emerge from the final tight corner of a series of hillside turns, we pass a sign, written in Greek. The sign looks like the sort of sign that would read, "Sea and food and fun this way…" and within the minute the sea and cliffs of our lunchtime destination do nothing to discourage such an opinion.

This is Agios Fokas Bay and it is a *proper* holiday destination. Just beyond a low stonewall, a single-file car park alongside the beach contains a series of further signs pointing to…*other things* (in Greek). There are several cars parked, and people are taking in the sun and swimming. Beyond the wall, gardens contain several small trees and around and further beyond are apartments and chalets. Across the way is a stone archway leading to a single-story modern stone building with a large covered terrace. From the sights, sounds, and aromas that meet us as we walk in that general direction, I suspect we will be taking lunch there.

After the relatively sombre locations we have visited today, this is a most-welcomed touch of geniality. There are sunshades on the beach (of the natural reed and palm leaf variety) and a few (just a few) sunbeds underneath; thankfully – nothing of the "industry" of the Athens resort, and without the end-of-season feel of our first island location: this place feels to be *perfect*.

Karina makes enquiries with the restaurant and returns to inform us it will be about forty-five minutes until they will be ready. This will give us about half an hour in the sea – the *us* being inclusive of Henri who, in fact, is first in the water, with Marie-Hélène close behind. The water is warmer here; clearer as well and it really *feels* better. Renna soon joins us and then Madelyn – whose rejoice of the experience only adds further to my suspicions regarding the other coastline. Feeling refreshed enough to head back to shore and with a mind to drying off under the sun, I am joined presently by Marie-Hélène who immediately moves her belongings from just a few metres away, to directly beside mine. She has not spoken about the heart-stone since I gave it to her, but as I lay down to dry, she lays close by me and that speaks enough.

Seated for lunch in the shade, we could not ask for a better location. Having considered our menus for some minutes, Marie-Hélène and I settle on different dishes so that we can share each other's and thus have a fuller experience. Having delivered our orders, Jo-Anne comes over and bends slightly to engage me. "Wayne, I found this, and I feel I would like to give it to you," she says quietly – taking from her side, a palm-sized pale cream stone and laying it on the table in front of me. "When I saw this stone, I thought of you – of Marie-Hélène and you. You look so at peace and happy together. I think it is *so* lovely that you have met. Look," she says, tracing the broad outline of the stone with her forefinger. "Doesn't it look almost like a heart?" (!)

I look, it does, and similarly to mine – it *suggests* the heart shape more than accurately depicting it, and so resembles the one I have given Marie-Hélène more than any ordinary heart shape could.

"Thank you. This is very special Jo-Anne and for reasons you'll not guess because, just a little earlier in the car I gave Marie-Hélène a small heart-shaped stone I had been guided to find in the sea after coming out of the chapel. It had felt strange to give it straightaway, but now that something so similar has come back to me, it all seems perfect. Thank you."

"Oh Wayne, that is so lovely. I'm so sure you both deserve it; you're both lovely."

With that, Jo-Anne puts her arm behind me and with a hand on my shoulder, she pulls me into a gentle side-on hug. On her release, our eyes meet and in a moment of mutual understanding, our eyes briefly close as we each make an almost imperceptible movement towards a bow.

"Oh, what is it, what does she tell you?" Marie-Hélène asks.

Showing her the stone: "She gave me this…" I submit.

"Oh, how special. Does she know what you gave me? Did you show her already – before?"

"No, no one else knows of the stone I gave you, and yes – it is special. Something about you and me – something about us – *is* special." With that, Marie-Hélène reaches for my hand and holds on tightly…until the food comes.

After a week of cuisine based around Greek salad and slow-roasted vegetables (as fond of it as I am) I very much welcome the fish with vegetables today. It has also been nearly six hours since breakfast, so for the first time in ages, I am feeling (almost) hungry.

Having thoroughly enjoyed lunch, I excuse myself from the table to find the toilets. There is a sign at the edge of the terrace written in Greek and underwritten in French "*Toilettes*" (?) and I follow it through a small gate in wooden-picket fencing towards the apartments. On the way, I pass a kindly looking young man standing a little uncomfortably. I acknowledge him with a smile and a nod.

Greeted by fierce sunlight as I exit, I shade my eyes looking for the best route back to the terrace, and I pass the same young man who has remained where I last saw him. Realising that *this* may be the 'son' that Karina had mentioned, I re-deliver a smile with more-sincere purpose, but it seems too much – for he turns slightly as if shying away. After closing the gate behind me I look back; he looks okay. I suppose there are worse places to call home than this, and having occasional contact with others is probably a good thing. Perhaps everyone with such similar challenges, and who is not a danger to themselves or others, deserves such a place within the wider community.

With neither Marie-Hélène nor I having ever experienced the cramping after eating that our parents had often warned of, we take the risk of entering the water with full stomachs so that we might have longer to explore. We set off towards a small headland about two to three hundred metres away on the left. Marie-Hélène proposes I lead and I do so happily – but with some interest, I note I have set a relatively a gentle pace. (Perhaps some rules/fears/conditioning go much deeper than I would like to accept.)

Everything below the surface here is more vibrant and perfuse including the sea-life of the fishy kind, but interestingly – not *so* very much more. Having reached the tip of the headland as agreed I look up to share my experience with Marie-Hélène…but she is no-where I…oh, there she is, right over to my side and some way ahead (!) I am beginning to get used to this general scenario now, and it is not long before she takes stock of her relative position and comes straight over.

"Oh, sorry," she says, slightly out of breath. "I saw some fish! It is so much nicer here – don't you agree?"

I smile. "Yes, I agree."

Seeing an inviting bay with a small beach ahead of us, we decide to swim on. Once near enough to the beach to confirm the existence of a suitable exit route, we agree to thread our way through the rocky shallows and get out. Having departed the water, we fall immediately into one another's arms. Agreeing to just a short rest, because we want to make the most of this – our best snorkelling opportunity so far, we have only a quick cuddle; just for a…

Some fifteen minutes later (!) we walk back into the water hand-in-hand until the rocky seabed causes us to stumble. Marie-Hélène opts for careful walking until waist-depth and then takes a plunge, while I do the usual: squatting down in the water and floating out horizontally. We spot a collection of small rocky islets another few hundred metres on, and we decide to set that as our next port of call. Upon reaching the islets, we continue to swim completely around them before returning but then spot another cluster. "Come, let's go look," Marie-Hélène says, still charged with the hope of finding something more. It transpires there is nothing different at all, but what we do find is that we have swum quite some way further than we had first anticipated. Being due to join the others for a walk to a clifftop chapel later, we opt for the shortest route back – straight across the bay.

Having set off first (of course), I then think better and make a case for bringing up the rear to monitor any changes in our respective positions that could indicate hazardous currents. The experience of the return swim evolves into being a very enjoyable one (and not only for the reason of watching Marie-Hélène). The steady mid-speed front crawl we are doing becomes almost like a meditation, my mind becoming peaceful and yet very much focussed, and my body feeling both efficient and productive. I find myself catching up with and out-pacing Marie-Hélène, and feeling confident that there are no perilous currents – just a gentle on-shore breeze – I decide to settle that bit deeper into my own pace. Looking down now as I dig-in, I notice the seabed sloping away until I can no longer see the bottom at all – suggesting we must be in a depth of at least ten to fifteen metres. Looking up, it seems we are about halfway back, but having lost sight of the seabed, and seeing we are about two hundred metres off-shore, I am in high spirit and quite impressed with our exploit.

When I next look up, we are about two-thirds of the way back and mid-way between the last headland and our destination. The sense of time and constancy lends me to focusing on the differing efficiencies of my arms and legs and trying to balance them. It feels so good to have my body doing what it was made for: being physical. With a further change of focus, I sense the water flow over the different parts of my body, comparing where it flows smoothly and where there are eddy-currents – how my flesh is being pliable in sympathy with the varying water pressures. For the briefest moment it is as if I am an aquatic mammal – a porpoise or such – with my whole body being made for moving at speed in water – but only for a moment, because I then notice the seabed coming back into focus. Lifting my head, it seems Marie-Hélène has drifted a little – or maybe it is I, yes – *I* have headed off slightly to the left.

Still exhilarated, my head goes down again as I seek to obtain maximum final speed. My lungs and heart now feel to be being taxed (just as it should be), and shortly after my arms and legs begin to complain (as one would expect). My arms, despite their complaining, are holding out surprisingly well, but unexpectedly, my shoulders are feeling the strain, and before long I feel the muscles pulling deep in my torso; (this is new).

Within fifty metres it all changes; in my ego-driven state I am blissfully ignorant of just how much my pace has dropped off. In fact, my over-commitment to "good exercise" has depleted me so much that I am left to sense rather than see the shore. I have not even noticed that I am already in relative shallows – it only coming to my attention when I look up to find Marie-Hélène standing directly beside me.

"Wasn't that *good*. How are you?" she asks.

"I am good (panting) now, yes – I am good," I confirm. It is clear Marie-Hélène got here ahead and has walked to meet me, and I readily confess to the heavy toll the swimming has made on my body. In contrast, I find my breath returning quickly and my heartbeat settling similarly – indicating that at least my cycling and dancing continues to benefit me (and in addition, indicating that, as one ego becomes reduced, another already waits in the shadows). In comparison, Marie-Hélène's face is red and bares-clearly the shape of her mask, but she does not appear so depleted.

After drying and changing, we see our friends are already gathering. We were supposed to meet around five o'clock for the short walk up to the family chapel; "family" as in: belonging to the family who runs the restaurant and apartments here. It is just past five by the time we meet at the car park, but we are not the last to arrive. Before we set off, we are politely advised that – whilst indeed, all chapels are sacred, the family use the chapel daily and so are particularly sensitive to its use by visitors. We are requested, therefore, to enter one at a time, and for a short while only – mindful of the number to follow.

It is just five minutes' walk up to the top of the hill, and having arrived there alone I briefly survey the chapel, then find myself enticed by the cliff edge. The thrill of height and the opportunity to survey the area of our recent swimming expedition keep me focussed for some time. Marie-Hélène joins me and we sit together on a rock, looking quietly out to sea.

We take turns in the chapel. Unusually, we speak very little on exit with most communication being made simply through eye contact, or with small gestures of hands laid on shoulders that would seem to say, "Me to, with you". Following Marie-Hélène, I am one of the last to go inside the chapel.

It is *so* different compared to the others. It could be that I am just not able to tune-in because of my tiredness after earlier, but I would speculate that the regular dedicated and specific intentions of the one family has – sort of – "tuned" the space for them, but at the same time "detuned" it for others. In any event, I do not feel the inclination to stay very long, and having offered my wish that all who visit may be grounded in peace, I make a quiet exit.

Marie-Hélène sits close to where she had been before, and on approach, I receive a smile and she pats the rock at her side. She leans her head onto my shoulder, and I immediately and unreservedly recognise the blessing of this day in its entirety.

We depart shortly afterwards going back down the dusty hill, weaving between rocks and brambles and the occasional aromatic herbaceous plant. Marie-Hélène has her hand around my upper arm, which looks polite and friend-like, but most-fortunately feels somewhat more intimate to me (and I suspect to her as well).

In the car Jo-Anne tells us we are now going to *try* to find yet another chapel midway between here and the islands main port, which is our final point on the tour, and the place from where we will depart next week.

We come across the chapel car park with only a few minor detours and just one U-turn. When we reach the chapel itself and take the further few steps to the end of its terrace, the view is quite breath-taking. We are high up, and the sun is in its final throes – producing beautiful golden ripples on the sea. Looking out, I take in the view of a big island that I understand to be Naroupia. The available vistas call for several photographs by all, and moves me to take a panoramic looking seaward, and a silhouette of a lone tree.

I hope I do not appear too disinterested and certainly not disrespectful to the others, but I do not find myself particularly present just now; I would rather be somewhere else. Perhaps I am "all chapelled out", because I spend a relatively short time inside this one, but perhaps – also, it is because I cannot hold back the thought any longer: there are only *three* days before I say goodbye to Marie-Hélène.

I feel so very hopeful that we will have some meaningful and loving future, but we have not really talked about it and just now, I am feeling lost. I am sensing the change to come, and we have so little history from which to cast hopes into the future. I – we – can only be sure of *this* now. [32]

Accepting I am where I am, I therefore do what I always *try* to do at times like this: sit and wait for the emotion to bottom-out, knowing I will start to rise again – with time.

When Marie-Hélène joins me in the car, she senses there is something on my mind and asks me what is happening. I reply that I have had a few unhappy thoughts about the retreat ending soon and then after a pause, I add it might also be because I require some nutrition. (It is, after all, nearly seven.)

"What, with all you eat for lunch? Do you mean it?" she taunts me, smiling.

I was half-expecting some such response, but never the less continue to marvel at how this woman can interject in such ways as to lift me and warm me so. It is just what I need and once again, I am on a rising wave. I continue on the subject of nutrition, saying how it would seem that, regardless of how much I eat

---

[32] See Appendix II: I – we – can only be sure of this now (the now is all we ever really have)

– that is, how much I have eaten earlier – my body still seeks a fresh energy intake at intervals that are fairly much set around the four-hour mark.

The next part of the tour proceeds similarly to the last – with some backtracking and turning around – but soon enough Jo-Anne recognises she is close to where she wants to be, and there is a roadside parking as well. The port of Linaria is the islands' main port and I think – the largest town. It is located on the opposite coast from where we are staying, and it appears to be at the opposite end of the social spectrum as well. There are many large and modern buildings, thriving shopping areas, busy industries and tourism; all the signs of wealth and liquidity that appear absent elsewhere in Skyros, and I surmise this is where most of the Skyros Town visitors came from the other night.

Before exiting the car, Jo-Anne advises that if we would like to have an evening-dip, we should take our swimming gear with us now. Marie-Hélène and I decide we have had a good portion of water and sun today, and that a more leisurely and altogether-drier evening would be preferable. Jo-Anne leads us on a route that provides a very good view of the bay and the port. There is a ferry in the dock and it is unloading its cargo; cars are driving off, people are boarding (…)

With the sea still about twenty or so metres below, we turn at a signpost that invites visitors to drink and dine with sea views. We head down a slope and then a series of steps until we reach a small terrace with tables, chairs, and further on – bars and a kitchen. Looking around, I see steps to other terraces, service areas, and it strikes me: this whole café-restaurant has been built on the cliff-face itself. There are several sunshades – large square-modern canvas ones – from which some lights hang and create a surprisingly cosy feel to the otherwise exposed position.

To the far side of our terrace are more steps going down in two directions and I suspect that at least one will end up at the sea.

"Now, I do not think that we will necessarily have our evening meal here," Jo-Anne postulates, "…although you can stay to eat here later if you choose; anyway, I thought we might have a drink here and perhaps a little snack if some of you are peckish. There is a lovely view of the bay and it gets even better as the sun sets. Also, if you want, you can join me in a little swim in a while. I always like to swim here, it is something very special," she offers. No one volunteers to join in, but most of us are enthused sufficiently to watch.

The sun has set and the air temperature has reduced noticeably. Nevertheless, we aspire to the "little drink" and a few nibbles (as it happens) and before long we are all drawn to review the 'lite bite' menus. Karina helps with the ordering and we are quickly served tasty morsels including deep-fried breaded mushrooms and prawns and some mini pastry savouries. I concur to the purchase of two jugs of Spritz (which seems to be a fruity sparkling wine). I say "concur"; however, it would be more accurate to say that when asked – I had not declined, but it is fun – the alcohol going straight to my head after only a third of the glass.

From the port across the bay, a horn sounds, and with the commotion of loading and unloading having subsided, our attention goes to the near-silent departure of the ferry.

Jo-Anne is *so* right: with the sunset colours now fading to dusk, we witness the lights progressively switching on around the bay. As night ensues, the dull lamps become starbursts of light producing a myriad of beautiful shapes and colours off of the seas' surface. Golds, yellows, greens and blues shine and ripple before us, and with the changing light, we see the spot lit bell tower of a church high above the port.

We all take a "few" shots (…again…) but this time I go further – exiting via steps to a lower level that offers less background light and more water reflections. Marie-Hélène joins me, resting at my left side, head on my shoulder. With my arms folded and resting on the handrail, her left-hand threads up under my crossed arms where inconspicuously — it finds mine, and her right hand is wrapped around my upper arm – just as friends would (just as lovers do).

When we return to our seats, Jo-Anne has already changed. "Look, she really *is* going swimming," remarks Marie-Hélène. We follow Jo-Anne down a series of steep steps of dark wood and stainless steel and shortly see water and rocks below. The strong floodlighting here penetrates the water to produce the most beautiful rippling patterns of green and brown that remind me of a tortoise shell. There is a small row-boat tied off on a buoy several metres out, and just across from that some manner of floating sun-bed – or something – both bobbing around with their shapes and colours in stark contrast to the dark green of the sea. It is almost as if I am looking upon a shop window display, or a film set (…oh, I must just — camera, once again).

Jo-Anne re-enters our view and steps out onto a wooden platform where she deposits her towel and sits a while – her feet dangling in the water, entertaining reflections of a different nature. She smoothly enters the water, the light reflecting from her relatively pale complexion joining the similarly contrasting shapes of the rowboat and sun-bed; a most-memorable picture ("click").

Recognising myself as a voyeur, and deciding it proper to allow Jo-Anne some privacy, I turn back. Upon climbing the steps, I find myself reflecting on my motivation; is there something else in my thoughts and emotions? I know I have a sensitivity to group dynamics leftover from times when group minds did too often seem to be set against me. I suppose my relaxed open state of mind may be fertile soil for the monkey mind, and of course with it having been active earlier…is it starting up again on what is to take place in a few days?

Maybe I will just sit quietly for a while.

I am not alone for long; the group emerge onto the terrace where I learn that some are ready to go explore the quayside shops and restaurants. Others, however, are planning on heading back to the accommodation to get a good nights' sleep. Marie-Hélène and I decide that we can always sleep another time (perhaps), and to take this opportunity to discover the place further. With Henri, Rachel and Karina also opting to stay, Jo-Anne will take one car, and Henri – under Karina's guidance – will drive us in the other.

The quayside is teaming with social life. Many cruisers and fine yachts moored here are lit up below the waterline and they make for another photo opportunity; or two. Whilst it is pleasing – because of the struggling Greek economy – to see so many shops doing business, I am not particularly enjoying this part of the island tour: browsing art galleries, trinket shops and jewellers. After two more gift-shops, it is enough and I return to the quayside, and to the colours and the gentle rhythmical lapping of water.

When Henri, Rachel, and Marie-Hélène exit the last of the shops, I walk over to join them and we set off to discover which restaurant will receive our custom. With the hour moving on (it is now nine) we settle at the first "nice" looking place and quickly focus on the menu. Karina joins us just in time to place our orders, and having placed them, conversation ensues on the rich memories of the day. Shortly after, the bread, oil and drinks arrive and as we share them, we finish talking about the day…and then move on to the bountiful gift shops… and then a few jokes, and then having 'shared' until the bread and oils have run dry the subject turns to: "Where is the main course?"

Henri beckons over the waiter who tells us that one order is taking rather longer to prepare than the others: as it happens – my squid. We ask that whatever is ready — be brought straight away so we can at least begin sharing something.

Karina's comes first: breaded fish-bites with mayonnaise dip and chips – but they do not last long with five of us. Next comes some chicken and pasta dishes, but given their meagre proportions, more chips are ordered. Some *forty minutes* after placing the order, the waiter confesses that in fact, they had to send out for the squid! Eventually, about an hour after placing the order, my squid arrives…and some more chips, but with squid not being so widely favoured it is left for me and Henri to finish up.

The return journey is completed trouble-free, with Karina knowing precisely where to turn, and the distance being simply the width of the island at its narrowest point (as had been so wisely planned).

There is no discussion of sleeping arrangements when we finally get back (for Marie-Hélène and me, anyway), we simply want to have the maximum amount of time together (and then to sleep if we are able, afterwards). My "cunning plan" is to place a blanket on the floor between the two beds, and position both single mattresses together on the floor. The mattresses make a very good fit between the fixed bed frames, and the sheet from my bed is wide enough to cover us both. (In the event, we end up lying so closely that we only take up the width of a single mattress; 'ho-hum'.)

Tea-lights are set either side on the bedside cabinets behind us, and another on the table down past our feet, and I recline – suitably impressed with the overall effect. There is, as one might expect, some delay between setting-out the bedding and proceeding to sleep on it – *mostly* due to the odd hour or so of lovemaking. Only "*mostly*" because – as full-on, beautiful, torrid etc. as our lovemaking is, we would seem to have company. It starts with a buzzing and flitting beside my ear, but it subsides as quickly as it had arrived, and my attention returns to the activities that now find our bedding somewhat dishevelled.

There then comes another momentary interruption: "Ouch!" I call out, shaking my leg.

"What – what is it?" Marie-Hélène quickly retorts.

"I think…I think I may have just been bitten on my ankle."

"No – really!" she exclaims. "Do you know what it is – show me."

"It will probably just be a mosquito. I had a few in here a couple of nights back, but they didn't trouble me so much (!)" I start to re-arrange the sheet to hide our exposed skin. "I didn't get stung the other night. Mosquitoes do not usually bite me, so I am certainly not going to be bothered tonight. Now, where were we…?" With bedding and bodies rearranged, we continue largely as we left off – though with a little more care, to keep the sheet in place.

"Ouch!"

This time instead of twitching my leg, I make straight to slap the ankle.

"Hah – have they bitten you again?" Marie-Hélène exclaims. "Honestly – you British man, you are just too sensitive to these foreign insects. I suppose you do not have them in England?"

"Actually, I do. We have them quite regularly in warmer months and they can be quite a menace in Scotland in late summer, but it is rare for me to be bitten." Putting on the light and pulling back the sheet, I swivel round in seated position to get a better look. Sure enough, on my right ankle there are two small red lumps. "Ooow, they are sore?" she enquires, having raised herself and bent over to see for herself.

"Actually, not particularly – not yet anyway, I wonder…" I look back down the bed and there is the offender. "It must have been trapped under the sheet when I had flapped it around earlier. At least this one will not sting me again," I say, picking it up by a leg and taking it to the toilet where I unfasten the fly-screen to the smallest window and return it to the night.

Some while later, we are lying on our sides with Marie-Hélène spooned into me, wrapped in my arms – with a single flickering flame casting soft shadows upon the walls, and…I start to feel some itching. I start fidgeting – rubbing one foot upon the other; then reaching down to rub it with my hand, and then rubbing again…

"Are you alright; are you bitten again?" she asks me sleepily.

"I don't think so, I think it's just becoming a little bit itchy," I reply. "Sorry to disturb you."

"That's alright. No problem," she assures me, nestling against me again.

Some time passes in silence, but then half-asleep, I recommence fidgeting, and then again until, "Oh sorry – I think I just need to have another look." Sliding out from under the sheet, I move to the bottom corner of the mattress and turning my ankle to make the most of the candlelight I begin to investigate the cause of the itching. I am surprised to see two *big* red circles, nearly a centimetre in diameter, raised and oozing like mini volcanoes.

"Oh, it looks like I am rather sensitive to these mosquitoes," I say with understated tone.

"Come, come let me see," Marie-Hélène says, putting the light on and kneeling beside me. "Oh – *oh*! Have you had these just tonight? They already look infected to me. Come, see if I can help with this," she offers, looking for her handbag, searching for something. "Ah, of course – I have left it in my room." Then turning to me she continues, "I thought I had some lavande oil with me, but I forgot – have forgotten – it is left back at the room. It is a pity; it is so good for bites. Tomorrow morning, I will fetch it; it will help." Then, turning back to my ankle Marie-Hélène asks, "Are you sure – just tonight, these look so big and sore?"

"Yes, just tonight," I confirm.

I go to the toilet and squeeze some toothpaste onto my finger, then carefully blob it onto the bites. "I'm pretty sure that toothpaste is supposed to be of some help…I'll let you know," I say humorously – trying to reassure her, and perhaps myself also.

It transpires that the toothpaste is of use because, after some further cuddling, we both fall into a good sleep…until the sprinklers come on…and until the first birdsong begins – and the dawn that then follows.

Reassuring as ever, Marie-Hélène stirs, nuzzles into me and then rolls on top – which is *fine*, and becomes very fine; *again*.

A "New" New Morning
(The Past Continues to Unlock the Future)

The experience of waking up this morning is a very different one. I have already woken three or four times, but on each occasion, it was for various reasons ranging from turning over, recovering the sheets, kissing and cuddling…etc. However, with the sun streaming through the window, it is clear to me that I will not – *we* will not – be sleeping any further. It is not this aspect, however, that makes the morning different, and it is not that I have slept for any considerable length of time – although when I slept, it was very sound: the difference this morning is that when I woke, I woke – *not* alone.

Still tucked up close with Marie-Hélène's back spooned into me, she murmurs, "Good morning." I am not sure which comes first: if my swelling has started her moving, or if her moving has started me swelling. Or perhaps both actions were initiated by waking with the memories and scents of the night just past, but regardless and following a little more wiggling – Marie-Hélène's sighs become a clear reply to my gentle undulations until, "No, it will not do!" she erupts. Hurriedly, Marie-Hélène pulls away and throwing back the sheet climbs atop me. With an intense and purposeful look, she lines me up and lowers herself squarely, surely and oh-so-deeply. "Ooooh," we call out in unison.

Gently at first, and then not so gently; slowly and then not so slowly, our movements soon take us to a point beyond all control, and with her hands on my chest, nails pressed into me and her head thrown back, Marie-Hélène again becomes lost to her rhythm. I witness the expression of her beauty and passion until her rocking gradually subsides, her head comes upright and her mouth searches for air. Her eyes open wide to stare at me: through me. Her mouth hangs open still for a moment longer, then turns up at the edges into a broad smile that spreads to light up her blue-grey eyes.

"How is it you can be ready for me – *again*?" Marie-Hélène asks. "Never did I think you were like this! I first saw you at breakfast in Athens as such a gentle speaking, quiet man. I could never have assumed you had such passion; that you – that we – could be like this. Where is my quiet English Man?" For a moment, she looks serious; as if questioning me, or at least questioning herself, but the moment passes and Marie-Hélène is again full of smiles. As she rests onto my chest, my arms wrap around her, pulling her into a gentle rocking motion – our earlier rhythms still seeking to govern us. I reach out to pull the sheet over (not so much to keep warm, more just to keep the world at bay a little bit longer) but all at once, we start laughing. Joy in abundance; joy that must not be contained – that must be expressed for no other reason than simply *to let it be.*

"I did not expect this either," I say. "What, what do you mean?" she enquires.

"*This;* I did not expect – when we were laying on the beach talking before leaving the other accommodation a few days back, and not knowing how we might see one another – that we would be making love and spending nights together like this!"

"Yes, we are so lucky." Marie-Hélène agrees. "And the accommodation, with you here in your *Chateau*: can you imagine if you just had an apartment? Do you think we could have done all this – wondering if everyone would be hearing us – can you imagine! We are very lucky."

"But if we do not get up soon," I interject, "we will be lucky *not* to give the game away."

"Okay, we shower and then we go, and you make the eggs – *remember!*" she reminds me. "Oh-oh-oh, we have the beach first. I must go and change," she continues, laughing as she goes. "Then, I shall bring the fruits here to prepare them, and then we shall go to breakfast together."

Down on the beach, the amount of cloud on the horizon holds back the sun until after our yoga and meditation. However, there is a balance, because as we enter the water for our customary morning dip, we receive the first morning rays directly upon our faces.

Marie-Hélène starts swimming almost immediately she is deep enough, but I instead continue to walk ever more slowly, deeper and deeper into the sea until – as my head submerges – I start to sense the "underwater" all around me; like a sea-diver of old. All at once, I know I have the basis of a visualisation with which to lead the group after breakfast. (I had forgotten all about that until just now: that was lucky.)

Walking down the garden path together, Marie-Hélène carrying the fruit prepared in my kitchen and I the scrambled eggs, I bring her attention to the bees' morning chorus and she stops to take it in. She appreciates the interlude greatly.

Breakfast just *is*…again, and this morning I find myself particularly thankful that despite the variable content of the mornings and afternoons, the breakfast remains a reliable constant. During breakfast, Doris appears, offers her apologies for interrupting us, and asks if I would mind swapping roles for the bell ringing, because she'd really like to ring the large one at the house today. I agree and she happily passes me her hand-bell.

At ECOS we start by offering our general "happy birthday" wishes to Jo-Anne, but it is then suggested that we hold-over all further "niceties" until the party gathering later in the evening, and then it is straight over to me…

"Close your eyes,
Be aware of your breathing…"

(…and a while later…) [33]

"…Back on shore, we come out in a line – just as had entered: hand in hand,
Opening our eyes now to clear our vision, we give thanks to those around us
who have shared this experience – this day.
– Thank you."

Following a protracted – almost palpable – silence, minds and then bodies coalesce around the 'now' and we exchange smiles as we become re-acquainted with our physicality.

"Thank you, Wayne, that was truly a special gift for my birthday," Jo-Anne says. "I will remember that."

"Thank you," I reply, not expecting the accolade. "I knew when I was in the sea this morning that I would find a watery theme for the meditation, but I had not known quite what to expect."

Staying on the subject of her birthday, Jo-Anne tells us about the timing for the evening meal, after which she reminds us of the workshops' recommencement today at ten o'clock, and then ECOS closes. Just as I am about to leave, I become aware that Beryl is looking directly at me and smiling gently. I am about to disengage when I realise the nature of her regard: as an invite. I

---

[33] See Appendix III for the complete guided visualisation.

offer my attention, and as the connection with her is made, I instantly receive her silent profound thanks. I return the smile, and we are done.

Upon making a move, Marie-Hélène approaches. "So, when did you decide to do – to say – all that? You have not said anything about it. Did you just have the words this morning?"

"Well, yes – that is how it happened essentially: I had a small idea come to me this morning when we were at the beach and I sort of just 'knew' that I would find the words when I needed to."

"I don't know how it is done: how you do it?"

"It may sound strange, but *I* enjoyed listening to it as well. I didn't know exactly where it was going or what I would be saying more than the next line ahead."

"Really? It was so lovely, but you know – I am not so sure how much I can remember just now. I do not think I was sleeping, but I only remember following you somewhere and being very moved by what was happening. But I cannot remember what you were saying, so please – do not ask me to tell you about it."

"I expect I will have to wait until I write the story of our meeting here on Skyros before I can find the whole meditation again," I say (mostly) in jest.

"So, you think you are going to write about us, about our meeting?"

"Yes, I think so. I have had this feeling ever since the idea first came to me so strongly when we were on our way back from the Mill. Do you remember?"

"Yes, but how will you do it, you are not making any notes? I suppose you can put into it what you want: it will be your story."

"I am hoping I will be inspired; that the words will come to me intuitively – as with *nucreationstory*, and like the guided visualisation just now."

"I will be very interested to read it – if you will let me see?" she says teasingly.

"You would?" I probe.

"Yes – of course; it will be *our* story," she says, taking and squeezing my hand and coming just close enough to leave her scent hanging in the air.

At nine-forty I head to the grassed area to the side of the chalets with the hand-bell. Once there I spend some minutes trying (again) to befriend the miniature pony corralled on the land adjacent. I offer it some grass which it is decidedly not interested in, and then I watch as the pony plods slowly away – "Eeyore" fashion.

I ring the bell – a pathetic result; unlikely to gain the attention of anyone. I ring it again – repeatedly – and decide I should walk up and down the grass (ah – and now I know why Doris had…)

"Did I hear a bell?" Rachel enquires, popping her head out and speaking in my general direction.

"I hope so," I reply.

"Don't worry, Henri and I often don't hear anything," Rachel confides. "We usually keep a lookout and wait for the one at the *Chateau.* Will you be ringing that one too?"

"No, that will be for Doris today."

"Oh, but you must go and greet us! That is *so nice,*" she implores. "Okay, thank you – yes, I will do that."

Rachel withdraws to her apartment and I make for the veranda – via the bees (of course).

"*Yod-hey… Shin…Vav-hey,*" we chant together.

I cannot help but smile to myself. There would have been a time when I might have pictured a spiritual retreat as being: people sitting together in comfortable clothing, cross-legged on cushions, smiling happily, smelling incense sticks and chanting – *exactly* like this!

Ah – perceptions: they can be so accurate and yet, *so* misleading.

I once heard: "*Do not simply believe anything; the truth will exist whether you believe it or not, whereas the lies will fade away if you do not empower it with your belief. But listen to everything because the truth is always there – somewhere.*" (But I don't remember from where I heard it.)

"*Yod-hey… Shin…Vav-hey,*" we continue.

This is not "belief", this is *experience*. However, I will admit to having quite some expectation because of the previous workshops I've attended, and I suppose expectation can be of similar effect as belief, so perhaps I shall take a healthy dose of scepticism to keep the balance.

"*Yod-hey… Shin…Vav-hey.*"

Beginning to enjoy experimenting with the harmonies I go up and down the scales, and having set my sights on a new higher harmonic – I go again with some gusto: "*Yod-hey... Shin...Vav...*" – only to find everyone else has finished (!)

"Journey to the Future" I write in my journal...... and Karina speaks to lead us again...

"Today you meet your guide on a path across a green field and you walk together for a time."

"You walk with them up a hill that leads us away, for a time, from our present, and it leads us just for a short while, off towards the future.

Partway up the hill, you find a signpost: 'The Future,' it reads – and it is pointing up-hill, further-up, where you cannot yet go.

If you wait a while and look into the mists that are there, you might in some way just sense a little of what might come.

Be open to your senses – to sounds, voices and noises, to colours, shapes and objects, to feelings, thoughts and ideas.

Just wait, stand, or perhaps just sit a while. Be open..."

Despite my just recently absorbed scepticism, the content of my senses comes with such vigour that I perceive no separation between mind and matter as I write...

My signpost sets me towards a future where I am Teaching and Healing in small groups not just 1 to 1.

I have Marie-Hélène in my life and there is a feeling of our individual flames burning as one which lifts hopes & aspirations of others.

However, before I have time to consider and reflect on anything further, Karina speaks again...

"This is just one perspective of one future, and it is taken from a viewpoint that is not so far removed from where we are now. It is from the viewpoint of your earth-bound self, the self that yet carries the memories of pain and suffering past, and still bears some burden of pain now, so walk – walk with your Life Angel now, walk up and through those mists. Release the confines of your earth-bound self, find your true shining-self, the self that is you without the burden of past, the shining self that is available to you when you have let go and learnt all you need to learn in the present."

"What signposts are there now; what is the future for your true bright shining-self..." I write some more...

My life-angel /signpost has set a path where Marie-Hélène is using colour within inspired creative artworks that lift the hearts and open the minds of those that see them, and through their connection with the paintings, their imaginations are empowered and they are drawn to find their path to self-development.

… and Karina continues…

"So, your Life Angel has helped you perceive what is available to you – not now, but in a future now, and you turn and walk back down the hill together to the place where you had found the first signpost. However, beyond the signpost, you now see a lake."

It is a vast and still lake, with a silvery surface just like a mirror. It is showing you – in its stillness – just how calm your mind is now, and just like your mind, the surface of this silvery lake is capable of reflecting *Thought.*

The lake is vast and so it is capable of reflecting all thought.

And the shoreline that surrounds the lake where you stand stretches into the distance and is also very, very vast, and it represents *Time.*

It is *all* so vast and so still that the lake reflects all thought upon the shore that stretches to every future.

You go to the edge of the silvery lake, and peering in you see the reflection of your True Shining Self.

There: *Your* True Shining Self, looking right back at you from the lake of all thought that is at the shore of all futures.

Looking out across the lakes' surface now, you know that the release of the smallest essence of true-intention will ripple out across the vast surface of the lake, across all space and all time.

So, sit now on the shoreline at this vast, silvery lake and ask your Life Angel, just one question…

'What are you, personality – to stop me accessing my future?'

Ask it now with me: *'What are you, personality – to stop me accessing my future?'* Wait a while, and when you feel the answer, you will also know instinctually what is to be done to let go of that burden.

So, look immediately around you now on the shore, and find a pebble that represents your burden, or find a stone or maybe a rock; and pick up that pebble, or stone or levitate that rock that is the burden you have carried so long, and knowing what it is that you must do to let go of that burden completely, cast it out now, way-out, out into the lake. And watch the ripples spread…

The ripples depart from the centre in concentric circles and all directions and slowly decrease in height, but watch as they spread ever wider and wider.

Wider and ever wider the ripples spread across until they cover the entirety of the silvery lake that is the reflection of all thought towards the shore of all future.

"Wider and wider they spread until they wash-up finally – on every part of every shoreline…"

We are invited to remain silent; not to say anything about our burden, or about our intention.

We are invited to sit and wait at the lake as our Life Angels recede, and when we are ready – to leave the lake and then to simply open our eyes and give thanks.

Karina asks that we write in our journals the words that best capture what we experienced at the first signpost, at the second signpost as our Shining Self, and what intention we gave as we cast the pebble into the lake. Writing about the first two signposts is relatively easy – it is all still in my minds-eye, but when it comes to what happened at the silvery lake, I find myself in conflict with what I had witnessed myself doing. At the lake, I had picked up a beautiful green pebble and sent it skipping out across the surface of the lake into the far distance. I had seen its multiple ripples as it bounced and skipped over its silveriness and felt much joy as I watched it go: its ripples spreading everywhere. I had done this because – while sitting by the lake – I had not felt any burden at all, so I had simply asked, "So, what shall I do?"

However, there had been no reply, and therefore, I had watched the ripples spread and fade and sat feeling somewhat deflated.

All at once, as I am sat still on the shaded patio of the chateau, comes a reply – almost like an echo from the shores around the lake…

"The journey is as Twin Flames."

I cannot help but smile, for when I had envisioned myself patient beside the lake, I had received nothing, yet when not looking for any answer – I get one. Sensing the space remaining open to me, I offer a further query: "So, when does it start – soon?" To which I receive…

"No – it's already started."

As I wait, focussed on that open space, there comes a sensation that starts as "happy", but it keeps shifting, changing, growing – right through "excitement" – to arrive at *"elation"*. Being new to my vocabulary, the word elation floats along with the sensation...until the sense of space closes and *"elation"* goes with it.

I look to my side to find Marie-Hélène smiling at me, and before I know it, a definite smile of my own is beaming back at her.

"What?" she says. "What is it – you will tell me?"

"Yes," I say. "I will tell you, but later – not just now."

Karina gives us just one instruction for our homework today: "Like before, put into the picture, that which represents: that which took place this morning, after which we are invited to reassemble. I am not-at-all sure why we are meeting again, but then again, I am practising to think less, so – let's do lunch."

Strolling down the beach today with Marie-Hélène on my arm, the sun feels a little cooler, the sea is not so inviting, and I know that we will be parting in a few days. Nevertheless, all of that is just fine: my *now* is just fine, in fact – pretty damn good actually. I now understand that my perception of the future does not have to be one held subject to fear, but can be a perception that I *engage* with: by living my intention for my future – *now*.

Lunch is – *good*. [34]

Walking back along the alleyway that leads from the main road to the beach, I have adopted another new perception regarding the over-ripe squashed figs: I need not feel corralled into accepting societies' general perceptions of, and the symbols generally associated with, the terms "excess" and "waste". Instead, I can use "abundance" and I can find cause for celebration. So-much can be gained, it seems, simply from considering and adjusting ones' perspective.

On the beach, that most-special beauty that is Marie-Hélène declares that she has no interest in entering the sea today, and may avoid doing so for the

---

[34] Trying to describe once again the simple lunchtime pleasures of Skyros could only risk diluting the truth. The best I can offer is that you close your eyes for a short while after reading the following: sun, breeze, fresh-baked bread, olive oil, sundried tomatoes, over-ripe figs, roasted aubergines and peppers, salt and *Feta*...then, dwell in what-so-ever sensory perceptions you may find – and return when you please. ☺

remainder of the retreat. Feeling congested in her ears and her throat, Marie-Hélène tells me she does not want to risk making it worse. Actually, after such a long lunch, and with the painting to come and then the meeting, we will probably have quite a full afternoon anyway.

At the communal area, I am pleased to find most of the paint tubes yet unopened, and the pallets clean and dry. (Things can change.)

Marie-Hélène joins me shortly after and together we try hard to "create" without thinking *too* much. The result is that I add two new features: a swirling ball of colours in the top-right corner, and a silvery-white oval shape in the upper-centre – though, I then add a little gold in the middle…and then some ripples either side in blue, green, red and yellow…and perhaps *just* a few curly wisps at the sides to show vibrancy. Perhaps this silvery oval is the "shining me" (or a defocused Easter egg!). The overall effect is as if some part of every feature and colour is peeling away and moving towards a common direction (?)

Marie-Hélène finishes around the same time, and knowing that our work is complete, we lay our finished pieces side by side. They look so different: at least, in terms of the main colours and in that mine seems "busy" with motives/themes, whilst Marie-Hélène's appears comparatively simple and more generally calm. We identify a few similar features however – a small swirling spiral of colour in mine and a similar but much bigger ball of spiralling colours in Marie-Hélène's.

In addition, the golden-yellow that covers so much of Marie-Hélène's painting, is in the centre of my "hearts", and it is the same colour as my yellow flower. Then, together we notice that while the outer-most of my two concentric hearts is blue (being "my" colour) the inner heart is red – the same red as the second predominant colour in Marie-Hélène's painting. Oh, and the spiral of my "past" is red as well…and the cushions in my "distant past" are mostly in red. Then, as we together look closer at Marie-Hélène's painting, we note there is one feature – and only one feature – that is of a single colour: a seven-pointed star that happens to be the same shade of blue as "my" heart. (*Perception!*)

There is one other variance between the two paintings: Marie-Hélène's has words at the bottom: "Each day is a new beginning with much hope and love."

"So, what is it we do until four-thirty, when we all meet again?" she asks. "Simples, we go to the *Chateau* for tea – of course," I reply.

"Of *course!*" Marie-Hélène agrees.

Back in our group, back on our cushions, Karina moves us on with little introduction, inviting that we close our eyes, and in our minds-eye – sit back 'on the grass' somewhere near to where we had felt our Life Angels this morning. We are to request that our Life Angels now take us deeper in meditation to discover something of the meanings contained in our painting…

A spiral goes into my past, to the little boy that felt unworthy/not sufficient. My Angel is trying to help me see the gift that was within my suffering.

I was not the girl that my mother had wished I'd been born as, but in being different I did not fit into her plan, desires, or conditioning which set me free to be more as I am…and that learning has been with me my whole life.

My tears start – unbidden, unexpected – and even though brimming over with emotion, I yet find more within me to be written…

Not feeling I must fit into the space – the box, as given-me by society/others, finding instead "me" in all that I do.

I receive with thanks that gift from my little boy and return my love to my little boy to heal that pain that has sustained that guidance all my life.

(Perception.)

There is much truth in what I have written. Having decided – albeit the hard way – to stay away from groups as a youngster, I had avoided being (mis)directed by group thought/belief, yet when the need has arisen, I have still been able to *choose* to rally towards a positive objective with any team. It is perhaps why I have been able to observe life, observe myself, and why I have started to find a sense of underlying "truth" in many belief systems. Now I can see the flip side of that life-experience that earlier in the week had been the memories of "not fitting in / not being worthy". There are now other perceptions available: the wider perspective that enables greater objectivity, and when necessary: the confidence to stand out – to be outstanding. Furthermore, it is time that I recognise just how much has changed over the years, for after all – here I am, happy being myself *and* being within the group. (Things change; all things can change.)

We depart the veranda relatively quietly and slowly, but having just been reminded of Jo-Anne's birthday celebration later, there is a sense of "life going on regardless"…and so there should be; because it just – *does.*

At seven forty-five, we gather on the grass beside the apartments.

The sun has dropped below the hills inland, but there remains enough light to take the obligatory "dressed up – going to a party" photos.

The light is fading as we walk down the beach as a group, until – as we get to the far end and close to where we are to go inland to the road – there is no longer any blue sky beyond the whitewash buildings. Instead, there are lights from windows and on verandas, their shimmering reflections on the sea interrupted by the gentle waves folding one after the other. (*Things change and change can bring something new and beautiful.*)

Marie-Hélène tugs gently on my arm, and with shoulders still touching we drop back from the others; "So, what was it you were going to tell me earlier?" she asks. "This morning – you were smiling so much, but you never told me. What was it?" I tell her about my life-angel, the signposts, about the lake and about the messages I had sensed being offered me about my life journey and of our journey as twin flames.

"And – so, what do you make of this?" Marie-Hélène asks simply. I am not sure quite how to answer, but before I can worry, she continues: "I know something is happening; I feel it, but I cannot describe it like you," she says, and with those few words, she immediately eases at least half of my burden. "Come *on* – be light," she continues. "Sorry," I reply. "Yes, you are right – sorry; it's just that, sometimes I feel so much is happening – so quickly – that I am having difficulty in accepting it all; accepting that it can all be – really; just *so* good," I confess (to us both).

"Yes, yes of course it can. I know it. Be *light,"* she says again, moving aside and reaching down to take my hand firmly. "Come on, we have a party!"

I am *so* in love.

It is somewhat after eleven o'clock by the time the party ends. Walking back along the beach, Marie-Hélène is just ahead of me and despite the relative fun-filled evening, I have returned to pondering over "the number of days left". I dare say that with Marie-Hélène having conversed widely this evening, she is busy in pulling together the remaining threads of topics left unfinished. She has her white top pulled firmly around her and clasps her handbag tightly to her front with both shoulders held forward against the breeze. Is it just me, or is the end of summer even more evident this evening (?)

Marie-Hélène looks back to me and then, just outside of the entrance, she slows for me to catch up. Knowing that we are aiming to spend the whole night together, she tells me she has prepared a few pre-requisites and has already said her 'goodnights' to Rachel and Henri. I wait in the cool night air while she gets her overnight bag from her apartment, and when she re-joins me and we depart together to the chateau, I submit to the feeling of being proud.

By the time the tea is brewed and poured into our glasses, which produces vapour trails that wisp up into the dimly lit lounge, it is somewhat closer to twelve than I had supposed. Whenever I had glanced at Marie-Hélène during the evening she appeared to have been talking virulently. It is quite a contrast, therefore, to now behold her stretched out on the sofa in her white butterfly dress and quite – quite quiet. I almost do not want to disturb her…almost.

"Shall we drink then?" I suggest.

"What, is it ready? You do not like it so hot usually?"

"I think it is ready enough for you, and I will probably take mine upstairs."

"Ohhh, I see; you want to get to sleep already," she teases.

"No, not necessarily, but it would be good to sleep at some time tonight, and I am thinking that the earlier we get to bed, the *longer* we might be able to sleep – and things."

"Okay, so I go to bed now," she teases; at least – I *suspect* she teases (I hope she teases).

Marie-Hélène rises from the cushions with her dress clinging and looks directly at me. Her smile reaches out to assure me that yes, she was teasing. Preparing for bed together is starting to feel (almost) normal. From her overnight bag, she extracts pads and lotions, and commences her pre-bed routines. I work happily around her: doing my teeth, freshening my face and neck and using the toilet until…in mid-stream: I stop – to witness myself using the toilet *with* Marie-Hélène in the bathroom!

I say nothing. I look at her; she seems oblivious. (Well, at least I am sat down.) "Sorry, but I must tell you this," I announce. "I have just caught myself using the toilet with you here."

"Yes, it is normal. Are you worried by it?" she queries, continuing to wipe a pad around her eyes without pause. "You want I should leave?" she casually offers.

"No – no, I'm fine. It's just, it has usually taken some months in a relationship, before doing something like this."

"And?" she queries, still looking into the mirror.

"With you, it has taken only a few days," I remark.

"So, it is alright?" she queries further.

"Yes," I say, "Yes, it is all – alright," I confirm.

"May-be, we have done all this before," says Marie-Hélène, casually shaking lavender water onto another pad. There is no sense of joking, of taking-the-mickey or anything, and there is no follow-up. (Yes, may-be.)

In bed (on the floor), and with Marie-Hélène's head tucked under my chin and her body laid loosely over mine, a candle holds our faces in its half-light. This certainly feels most natural, as if we have been doing *this* before as well. We remain silent for quite some time; silent in voice – yet in another way so-active in the awareness of our "togetherness" – our energetic connection; as if the slightest tender touch or the smallest sensual kiss may light the fuse…and it does. Accordingly, the "fireworks" are as bright and wide, and as varied in shape and pattern, as has been the case every evening, night, or day. The crescendos peak as high as ever and the appreciation of the participants is as complete as ever it could be until finally, I am brought down to earth sharply, by the discovery that we have company: mosquitoes!

This evening at least, I have not felt anything until "after". Additionally, Marie-Hélène has brought with her the much-talked-about "lavande spray" which, under the brightness of the room light, she endeavours to apply with some accuracy. She touches the oil onto the first bite. "One," she says; "Oww," I respond. "Two," she says, "Ouch" comes my reply. "Three"… "Aaaaah…" – my final response then prompting her to spray the entirety of both ankles before collapsing back onto the bed in mirth. "How? Why is it, that I have not been bitten at all, and you have all these – and from just tonight!" Marie-Hélène exclaims.

"I don't think they are all from tonight; from their size, I think that some mosquitoes have returned for second helpings."

Securing the largest sheet under the bottom edges of the mattresses and the pillows at the top two corners, we hide underneath like in a tent. We have kept an opening wide enough to bring in the much-needed oxygen, but it also admits the occasional buzzing-biting visitor (though only to visit me, it seems.)

The Big Reveal
("Where, Therefore, Does It Leave Us?")

Each morning in Greece seems to have been outstanding in some way or another. Today, it is that Marie-Hélène and I have not only gone to bed together, but that we had actually *slept* and thus wake up together. With no interest in escaping this new experience just yet, we simply take sips from the bottle of water beside the bed and nuzzle into one another, drifting back to sleep. [35]

When next we wake, it is to take turns in the bathroom "freshening" our mouths (…all things considered). I also take the opportunity to check my bites. Thankfully, there are no new ones, and they are not as itchy as I had expected (thanks, no doubt to the lavender – sorry, "*lavande*").

Sometime later, we stir again – moving leisurely one against the other. This time, however, the preoccupation with sleeping together appears absent, and with all senses firing, the moving turns into caressing and the caressing into stimulation, and by this route, we return to what we *so* enjoy…

In the shower – still together, but with my mind drifting independently, I compare my situation to that Sunday morning in Athens, during breakfast, when I had simply admired a certain beauty – briefly, and from afar. I could never have foreseen that just two days later we would be kissing in the waves beside the Mill, joining so intimately that evening, and becoming so relaxed and familiar that we would now shower like this. Additionally, every day since Athens I have witnessed something new about Marie-Hélène that has moved me to recount my blessings. She has a way of asking a straight and searching question – so beautifully, and offers very pertinent interjections in such a direct yet polite manner, that I am brought down to earth by the truth so revealed. Sometimes it is just in how she has laughed, simply laughed – out-loud: with me, at me, at herself and with others. Sometimes it has simply been the way I have felt her looking at me – into me; through my "veils" to the soul within. One of the most

---

[35] I must confess, my knowledge that it is the morning is based on the fact that it was already the early hours when I had last switched the light off.

astounding experiences, is the sense of wondrous peace that first came when our lips touched at the Mill; the same peace that has befallen me at some point every day – including sometimes when we are simply at rest – *being* together.

A mix of such similar undisclosed thoughts continues to circulate within my mind – as now – I observe her walking just ahead of me: our fruit, eggs, toast, and tea in our hands; walking the garden path towards breakfast. Upon reaching the bees and hearing their energetic and harmonious chorus, I am given to such a state of emotion that I am left with one undeniable realisation, from which there is only one course of action that can fairly express all the truth that lies within me. I come to a halt; "Marie-Hélène…"

"Yes?" she turns, smiling. "I love you."

Marie-Hélène stops walking as if she is about to say something, then turns back as if to move on, but instead, pausing and turning her torso half towards me, she lowers her face in a gentle smile that reveals both her acceptance and her pleasure. No more needs saying, no more needs to be heard, she/I – we, *know*.

As we sit eating breakfast, I realise what being light-hearted truly feels like. What with waking with Marie-Hélène this morning, preparing food together, being propelled towards joyous confession by the bees, and having been welcomed by such kindly people with whom we now share our food – I am in bliss. No more thinking; just living.

It transpires that I am perhaps just a little too lost to the gravity of "breakfast" and seemingly, the others are as well, because as we are yet sipping our teas in the early sunshine, we see the group already gathering for ECOS. Fortunately, we are now well practised and we quickly clear away the necessary items to Rachel and Henri's sink – for later.

In today's ECOS, the final one, Jo-Anne starts by thanking us for last night's celebration and then extends her gratitude to those who have joined her at sunrise each day – expressing her understanding towards those who could not make it this morning. Marie-Hélène and I look at one another realising neither of us had thought of going to the beach at all! Looking coyly around the table, I see what appear to be stifled grins (perhaps, because the two people who had been together on the beach every morning, were the very same two not present this morning.)

With today also being the final workshop day, tomorrow – we are reminded – is *free*. Our journeys home on Thursday will entail the ferry back to Athens – well, two ferries to be precise, but there will be more about that later. Jo-Anne reminds us to take our paintings to the veranda together with our journals, and advises that the duration of this final workshop is somewhat unpredictable and could extend into the afternoon. With a certain sense of intrigue, and with traces of knowing smiles still on a few faces, we depart.

Sitting together on the veranda, Karina informs us that the main objective today is: to review our paintings. A "show and tell" with our paintings was pretty much expected but – the whole morning? It transpires that we are about to explore the hypothesis that such inspired illustrations as ours may contain yet greater intrinsic meanings. We are told that the specific and relative positions of various features – along with their shape and colour – can be quite revealing, and that the comparison of one person's work with another's can sometimes be rather interesting as well.

Marie-Hélène and I look briefly at each other. I am aware my painting already exhibits quite a clear orientation of features towards one corner, but what might it suggest about my future, and what might our paintings say about *our* future? Hopeful that the exercise might provide even greater uplift, but fearful of it stretching the reality so far that the bubble might burst, it would seem my monkey mind has appeared on the scene and is feeding robustly. Surely though, nothing that has happened these past days can be taken from us; the way we feel towards each other is unlikely to be wreaked by any "sometimes" theory – but all the same…

Having instructed us on the code for deciphering our paintings, and having each reviewed our paintings with the code in mind, Karina then invites us to take turns describing what we think has been revealed. Of course, as soon as Karina ventures: "So, who would like to…" I am there. "Ah, Wayne…" invites Karina.

Scanning the faces now turned at me, I tender my justification: "I know, I am offering to go first again, but – I am *so* excited. In my painting, I can see so many features in – well – very *interesting* positions, and having never heard anything about this theory before, I am so *ready* to share it with you – does anyone mind?"

There is no opposition, which (*thank-you – monkey mind*) gives me to thinking: "S*o what have I opened myself to?*"

"Right then, Wayne," Karina counsels. "There is no need to rush, just take your time, and if you get lost or stuck just pause and 'tune-in' like I know you can, and I sure you will receive some help."

My corner already makes me well placed to give a presentation, and so – okay…

"So, on the first day, in pencil, I had started by drawing a heart shape, and then another heart shape, one inside the other, down at the left – here. Next, I found myself drawing a brick wall either side of the hearts and some heavy wooden gates – partially open, perhaps showing there is a route for two hearts to come together(?) After we had meditated, I recall talking about this with Rachel – didn't I Rachel(?)(she nods) that morning…oh no – last week now, and I had thought maybe the retreat might show me the way to opening the gates. Oh…"

I pause to steady my emotions, realising that the retreat has not just opened the gates – but taken me clear through!

"The next stage was the painting-over of the drawing – with this lilac-lavender wash over…"

I stop and look at Marie-Hélène: thinking *lavender/lavande*…and my eyes become moist.

"So then, I had chosen a small yellow flower when we went into the garden, feeling it to be a pure symbol of beauty, of life and living; it doesn't strive to be beautiful – it just is; and the colour – the yellow, felt very important as well."

All heads turn at this point, and my eyes follow theirs – to Marie-Hélène's painting leant against the wall – virtually all yellow…and I am now with tears.

"Anyway, the yellow flower is placed almost in the middle, halfway up the left here, just above the two hearts, sort of partly in 'my past' and partly in 'my present'…"

"So, the next day, I had worked largely on my childhood and although what came to me was very powerful, all I could come up with was this small spiral up left here, and it's sort of winding outwards into – 'now', I guess; and with deep red symbolising something out of the past – red being the root chakra."

"But while painting this part, I felt there was something still missing; and I found myself given to bringing forth something of the hearts from my pencil drawing – here in red and green-blue, just below the flower."

"Then I felt the need to represent something at the core of them – like at the centre of everything, a driving or guiding force – but actually, now I can see how the stem of the flower goes into both hearts, linking them…bringing them together."

I have to pause again.

"Well done, Wayne," Karina reassures. "Go on when you are ready."

"Then, when it came to our distant past, I found that the lavender brushstrokes had already started representing a movement to the right, and so the cloth and cushions depicted here – took on the same lean which – as I would understand it now: takes it all into the 'future'."

"Then here, this – this sort of drifting vibrating white and gold energy in the centre, with blue and green around it; this represents the life-angel having been present throughout all of my existence – past, present and future, and then here in the top right, this multi-coloured swirling ball – which the code says is in the direction of "future" – feels like all the lessons from my past are shown to be present in a beautiful pallet from which I can dip-into for ever-on."

"I'm really surprised just how much my painting fits in with the code, and how much further meaning it would seem to be revealing; so much reflected in my painting; so – so surprised…"

"And you have not come across that before?" Karina asks.

"No, not at all. It is so simple: dividing the canvas into quarters – I'm sure that I would have remembered it," I deduce.

"Well, that was lovely Wayne," says Karina. "I think you brought out almost everything that I would have done. Well done."

Karina turns to address the group, "Who's next – ah Beryl…thank you…"

There is little delay between one presentation and another, with everyone seeming to have been encouraged by my enthusiasm. When it is Marie-Hélène's turn, she shares how there is a lot – *a lot* – of yellow in her painting, and quite a lot of shimmering golden-oranges as well, but mostly it is yellow. Just above the centre, like a rising sun, there is a big ball of swirling colour. It seems to be taking on something of all the colours from around it: blues, reds and oranges, green-wisps, and golden/yellow spots. In the foreground, there is what appears as a calm sea (of yellow) with gentle ripples of blue across its entire expanse, and a shimmering reflection of the swirling ball above it.

EACH DAY IS A NEW BEGINNING
WITH MUCH HOPE AND LOVE

Whilst the top half has mostly yellow and orange rays, there are two other features: a golden/orange crescent at the top right and a blue star in the top left which seems to have a gold/white light behind it.

Karina advises us that the four-section cypher should not always be applied too-strictly or be taken too seriously. "But here," she points to Marie-Hélène's painting, "…even with the colours being a most striking feature, and this big ball of many and mixed colours radiating energy to everything else – there are a few other things that stand out. For instance, one could interpret that both the distant past and the now appear as being quiet and calm. Also, whilst our attention may easily be drawn towards a feature in blue relating to the past, there seems to be quite a lot of the same blue across a lot of the foreground. And one might also see, from the crescent in the top right, the potential for a new dawn, a shining future," she speculates.

Everyone finds something in the deciphering, and some, like me, have been quite astounded. Karina had been right about many things, including that the process of the morning may last some time, because come-lunchtime, there are still three paintings to be shared. Therefore, we all agree to continue here after lunch.

This lunch is "the final lunch"; there are no more to be eaten at this taverna – therefore, it is enough to say we all have "another lovely Greek lunch".

As I walk back along the beach, I contemplate just how much change I have been experiencing recently: the changes in weather, changes in our location, and certainly – my perceptions of me/my life have changed, and so much; and now the end of the holiday is in sight. It would seem, the way I have gauged life – by what things change and what stays the same – has never brought much real joy, and in truth – little satisfaction. It would seem in fact, that by the very act of trying to measure a thing, I consign it to history i.e., it is something now passed and cannot be experienced *now*. So perhaps it is better, therefore, for life to be gauged by the freedom and accessibility of the "now" at any moment – for whatever that moment holds. Additionally, perhaps what I have called "pain" and what I have assumed has been "pain-now" is not new pain at all, but mostly, if not entirely, the re-creation of past pain – the true cause having already passed. In some ways, I have perhaps unwittingly *agreed* to carry forward this pain – subconsciously at least, because I have thought the pain, or at least – the self-images/identities that suffered pain, *were me*. On reflection: what burdens I have carried! (What burdens we have all carried!)

The emotions that originated from past experiences of pain, would now seem to be the signposts showing the information I need to reflect upon – so that I can form a new and truer understanding of myself. A new understanding *now* of what I had experienced *then*. A different perception of the un-truths I have carried with me; boxed away – until now.

The structure of the retreat has been very carefully organised, but the role of Karina as both emissary and catalyst, and her knowledge and experience – her very *vibration* – has been crucial. Having gained confidence from the experience of previous retreat processes, I suppose I have come to Skyros at a point when the development of my inner world was already underway, but I think there is yet a more pivotal factor that has contributed to the eminence of this retreat. Depicted by the original intertwined hearts in my painting, the pivotal factor is my association with Marie-Hélène.

I both see and *sense* Marie-Hélène's beauty within and without – the wonderful mix of her fundamental elements, characteristics colours; if you like – her essential Being. However, whilst the "pivotal factor" includes all these elements, the picture is only completed by "my association" with Marie-Hélène i.e., the involvement of the essential Being that is me. It is in the sympathetic difference in our colours, *our* vibrations – which brings us to balance one another, to meet in the centre. When in balance, there is no hiding – no misalignment of intentions that can accommodate untruth, no disconnected energy on which misperceptions can be feed, no space that can be used to shut-away that which is uncomfortable, painful, or threatening.

Out of all things, out of all my knowledge and my experiences, it is this particular "knowing" that gives me the most hope and confidence, to take steps towards my true-shining self, in the full shining now. It is also clear, that the steps show themselves whenever I engage with Marie-Hélène as I have here on Skyros: expressing, sharing, investigating, learning from, and celebrating: *truth*. In addition, if there is a balance for one, then there is such a similar-opposing balance for the other, and thus the future would appear to be so very bright and shining for us both – apart from one thing: the agent that enables each of us to choose between living by truth – or not: Free-will. [36]

Where, therefore, does all this leave us – Marie-Hélène and me? I suppose, it places us in much the same general situation as everybody: with choices – everyday choices, and all of them are like stepping-stones. [37] Small steps in any direction may not appear to make much difference, but if we choose not to take responsibility for the direction the steps are heading, we risk these many small stepping-stones leading to deeper water – unknown depths – where we then have the choice to turn back…or take the plunge.

---

[36] Life can be a complicated journey where Free-will takes the role of the navigator and driver – which sounds right and fine, other than the fact that in the back-seat (and sometimes in the passenger seat) sits the main protagonist: the ego "I". See Appendix II: Free Will…and the ego "I".

[37] See Appendix II: Choices are like stepping stones

Anyway, that is all I think I care to say – just now…*correction* – that is all I would say *if* I was talking and *if* I was going to express myself. Instead, however, I am walking hand in arm with her that vibrates in balance with me, and all of *this* is somewhere in my mind, to be expressed…some other time.

Of course, it is by free will that – instead of sharing all of these thoughts with Marie-Hélène right now – I have elected to defer the experience to another time. Maybe I will be able to gather my thoughts in such a way that I might present them better another time, but I sense there may be some subterfuge here – whereby the deferment may be repeated and repeated to completely avoid "another time". Perhaps my monkey mind is in the background whispering, "I risk scaring her off with such bright and bold assertions."

However, if do not share my truth, I may be denying Marie-Hélène the opportunity to recognise such a truth within her. Alternatively, there is another course of thought: that I need not say anything because she will just *know* it; or does this just feed back into "avoiding the risk" as before?

One thing I am perhaps more certain of now, is that all of *this* thinking is certainly the route by which free-will can become over-influenced by ego, which in turn may have already been "misinformed" by copious interjections from the monkey-mind (conceptually speaking).

We have reached the end of the beach.

Consequently, have I gained from the action of "thinking for the purpose of discerning truth" only to lose from the inaction of not speaking it? Alternatively, perhaps the energy given to "right thought" is *enough* in itself – for I have not spoken an *untruth* by saying nothing? On the other hand, does the river of life – ultimately – wash one along if one floats too long without positive action, and may I find myself – in any event – at the edge of the same depths, or worse still – a waterfall!

For sure, too much thinking now means I will not engage *with* the now – which is where I (think) I should seek to be.

"So, Marie-Hélène, what would you like to do later this afternoon?"

"Later – what later is that?" she jests. "We have more paintings to go through and then it will be time for eating again. Oh, I do not think I am so good for all this eating. I should like to swim, but even if we had the time, I do not feel like swimming here. I still feel like I am coming down with something – something in my throat, and the water here is – not so good. It would not be good to put my head under again – I feel it."

"Oh Marie-Hélène, I hope it is nothing in the seawater here, but – thinking about it, there are not many that use the sea as we have, and none of those who have been here before seem to use it at all. I wonder if they know something we do not? Do you remember back at the other place, when Nikko passed on those Skyros bags?" I continue.

"Oh, do you mean the ones we paid for – only to find we would be given one when we got here! Yes." Marie-Hélène retorts.

"Yes, that's true, though I think I will try and forget that bit – anyway, he said then that the money would go towards cleaning up the island and making its inhabitants more environmentally aware. M'mm, I do not feel inclined to swim anymore either."

Outside her apartment, Marie-Hélène turns to me; "I think I will just go and clean my teeth, and then I may – *may* I – come up to the chateau until it is time for us all to meet again? That is if I do not end up talking too long."

"Yes, yes please do. I will see you in a bit then – bye-bye," I reply, blowing a kiss.

It is almost two hours into the afternoon workshop before Karina finally announces the ending of the retreat. In concluding, Karina recaps the processes we have experienced, saying that Jo-Anne and she both believe the qualities of the island enhance the process of the retreat. Karina assures us, that the same sort of learning and healing can take place in other retreats, and also in courses in Glastonbury, and that Jo-Anne will be seeking to organise meetings of her own and other events in the New Year.

We are reminded that tomorrow morning is set aside for a general clean up within our accommodation and the gathering together of our belongings, ready for the final packing before an early departure on Thursday morning. After the clearing up tomorrow, the rest of the day is free for us. It is suggested that we consider a return to Skyros Town for lunch and holiday shopping; it should be enjoyable in itself, and would also be a way of giving something back to the island. Most of us agree, and Jo-Anne offers to order a couple of taxis.

We are then informed of a suggestion – an invitation – from the family that runs our taverna, to eat a final group meal there tomorrow evening, and with a gathering afterwards in which we can share meditations and prayers with them.

Finally, Karina hands out printed cards containing two extracts from transcripts of inspired teachings gained via the London group meetings. One extract is a visualisation following the line of "how it may be possible to understand better – the concept of *now* and that everything is happening in the now". It is good to read (and poignant as well) but it is the second one that catches my attention the most. Concerning the concept of passing over from this life into spiritual life, it is read aloud…

"It will be like a field spread before you. A field of flowers, wonderful golden flowers, etched here and there with lavender."

"Even amongst the lavender, there will be green, green of a shade you have not seen before."

"That green will travel to the edge of the field, and as it travels it is transformed into lovely little shrubs and small trees and the larger, beautiful trees that fold over towards the earth."

"You hear the birds within those trees and you see them."

"In your mind, you lie down in the grass and you smell the lavender and all the other beautiful plants that surround you, and you know that you have passed through the Doorway into a world of true peace and true enlightenment"

I cannot help but notice the recurrence of "yellow" and "lavender" in what is read – those being the principal colours in Marie-Hélène's and my paintings.

For the final time, we offer the collective prayer/intention, "God be in my head, and in my understanding…" and with that, the retreat finishes.

Neither Marie-Hélène nor I feel motivated to speak. Perhaps like me, Marie-Hélène is *feeling* the approaching end to the retreat – knowing it is another step towards the time we must say goodbye. We depart the veranda, taking our paintings with us.

In the communal area, where we gather to use up the leftovers from the final lunch, the mood is quieter than of late. It is still quite jolly however, for after all, along with the bread and feta, there remains from last night – some wine and *quite a few* Baklava.

After washing up, Marie-Hélène pops back to her apartment for a few extras before joining me in the chateau. Tonight, I plan to have the whole 'mosquitoes' situation sorted (*I* because Marie-Hélène has still not received a single bite). Thus, after our Greek Mountain Tea – and a few more photos from home – I, (not we) remain fully clothed throughout the toileting, after which I light the candles, undress and get *straight* under the covers. Marie-Hélène meanwhile has walked nonchalantly between bedroom and bathroom with various items of clothing and toiletries and now stands at the end of the mattresses – looking down at me mockingly. I can see she is searching deep for some new humour around the subject of "The poor Englishman and his mosquitoes".

Marie-Hélène wears (only) a large T-shirt reasoning, "I always wear something in bed – you know, it is not so warm here," and I wait for her to continue with something like: "Not like South of France," however, she follows with: "I do not know why I bother to put this on, it always comes off again so soon. I seem to stay so warm with you: why is that?" she asks. "What do you think: on or off? Are you planning to keep me warm tonight again?" she teases. "Oh, I think you will; move over," Marie-Hélène encourages, pulling off her T-shirt and pulling the sheet wide open.

Close at my side, she nuzzles her head once again just below my cheek, into my chest. "Oh, I feel *sooo* good in your arms," she says softly.

"Yes," I reply. "Yes, you do; and do you know something else that is good tonight: no mosquitoes."

It is true, none – anywhere to be seen or heard. Thus, and with the absence of a sheet leading to a significantly less carefree approach than yesterday, we find ourselves taking every advantage from the situation, seeking out every corner of the mattress, and every nook and cranny – elsewhere (…)

Synchronicité
(And the Long Walk Home to Find It)

I do not remember falling asleep this last evening/this morning, or whatever – but no matter, because having taken some water, and then visiting the bathroom to let some go, we return directly to snuggling in bed.

"You have no worries with not sleeping now?" Marie-Hélène asks. "No – it seems," I reply. "I'm not sure I have had time to think of it recently." (The truth, of course, is I rather prefer to proclaim the virtues of *not* sleeping just now.)

I look to the alarm clock, but cannot see it anywhere. I open my phone. "*Ahhh* – it is seven forty-five!"

"Oh, is it! Okay, we will clean your bedroom here first, and then I will leave and go prepare some fruits at my apartment. I do not bother today if I will wake someone, I think it is time that I use the apartment *also – too*…is it? No – *also*," she decides upon.

"There is no need for you to tidy up here," I say. "Just grab what you need for today."

"Oh yes, our last evening on the island. You know, with my throat and things and with not sleeping so much – I think my body will like to be home soon." Marie-Hélène then pauses, realising how her words might be misconstrued, but as our eyes meet, she knows nothing else needs to be said. She moves around like a veritable whirlwind through the bedroom and the bathroom, and as she disappears behind the lace curtains and down the wooden stairs, she calls out behind, "Wayne, remember – the eggs!"

Perhaps I should have been expecting it but *unexpectedly*, this *petit-déjeuner* is the most enjoyable breakfast yet. With this being the last breakfast together, we have an excess of fruit, yoghurt and plenty of "*honeeey*" (she still says), and additionally, no shortage of eggs, cheese and bread. Another pleasing feature of this breakfast is that with no morning ECOS, and no workshop, our minds are released to plan and ponder over the day ahead. There has been some discussion regarding meeting up as a group for lunch in Skyros town, and I have imparted my wish (to Marie-Hélène) that we walk back from town – alone. If only these two ideas materialise, I will be satisfied.

Passing by the bushes, there are only a few bees still working at *their* breakfast, and I regret not having taken the time to connect with them earlier. At the house, and after washing up, I take the cushions we have used on the veranda each day – back into the house, but leave a space on the couch for our evening tea and Marie-Hélène's favoured supine repose (*"position en repose supin"*). [Guess who found the App!]

I next repair (a variant of yet *another* French word) to tidy the bedroom. As I survey the disarranged bed linen, my earlier lightness dips somewhat at the thought of this next night being our last. I have begun to enjoy thinking in terms of *we*. In expectation of sadness, I am virtually willing myself to get down into the trough of this particular wave so that I might then experience the rise, however – the sadness does not come. Although, why should it? Whatever is to happen has not yet happened. At this point, who knows what is going to transpire. In the space where I had awaited sadness, instead comes a gentle background hum of quiet expectation (*but no bees this time*). As I further release myself from the expectation of sadness, I realise I have missed the bigger picture (*/painting*), and as I continue to accept this *unexpected* space, there follows the thought…

"I can take this Love that I am experiencing, with me – into the future"

Of *course*, I can carry my – our – new-found perception of love, throughout this day and tomorrows' travels, and back home with me into whatever "normal life" might now become. Likewise, Marie-Hélène can do the same – or at least, she can *choose* to do the same – assuming it is a good choice for either of us, because…well – might it not be easier to simply accept the last two weeks as a wonderful blessing? Like a gift that we have received here in Greece – unwrapped, explored and enjoyed, like a fragile magic snow-globe – but then left here so as not to risk breaking it later. It feels to be the less risky path, emotionally at least – but, is life meant to be measured simply by how easy it is? Surely, life is at its richest when it is lived deeply and powerfully, with its bounty being revealed within the depth and breadth of such meaning…

I have found such balance in *being* with Marie-Hélène as I have never known before…so – no more questioning: it is time to step forward into the world once more with my darling, and to do so without waiting for "an end" to anything.

Just before leaving the bedroom, I turn back to check that it looks clean and tidy enough to receive "my darling" later: "M'mm, it'll do."

The taxi journey into Skyros town lasts all of ten minutes, but I am already looking forward to the walk back [so much for not waiting for an end]. I have had the sensation of losing all sense of time these last days, so I am hoping a long walk might help me counter this; to *feel* the time that Marie-Hélène and I are sharing. Perhaps also, there are things to be said, or to be heard or both, whatever – I just want to *be* with her.

The four of us: Rachel, Henri, Marie-Hélène and I, are dropped off in a small car park just short of the town centre – we think, and before long, we indeed find ourselves in the environment made familiar by Nikko's tour. From whitewashed walls, pots of basil beside entrance doors and a café that Rachel thinks might be good for lunch, we look ahead to behold cascades of flowering vines and, as per – we take photos.

Shortly after, we find ourselves looking at the restaurant we had used last week, and where we have arranged to meet the others. Accordingly, just as we start to discuss where we might eat, we hear a "woo-hoo" from behind. It is Renna and Madelyn and they seem to have set their minds on the same café that Rachel had earmarked earlier.

Lunch becomes quite extended, with more time given to talking than eating, but that is fine – it is all helping to set a relaxed and light tone for the day. Lunch concludes with a few speciality pastries (of course) after which the majority of us visit the restroom before spilling out onto the main street.

It is quite a bit busier now – mostly with weekend shoppers, but also some locals going about their daily lives. We do not walk far before coming across a tree growing out from the pavement. It presents a big display of cerise-pink that fills the overhead space between the buildings, and the sunshine enters from the side to light the top of the tree – making the bright pink blossom *glow*. I invite Henri, Rachel and Marie-Hélène to pose underneath, and I take... (Yes, yet another).

On seeing that the main part of town is just ahead, and expecting that Marie-Hélène will – as before, and as many do – take some time in the shops, I ask if she would mind me taking one photo – just of her; she doesn't...

I have never enjoyed shopping for long stretches at a time and I rarely volunteer to do window-shopping, however, as we wander up a side street, I am content with looking on. Rachel moves towards a display of hats strung-out along the wall. She looks over to me and then approaches Marie-Hélène and beckons her before turning back: "Wayne, what do you think of these? I think a hat would suit you; I think that black one – there…" she trails off as she points out some straw trilbies in various colours.

To be honest, she is right, I can carry a hat quite well; a proper hat that is – not one like the blue and white one I've recently passed to Marie-Hélène (the hat which by the way has – on occasion – found people comparing me to Mr Bean!) However, I am not sure I *need* a hat just now, not when I am going home tomorrow. Out of politeness, I put it on briefly, but then Marie-Hélène comes over, picks up a black straw trilby, and replaces the one on my head declaring me, "Very smart!" I look at her for a sign that she is joking, but she is not. "Go on – find a mirror. Rachel was right you should try some on – really," she says, turning immediately to go into the shop. I try a few, then – not being convinced – I take the original black trilby into the shop to find a mirror. I have to agree: it looks quite good on me. From a point across the other side of the shop, where Marie-Hélène and Rachel are huddled around a small glass display, Rachel turns to me and says, "Oh, yes – but I think you should try a few more on; try some different colours, Wayne. Try some more of those that are outside." I oblige, and Rachel follows shortly after, taking me through virtually every style and colour including a tangerine one. I finish with a black straw trilby (much like the first), with an orange-coloured motive on its side. "*Interesting,*" I say aloud, but in turning to seek Rachel's opinion, I find she has gone back into the shop. Heading for the mirror again, I renter the shop to see Marie-Hélène at the counter and apparently in mid-purchase. Absorbed by my search for the right hat, I turn various ways in front of the mirror. Yes, it might serve both as a casual sun-hat *and* one I could wear for Salsa. It is a little pricey for a straw hat, but as Karina had said, it is a contribution towards the town.

At the counter where Rachel and Marie-Hélène had just been standing, I lay my hat on the glass-top and extract my wallet. Awaiting the receipt and the change, I notice – just below my hat – some interesting jewellery. They are for the most: silk-lace necklaces, bracelets, and wristbands of various colours – mostly black – but some are quite vibrantly coloured with burnished metal pendants and some have crystals. One catches my eye: a bracelet comprising a spiral shape on a woven bright pastel lemon wristband. The colour is not the strong yellow in Marie-Hélène's painting, but it is very nice all the same.

Realising that the others may already be some-way down the street, I leave to catch up. Having all-but caught up to everyone however, a nagging sensation befalls me – urging me to go back and buy Marie-Hélène something. Knowing she has such good taste, I am not wholly comfortable with the idea, but yes – it would be nice to get her *some*thing.

"Just a moment," I say to the other three, who all stop and turn to listen.

"Oh, the hat – Wayne, that looks *good,*" Rachel says, with quite some enthusiasm.

"Thanks – oh, sorry," I reply hurriedly. "Can you wait here a moment; I just need to go back."

Inside the shop, the young male shop-owner approaches me and in passable English invites me to examine the bracelet I had been looking at earlier. It looks quite delicate, and with it in its box is a card that in a creative font reads *"The Spiral"* and then in smaller text…

The path isn't a straight line: it's a spiral.

You continuously come back to the things you thought you understood, and see deeper truths…

The phrase is *very* meaningful. In fact, the spiral shape and the words together suddenly remind me of discussions in the workshops; and, as I think of it, there have been discussions about spirals at London group meetings *and* references to spirals in my writings…how wonderful!

Walking down the street, I now have a folded paper-bag in my pocket and – no doubt – a grin on my face. Regardless of the colour, I am sure Marie-Hélène will appreciate the spiral – and hopefully the words as well. I wonder when I should give it.

"Oh, you seem happy with your hat," Marie-Hélène exclaims. "Oh yes – yes, I am glad…I got the hat."

Upon reaching the bottom of the hill – close to where we had entered the town this morning – Rachel and Henri convey they are ready to walk back, and with Marie-Hélène in agreement we continue down-hill, looking for a signpost to the coast road. Once clear of the shops and cafés, Marie-Hélène pulls on me gently, and removing the bag from her shoulder says, "I am just checking if we have enough water with us." Then quietly – aside, "Actually, I would like that we walk back on our own, is that alright with you?"

Before I have the time to say anything, Rachel turns around: "I hope you don't mind Wayne and Marie-Hélène, but Henri and I would prefer to go at a good pace, and it will allow you-two to take your time."

"Oh yes – that's fine by me," I (economically) admit.

"Yes, we will meet you for dinner I expect," Marie-Hélène offers.

"Half-past seven on the grass then. *A plus tard!*" ["to later"] Rachel signs off, pulling on Henri's arm.

If I had the strings with which to puppeteer the world, I do not think I could have orchestrated this last-minute half as good as the reality I had just witnessed.

"Oh, she is wonderful – Rachel; she knows our time is precious," Marie-Hélène confides.

"So, have you told her – about us, I mean?"

"Not really, but she sees that I am very happy, and '*that man has something to teach you*' she has said to me; you remember!"

Approaching the roundabout last navigated in the taxi this morning, I gesture onwards, "There we go, that's the coast road."

"Are you sure?"

"Well, the sea is over there, and the road appears to be the only one so – yes – I think so," I say humorously.

"Ah, I need you; *Englishman*," she says, almost reprovingly (but not quite).

Reflecting on my good fortune re the gift, and our good fortune re the walk back, and then pondering on the shortest route to navigate the roundabout, we are stepping off the pavement into a roughly cobbled gutter when…I miss-step. My right foot turns, and pain sears through the outside of my ankle. Transferring my weight to the left foot, I hop clear of the roadside. Deep burning pains then take hold and I move to the nearby railings to steady myself.

Marie-Hélène is directly at my side. "Are you alright? You have hurt your ankle? I did not see; I only heard you. Are you alright Wayne? Please, say *something!*"

"Yes…I just have to…wait a bit and…breathe slowly and deeply…can't talk just now…sorry, give me a minute"

"Is there anything I can do to help, please?"

"No, just a minute…I…I just need to stay with my pain right now – to accept it – not reject it."

Moving my right hand down, I invite Reiki energy to flow and with my palm just clear of my ankle, I sense the point at which the flow is most apparent and hold the position. "Phew, that's better," I say with relief. "It's easing now."

Marie-Hélène gets out the water and I take a long swig.

"My ankle is maybe a little damaged," I speculate. "But the pain is just the nerves' response, so normally, if I *accept* the pain just for what it tells me about the physical trauma, I find much of the stress goes. If I fight against the pain, it is as if my rejection establishes it as a "thing" – giving it substance, and it just seems to invigorate the pain, with the pain-rejection-pain cycle serving only to prolong the discomfort." I explain.

"Where have you learnt this?"

"I think I read it first in one of the *Celestine Prophecy* books, but I guess I view it a bit like homoeopathy: if it makes a difference, that is enough – yes?"

Marie-Hélène suggests that we should call a taxi, but confiding I have done this a few times before, I assure her that the best thing for me is to use it – gently – but as normally as possible.

"As long as you are sure," she says, supporting my armpit to help me. "Sorry," I say, "but that does not help me; just hold my hand – I need to find my own balance. You know, I'm just wondering if Rachel and Henri had not offered to walk ahead, do you think this would have happened anyway, bringing about the same effect," I postulate, wondering if in some weirdly wonderful way I may have pre-programmed my mishap with my desire to walk back alone.

Having walked for about twenty minutes I notice we are quite close to the sea and on a small promontory. Glancing back, I bring us to a halt. We are gazing at *the* bay: where we had first walked alone, and at the little island chapel and to the headland where we had first kissed. Accordingly, we kiss again and walk on.

On coming to a small car park, and being that is a spot of quite some natural beauty, we decide to make use of the picnic bench (a prerequisite it seems, to tempt the general population to pause long enough to *be* with nature, and then – most usually, and unfortunately, as here – to trash it). Deciding that this must be about halfway back, we agree – despite the litter – to take a short rest break.

"Marie-Hélène, do you remember me saying, that someone called Helen had introduced me to *another* Helen who had, in turn, introduced me to the London group and that those and other subsequent events had led me to be here?"

"Yes…"

"Well, you know… isn't it a bit of *coincidence*: what with the two Helens, and you being called Marie-*Hélène*?"

"Yes, and remember also you have said about a meeting with that young lady Marylene – '*Mar-ylene*' – going to Glastonbury. Hah, that *is* funny!" she declares, but then halts abruptly. "Oh, Wayne – stop! Oh, there is something else – you could not know but – it is Rachel: her real name is Helen as well!"

"What do you…?"

"We are all just calling her Rachel because she would prefer…and do you know, if it was not for her persuasion, I would not have gone to Glastonbury and I would not be here at all! It is special – yes! Oh Wayne, you know: if it had not been for the extra days in Athens – that she had suggested, you know, I might not have been persuaded at all – really! Wayne, I have her to thank, *so much*!"

"Then I suppose, we have all these Helens to thank," I conclude. "Oh Wayne, where do we start."

Two bays and two promontories later, we find ourselves at the point where the road starts to depart the waterside to go behind/between the buildings we are now so familiar with. As always, we refrain from taking the simple route along the road to the apartments taking instead, the scenic route along the beach. However, before leaving the road, I recall the beach-episode: "It must have been about *here* where that car came around and shone its lights that startled us."

"Oh yes, under the stars," Marie-Hélène says softly, and kisses me on the cheek.

"Perhaps, we will do that again sometime… if you *like!*" she teases as she slips out of my hold and runs down the slope between the rocks and onto the sand sharing furtive smiles as she goes. I do my best to catch up, but with a weakened ankle I decide to ease back and delight in witnessing her joy as (like always) she radiates – and especially when she meets with sand and sea. Upon catching up, we both take off our footwear as hand in hand we walk the waterline, dodging the waves as we go (and for the most part, quite successfully).

Upon passing through the picket gate at the accommodation, an idea comes to me: "Marie-Hélène, earlier, back in town, do you remember – I went back into the shop?"

"Yes?"

"Well, it was because I saw something, I wanted to buy for you – no, more than that, I found something and *had* to buy it for you."

"Oh, what is it! Show me – *please*"

Extracting the promised package carefully from my pocket, I stare for a moment before handing it to her. Marie-Hélène carefully unfolds the paper bag. "Oh, it is lovely! Oh, the spiral…and what is this written… yes, it is just *so* true" she continues.

Then, suddenly full of excitement she roots around impetuously in her handbag. I have prepared myself for a hug or perhaps a modest peck on the cheek, but instead – holding the bracelet up to me – she says, "Oh, I cannot tell you – what I want to say just now. No, I need to show you – later, when I get dressed." Marie-Hélène continues sifting fervently through the contents of her bag, and then suddenly stills – as she reaches her goal. With her hand still deep in her bag, she exclaims, "Oh, I have bought a little something for you as well, but before I give it to you, I simply must tell you why I am so happy. When I was packing to come on holiday and I was thinking I should pack only sensible clothing, I suddenly decided to bring one special dress – just in case. Well, I have not used it yet, but tonight…" she says excitedly, "…tonight, I shall wear it, and tonight you shall see!"

"See what?" I ask her.

"But first," she continues unabated, "this is for you."

I notice the packaging being *quite* similar to that which had contained my gift (…ah!), and I open it to find – a fridge magnet (?)(!)

"Oh, I know," she says. "I know that a fridge magnet is just the sort of gift you said you *never* like to buy for anyone, but look – look at it, please," she says excitedly.

It is a small ceramic heart, largely blue – *my* blue, and it displays a similar heart-within-heart motive as is within my painting, and there is the outline of a golden-yellow inner heart with a green heart in the middle – the colour that comes from mixing blue and yellow. "A-ha, so *that* was what was happening when Rachel was going back and forth in the shop earlier," I enthuse.

I kiss Marie-Hélène squarely on the lips, but only briefly, because she is so full of glee she cannot hold still.

"So, what *is* it about the bracelet?" I plead.

"Tonight, tonight I shall wear it; oh, it is *lovely* – just wait, you will see!" Upon those words and still brimming-over, Marie-Hélène exits stage left (well – right actually, but…you-know).

I am in my room, deciding what to wear for the evening, when out loud, and to no one in particular, I say: "So, tonight I shall see…"

"Deciding what to wear." Ha! Who am I trying to fool? I have only one combination of top and trousers that remains clean and fresh-enough for this last supper. "The *last supper*," I reply (to myself). "I hope I am lighter than *that* this evening!"

On, therefore, goes my beige shorts and my cream (okay – light *beige*) short-sleeved top, and then a little aftershave and… "Now, where's my necklace?"

Ah there, yes – the pendant that came to me via *Godspell* and returned now to Greece (some years and quite some meditations later). As I lift it to my neck, I recall it has been many days since I had last put it on – in fact, quite a while since I have worn anything around my neck. Eager to discover Marie-Hélène's surprise, I am fiddling with the clasp behind my neck…easing, pushing, pulling when "clack" the metal pendant hits the tiled floor. The Greek/Pagan cross lay at my feet, however, not wanting to delay the forthcoming *revelation* (and interestingly, with no trace of frustration or sadness for the pendants' demise) I hastily put it into my pocket, and without further delay, go out into the half-light.

At five minutes to seven, (and for once, ahead of schedule) I am on the grass adjacent to Marie-Hélène's apartment. A moment later – following sounds of laughter from Rachel and Henri's apartment – Marie-Hélène emerges from the same, beaming wildly and wearing a beautiful dress; a light-bright, pastel *lemon-yellow* dress. *Now* I see why she was excited. Approaching, she puts both arms around my neck and almost heaving with exhilaration, she momentarily lowers her face to my chest, before pulling back and planting a hasty kiss on my lips.

"See – you see! That is why I could say nothing earlier – see! Look – look at that" she continues. "Look at the colour of the bracelet; it is the same – see! Of all the dresses I could have bought with me, I choose *this* one, and even though I have not brought much clothing, I have not thought to wear it – until tonight. And then you get me this!" she rejoices, displaying once again the perfectly colour-matched bracelet.

"You two!" Rachel calls. "Just turn around, let me take a picture of you both."

It takes three or four shots and the joining-in of others keen to capture the moment before Marie-Hélène can compose herself fully, whereupon "vivacious" changes to *elegant*. In the meantime, I just stand, wonder, and float with it all. (Yes, this…this is being light.)

Just before departing for dinner, Marie-Hélène asks I wait while she returns to the apartment. I follow but wait short of entering bathroom, from where I presently hear a light "hiss" of spray which is swiftly followed by the return of a familiar citrus-lemon odour. Marie-Hélène emerges and quite relaxed, puts her arms firmly around my waist and initiates a much-awaited, full, soft, lingering kiss.

"Thank you," she says. "The bracelet is *sooo* lovely."

"Please, before we go," I ask. "Just in case I forget to do this tomorrow, may I take a photograph of the bracelet against your dress? The colour match is just so astonishing."

Walking along the beach for the final time, everything feels – well, fine: no fears, no doubts, no concerns about what tomorrow may bring. Halfway along the beach, I reach into my pocket. "Marie-Hélène, would you mind – just a moment, please." I pull out the cross, which – if it has had any part in my coming here – has certainly done its work, and I hold it firmly in my fist. It came from Greece, and now it returns to stay…

"*May the energy that has brought this cross to the other side of Europe and back, now be absorbed by the sea to the eternal betterment of both,*" I pronounce, and with the action flowing perfectly from the words (wherever they came from) I propel the metal cross far out into the cool grey waters.

"Oh, was that your cross?"

"Yes, I think it has come home now."

We walk on, hand in hand.

The final evening at the taverna – is quite different. Following the food, the family who have hosted us so well – usher us into the main building where a space has been cleared. Karina sets a tea-light in the middle, and then proceeds to introduce the whole family: children, parents, sisters, grandparents and grandchildren, and then invites that we sit together in a short visualisation and prayer.

Karina speaks slowly and Nikko – who happily, has joined us for this final evening – interprets her words. The youngest granddaughter (not more than three or four) sits with us in the circle and keeps perfectly still, watching and listening. I suspect it is of no matter whether Karina's words are understood or not, because everybody present can surely *feel* the integrity and beauty in what she is saying.

By the time Karina finishes, there is hardly a dry eye amongst us, and even the tables on the terrace have quietened – the diners having turned to face our way.

What surely could follow? Well, what could be a better end to the evening than Greek dancing! Accordingly, with lively piped music, our hosts show us some of their local moves. What with the bowing, hopping, skipping and such, I am reluctant to let go of the peace I absorbed from the meditation, thus, I decline the invitations to participate. Instead, I watch on, pleasantly surprised to see Marie-Hélène celebrating with the utmost commitment and a corresponding amount of joy.

The evening continues in such a similar joyous fashion, with even some diners being drawn into the exuberance. As with all energetic parties, however, there comes a time when everything seems to naturally moderate and then diminish, and thus, looking quite complete, and a *little* bit tired, Marie-Hélène comes close and says, "Let's go home." (What a lovely thought.)

The Mosquitoes: Their Return
(And Leur Reprise)

The walk home is relatively protracted, with Marie-Hélène and I arriving back just after midnight. Marie-Hélène takes her time in her apartment, gathering her luggage and "things" in preparation for the morning's early start. At the chateau, we take our Greek Mountain tea in a similar un-rushed fashion and are in no hurry to go to bed either.

The subject of "life after Skyros" has been discussed – probably, at least once a day, but admittedly, most attention has been to the current moment: to what had seemed real in the Now. [38] However, as we rest in one another's arms – acutely aware of what the next day brings – it feels we are somewhat adrift regarding how to move-on from our wonderful time here on Skyros. Just now, I cannot see the course ahead.

While the moon moves through the sky somewhere above, the nature of our discussion becomes more occasional, then it becomes intermittent, and then it pauses. It feels like we are both riding the same emotional wave, descending towards an unfathomable low…when Marie-Hélène declares, "You know…" (Pause). "Having time together can be *made* to happen." (Another pause.) "It is simply a case of organising things," she affirms. Excitedly, we conclude that with information such as telephone numbers, addresses, airport locations, airlines and flight-times, we can bring our minds together to coordinate our diaries, and then our bodies can be brought together as well. "You see! It is no problem – just organisation!" she exclaims, and thereby, not only securing our buoyancy but completely turning the tide. (I love her.)

Even so, and as the wave inevitably passes, we yet find ourselves afloat on a somewhat skeletal raft of arrangements: while we can see a way to spend weekends together and occasional holiday breaks, it is clear that the future will inevitably find us wanting for something more. Consequently, and although we

---

[38] See Appendix II: Giving attention to what seems real – now

have the safe haven of one-another's arms before tomorrow's sailing, we yet feel somewhat at sea again, with "hope" now appearing to be our only way-point.

Neither of us has experienced such a relationship quite like the one we are now having, and thus we conclude: if this is a measure of the change that can occur, we must accept that we do not know *what else* might come our way. We have both experienced misfortune in our lives, but now we are open to change – engaging with new experiences and not trying to control things too-much; it is clear that life can also bring very *good* fortune. Consequently, our agreed policy becomes *not* to try and determine the complete shape of the future, because – if we base it on our previous experiences – we are not likely to create a space big and beautiful enough to contain the sort of good fortune that Skyros has brought us. Unwittingly, we would seem to have stumbled upon a new understanding of "faith"…

"The ability to perceive a space in the future – held open with 'not knowing', so that it may be filled with such wonderment as never known before."

Our talking has been productive, and so has much of the thinking, (which has not always been my experience) but nothing has held back time, and upon finding we are nearing the hour of dawn, we agree that we have done enough *thinking*. As our attention returns towards our current *position(s),* Marie-Hélène (or is it I), cause us to move each – one against the other.

"Oh, you're *here* then," Marie-Hélène says warmly, encouragingly.

"M'mm, I think I just might be," I reply, then – speculatively lifting the covers I announce, "Yep, that's me." With that, our bodies take over the energy-train that our minds had previously occupied, and without thought and planning of any discernible nature, we give time to experiencing the now – the best way we know.

"Maybe if we can sleep on the boat and the plane tomorrow, we do not need to sleep so much tonight, yes?" Marie-Hélène proposes.

"Yes, okay, let's *not* plan to sleep!"

"So, there is no problem now for us?"

"Nope, no problems, just some organisation," I affirm, pulling the bed sheet off in mock abandon. "No, no problems," I continue, as she receives me to a gentle sigh, "Just a little more organisa… *ouch!*"

"What, what is it?" Marie-Hélène responds.

"Hah! You won't believe it; I think I have been bitten!"

"What, *mosquitoes?*" she says. "Mosquitoes!" I confirm.

As I withdraw to scratch my ankle, we both start to laugh.

"So, maybe this is what happens if we do not plan enough. So much for faith," Marie-Hélène teases. "So, you do not *organise* enough to keep out the mosquitoes!" We both curl up now, holding our bellies and shaking with mirth.

"Hah, but what if this is just my *perception.* What if I now choose *not* to accept a space in the future where the mosquitoes can be?" I counter.

"What, what do you mean? You mean we must stop all this and hold the sheet over us so that Mosquitoes do not get you?"

"No, I mean: I can choose *not* to perceive them, and just go on regardless!" I enthuse, heroically pushing the sheet completely off the bed.

"M'mmm, I like this un-organisation," Marie-Hélène murmurs.

We thus entertain ourselves, albeit – with the sighs that float into the night air being occasionally interspersed with, "Ouch!", because even though I prefer to perceive the mosquitoes as *not* being there, they clearly – do not!

Having conceded that the mosquitoes – in being devoid of free will – cannot be persuaded otherwise, I hit upon a workable compromise: on each occasion the little b*…*s do now ("ouch") bite, I choose to perceive it all ("ouch"), as a cause for celebration – upon the reasoning that the presence of the mosquitoes is inseparable from what is Now, and, therefore, to deny their presence here-now ("ouch") would require me to obscure my own presence – here now, ("ouch") or indeed – *here* ("oooo-oh/aaaah")…now… (… "Ouch!")

The clock rings, and shortly after the alarm on my phone sounds, followed by Marie-Hélène's phone-alarm (organisation or *what*).

We have not slept much, but the other side of the coin is that we are both too thrilled, (/tired) for sadness to take hold. I am, however, most certainly *sore,* with the mosquitoes having been company to much celebration last night (…as one way of looking at things). Interestingly, however, it remains that Marie-Hélène is bite-free, and it is for the better because she now has the time to apply copious amounts of the *lavande.*

We have chosen not to set aside time for breakfast today, but to focus instead on preparing for the taxi departure (and the ferries and later on – the flights). Although Marie-Hélène had thought-ahead enough to bring her luggage to the chateau, she still chooses to depart the chateau now to do a final check of her apartment, "Just in case".

Having finished my packing, returning the mattresses (etc.) to their original positions, and making the house tidy, it is not yet seven o'clock: this is good. I load up my blue swim-bag with water, two large bananas, some nuts, and some bread and cheese, and with my suitcase and two bags in hand, I descend the wooden staircase for the final time. Placing all belongings on the veranda, I take a few photos of the rooms I have occupied so joyfully this last week. My phone comes out again on the garden path – for *the Chateau*. Despite the changes happening today, it would seem that the rest of Creation proceeds as normal. Accordingly, and with nature having made no adjustment to its timing, I pass between the bushes before the staging of the bees' chorus, and I feel the loss of their presence. In their memory, I frame a final shot that captures the house and the flowers that are now opening. In the two-seconds that the photo stays on the screen, I notice the sky is just starting to turn blue, and turning towards the sea I think upon the coloured sunrise that will also now escape me.

Leaving the garden behind, with bags knocking against my legs as I walk, I am prompted to accept I am truly taking back *more* than I had come with.

Beryl is sitting outside her apartment. She welcomes the offer of my well-used mask and snorkel, and I happily let them go.

Marie-Hélène comes out presently, clasping a bag of things she has recovered from her apartments' fridge, ("*Just...*"). The mini-bus arrives, luggage is loaded, and hugs and kisses are shared with those who remain. Some moist-eyes are experienced, mine included, but my eyes are just the start because as the mini-bus heads off across the island towards the port, I start to sense the tunnelling of my emotions, and where I might have expected some sadness to follow – instead comes numbness.

Not all of my senses are so consumed however, because I am presently aware of a certain sweet *odour*. It is not unpleasant, but it is pervasive to such an extent that I am determined to identify its source. The strength of the odour is so acute however, that it almost defeats my ability to establish what the odour smells *of*. Detecting that it is coming from the floor of the mini-bus, and from the direction of my feet, I am resigned to accept that it is the *lavande* and that Marie-Hélène must have excelled with the use of her favoured potion. Perhaps the others will assume that a bottle of lavender oil has leaked, and not suppose that I have bathed in it this morning.

With my lavender "hit" beginning to fade, my mind starts to recalibrate and I find some solace in the relatively still landscape…and then in the views of the coastal landscape, and then – as I see the port looming – my emotional landscape takes back-over and numbness returns. There feels to be a dam forming within me, a "holding-back" of much sentiment; but I do not feel ready to face whatever content is threatening to flood out.

At the port, there is quite a commotion. It seems that many people have chosen this day to leave the island. Alternatively, perhaps these may be commuters going off to work. On the other hand…ah, no, let's face it – I am attempting to divert my attention from my emotions. I find myself quietly mouthing the words, "I do not care," hoping that a "not bothered" attitude might counter the ever-rising pressure on the other side of my emotional dam. My ability to empathise reduces rapidly; my thoughts now encompassing only *my* group and *my* departure. The wall of the dam continues to pressurise and life beyond the window is reduced to a two-dimensional blur. As the volume and density of the emotions increase, they weigh against the wall causing it to bulge and stretch to the likeness of skin – so taught, so thin, that I can almost see the nature of the emotions on the other side. They have the greyness of fear and the sting of separation, and I know that if I were to say goodbye to Marie-Hélène just now, the dam would burst. I look at Marie-Hélène; she appears to be encountering a similar "greyness".

The mini-bus comes to a halt, Marie-Hélène and I recover our baggage, and as our eyes meet and we sense each other's disposition, we share a restrained smile. We carry our things over to the coach waiting to drive us onto the ferry – taking us to the next ferry, and then to the shores of Athens – for the flights this afternoon.

There are no remnants of any good humour from the night before. It all eludes me just now. Neither can I find any imagery to hitch a ride upon towards some notion of future happiness. Nothing about this "now" seems to be offering even a thread that leads me towards a lighter place.

Despite feeling forlorn, however, I realise do not want to waste this time, for these are my and Marie-Hélène's last few precious hours together. We have swapped addresses and home phone numbers and we intend to call each other tomorrow – to investigate the 'when' and 'wherefores' of flights…so this is not the end. Therefore, why all this – *greyness*?

Once on board the ferry, we walk with the others towards the upper levels – I assume – to be able to have a view of the port and say goodbye to the island. Walking the cold metal decks and up the rigid unforgiving steps, and smelling the diesel fume from the ship's engines – does nothing to lift my demeanour. I feel frustrated that the group is not settling anywhere, but I follow them all the same. I am trying hard to accept what is happing, not wanting to reflect the negativity as blame onto others, but I cannot help feeling that I would rather Marie-Hélène and I were elsewhere – alone. I need some sense of something *better*; better than grey and metal and fume…and the threat of goodbye.

Marie-Hélène asks me to watch her things while she finds the Ladies toilet and that I try to track the group if they move on. After one minute, however, I am ready to give up waiting for the group to settle. I have never found it easy to *follow* when there is no clear lead or plan. Therefore, intent on seeking somewhere "else" – and from where Marie-Hélène and I might see the port fade into the distance, I gather our things and set off. Where I set down offers little advantage over where we had just been, but being less subject to the influence of "the others" it seems to be something of a respite. I arrange our things in plain sight on and around a bench, and then move back to a mid-position from where I can see our things and still catch sight of Marie-Hélène's return.

There is a change in the volume of the ship's engines followed by a deep rumbling, and upon seeing plumes of black-blue smoke billowing out the funnels, I return to move our baggage in fear that all might be enveloped. There then follows a few shouts, and with a scraping sound as metal grinds metal the vehicle ramp folds up into the ship and we are off.

I look around to see if Marie-Hélène may be returning but there is no sign of her. Picking up her things, I decamp to a point near to some stairs that lead to the upper decks, and as I begin to set down once more, she comes out – with Rachel. They look as if they have been talking over something serious, because both their faces appear to be quite "set".

"Oh, you have moved our things?" Marie-Hélène remarks.

"Yes, well yours at least; I just need to go and get mine. Can you wait here?" "Yes, but when you come back, can we find somewhere; somewhere lighter and where we can be alone? I just want to be with you."

As Marie-Hélène looks to me for endorsement, her eyes disclose her sadness. Having recovered my things, we move to the next deck. Upon emerging into direct sunlight, I experience what Marie-Hélène had felt-for: and I immediately feel – well – *lighter*; as if the sunlight itself is feeding me: *"feeding me…"* – I have not eaten.

Hoping that some food might (also) benefit my emotional state, I find a packet of nuts and a large banana. Marie-Hélène has several nuts but declines the offer of the whole banana, taking instead a small and uncharacteristically dainty bite from the top as I hold it for her. She stares at me, and I'm not sure if is she eying me with suspicion, or trying to make a joke of it. In any event, the joke is not apparent. However, she proceeds to take another small bite and to hold it in her mouth, and then I do the same, and as we repeat such in turn, we realise our parts in a game of capturing the maximum of banana with the smallest of bites possible – and our moods lighten further. Creating humour around dining manners is something Marie-Hélène has done ever-since our first visit to the buffet tables (though perhaps not always knowingly) and it warms me greatly. With both of us smiling again I feel a sense of our reconnection and realise: *that* is what I have really missed. We have both been so wrapped up in ourselves, that we have forgotten the *"us"*.

Seeing there is yet another flight of steps to a higher deck, we decide to explore. We find ourselves on a small deck, and alone. There are several wood slatted park-bench type seats lined up and facing the sun, and we set down mid-way along. With a clear view to the left and rear, and a fair view ahead – looking around the side of the wheelhouse, we have the sun on our face and a breeze in our hair, and we feel – at last – able to settle.

I sit to the right of our three-seater and lay my rucksack against the thin side rail, and with that Marie-Hélène swivels around and leans her head back on my chest. It is all much brighter now – inside and out – and I resolve in future to remember how much my blood-sugar level can affect my emotions, and how much the simple sense of our connection can do the same.

A few minutes later, my "not so sad" lifts to something like contentedness, and as I venture to think to the days ahead I feel further uplifted by the prospect of unpacking some of these loving-memories.

"So, what do you think we will be doing in a week or a month's time," Marie-Hélène asks.

"I don't know, but I suspect that within the month I will be visiting you, or you will be visiting me," I venture.

"Yes, I know it. You do not seem so worried about the future now," Marie-Hélène observes.

"I guess the future will always have things in it that can be a challenge, but I can see that "challenge" itself, is very much a matter of perception," I offer.

"*Just organisation*," she ribs. "I told you, no problems!"

"Yes, just organisation," I consent.

There then follows something of a pause, before I continue, "But you know, I think we will still need to have realistic expectations, because when the organising has all been done and we have governed our expectations, it would be wise to assume that there are still enough "unknown-unknowns" for some of them to come and bite us. Though, I guess *if* and *when* they do, it will just be a case of deciding again: do we duck under the covers, or hold ourselves open to the maximum joy in the midst of whatever challenge may follow."

"You mean, like the mosquitoes in Skyros," Marie-Hélène offers.

"Yes, sort-of," I reply.

It transpires that the position of my backpack does not make for such good padding, and to relieve the discomfort I commence to readjust its position. This, in turn, disturbs Marie-Hélène who also moves, swivelling back around to a seated position, lifting her feet, bending her knees, and bringing both her legs round to tuck them at her left side. She completes her reorientation by repeated nuzzling until her head is just under my chin and partly on my chest.

One of my hands rests on Marie-Hélène's knee, the other partly cups her head, and wisps of her fragrant blonde hair blow freely across my face with each occasional breeze. I close my eyes and offer my face to the warming sun.

I can feel a space opening up inside of me: it feels like "future". It is clear, it is expansive, and I *know* it has the potential to present all manner of good.

"How long do we have before we get off?" she asks.

Forever – I am thinking.

(The End)[*]

---

[*] Sort-of ☺

Appendix I
The Process of Writing:
Mosquitoes in Skyros
(...And Discovering How My Mind Works)

Writing mostly at weekends, it took several days of work – setting out the thoughts and feelings that were bursting to be represented – before I realised that they were not coming to me in any particular order. Subsequently, I dedicated the next few weekends to the creation of a summary using keywords to represent all of the content that seemed to be inside of me, then putting it into a timeline and finally slotting it into a calendar to match the period over which everything took place.*

When I recommenced the "storytelling", I found myself assembling what came to me as poignant photo-like memories with their associated feelings, and then rushing to write down the surrounding follow-up memories that would immediately follow. All too often, however, when I sought to "interrogate" the follow-up memories – to gain more detail, the words would dry-up. Subsequently, I took to holding back on the "interrogation" and simply (*simply!*) allowed everything to flow in the "memories-with-feelings" format, and they poured-forth.

Unexpectedly, what came was not only words but – in my mind's eye – veritable pictures, often imbued with colour, sometimes with sound and aroma, but always with much emotion. I then proceeded to (*simply*) sense and write, and then to sense and write some more, and so I would proceed until the flow ceased. At this point, I would stop and read what I had written, usually to be impressed at just how much reality had been revealed.

---

* If you have read this "the writing of..." section first then yes – with this knowledge you could now skip straight to the end to see "what happened"; but if you do, you will be missing one of the most important life-truths – that time exists to purposefully separate and line up events *for a reason.*

This process, however, initially presented some challenges, partly because of the first-person voice (/tense) which was wholly new to me, and partly because the words came in such quantity that I could write several pages without a pause, only to find that what was written had holes/gaps in the narrative that prevented any sense of natural flow.

What I had effectively written was a selection of lovely but largely unconnected mini-chapters, and whilst they were very evocative individually, they did not make for good reading as a whole. What was missing from in between the "pictures in time" that the words represented, was all the *living* that takes place in reality.

Hoping to improve matters, I sat down one Saturday morning to reintroduce some interrogation and I adopted the process of at least once every page – pausing the writing, reading what was written, and then, if a hole or missing link was apparent – casting my mind in the direction of that "hole". Again, I was surprised this time – because upon "finding" a missing detail, even just a single missing moment in time, it would often be enough to bring forth plentiful words and pictures (…etc.) as if a bag of memory had been burst and the content could do nothing but spill out.

After some practice, when it appeared to me that a relevant part of the story was in fact missing, I found myself in a process more akin to asking and receiving than thinking/interrogating, and on many occasions, the clarity of what came to my mind's eye was so evocative and organised, that I could then "forward" or "rewind" simply to order. "Simply to order" is perhaps – a little misleading; perhaps a lot. An advantage in the asking and receiving process was that I was never short of words. The disadvantage, however, was that I was never short of words!

Then, another new challenge arose: if my mind wandered – even just a short while – away from the immediate "what happened next", into any other point in time, I would find my inspiration to have jumped straight to, and proceed directly from – that new point. It took a few weekends of repetition – suffering the difficulty (again) of slotting sub-sections of story into a common timeline – before I understood just *how* fickle and flirtatious the mind is.

In short, I had to be very careful about where in time I positioned my "questions" within the framing of *Mosquitoes*, and to accept that if my monkey-mind so wandered onto pastures new, that the words, pictures etc. that came to me would reflect *only* that new point in time. I also came to find a great new purpose for my meditation practice: to still my mind before starting to write (and occasionally during,) so that I could exercise some greater control of my thinking.

Of additional interest (well – to me, at any rate) was the fact that my mind always seemed to be working within some overall conceptual framework of understanding whereby, as I would read what I had written, a larger picture would come together – a bit like how one experiences the piecing-together of a jigsaw. This not only enhanced my overall understanding of the story, but also enabled me to return to the sections already written, with ever-more probing questions along the lines of, "So, what thoughts had taken place before 'this' was done?"

As the story progressed, my perception of how the (/my) mind worked, expanded similarly. Whereas I had sometimes taken life to be all about "the things that had been done", i.e., a series of events and experiences, wherein we encounter thoughts and emotions and make various decisions, I realised that a series of subconscious thoughts often occurred before all mindful thoughts/ actions, or perhaps to put it more accurately – thoughts *within* thoughts. Moreover, this did not just concern *Mosquitoes*, for as I continued writing, I found that I could also *ask and receive* regarding other aspects of my life: long past events, relationships etc.

For a while, I became sidetracked by the revelation of my mind's internal workings, and I starting to consider more deeply the "thoughts-within-thoughts" theory, which extrapolated to considering whether "frameworks-within-frameworks" might more accurately describe the process of "mind" when it is seeking to make sense of the world. * At this point, thankfully, I strayed (back) to my original purpose of writing – and continued with the story!

A side effect of all this thinking, however, was that it led me to reconsider the wisdom of my initial commitment, re "writing only truth" – but not for long. I realised the process I had adopted – of writing "answers to questions" – was born out of the intention to understand something about the power of truth, and because I was often coming across information and concepts in the story, that seemed both *true* and *new* (to me at least), the process itself deserved honouring. Therefore, I concluded that if information, pictures and the like – came to me

---

* It also begs the question: just *how* many levels of thought we humans might be able to access.

feeling as truth, and fitted in with my knowledge of life, who was I to determine what should be was *in* and what should be out? It just had to be all or nothing.

In editing *Mosquitoes in Skyros*, I have sought to preserve something of everything that a true experience of life involves; not just the main events, but all the thoughts, feelings, doubts and fears, joys and ecstasies – everything. [*]

Starting as a book that "just had to be written", *Mosquitoes* became a source of reflection and personal development for me both during and after its writing. The multi-faceted story has found me learning from myself, laughing and crying at and with myself, and to that end – the hundreds of hours put into its writing have pretty-much been repaid.

If it so happens that others who read *Mosquitoes* find themselves moved in any such similar and various ways, then so much the better.

(End of Appendix I)

---

[*] Please note, however, names and other personal details of others in the story have been changed.

Appendix II
The Particularly Interesting Footnotes

Presented here, are the footnotes arising from the story that deserve some further consideration/exploration. The content relates to topics that commonly arise during individual reflection and truth-full discussion in connection with personal or spiritual development, or in times of crisis. The footnotes expanded upon are investigated towards a deeper understanding, with occasional references back to the story when it serves.

The content seeks to nurture and feed the fertile mind and is particularly for those seeking to be more proactive in their life journey.

Suggestions for the use of this Appendix:

a) read *Mosquitoes* and follow the footnotes that capture your interest:
b) browse the contents page for Appendix II at the front of the book – and go where your heart leads;
c) or – now you are here – just read on…

Once again, I wrestle with the conflicting perceptions that stem from the subject of religion {p94}

In as much as most wisdom traditions promote the purpose of identifying and sharing truth, I by in large, respect the practice of religious faith. The continued search for *Truth,* however, often seems to be obscured by "belief" and the process of worship, and goodness may be further reduced by the power so many religion-based organisations seem to accumulate and weald. However, where "life" is respected and there is the acceptance of "a greater plan"/ "higher power", this surely signposts some common truth.

I have experienced so many meaningful perceptions, sensations and synchronicities, that it seems a natural conclusion to me, that some higher power, guardian intelligence, or higher-governing scheme of natural law must surely be involved. Something that is both within and beyond most wisdom-traditions, seems to impart both wonders and limitations to all life.

It might eventually transpire that the *natural law* I allude to, joins up with that other wisdom tradition "science" – that already ventures into multi-dimensional spaces...but I digress. It often seems that at the same time as religious practice binds many together, it immediately separates them from others. Most wisdom traditions – with their favoured teachings, favoured icons and such – would seem to demand its followers accept just *one* particular line of truth, apparently ignorant of, or perhaps scared of the obvious: that some even-greater truth must surely lie behind them all. (If only we could let go our addiction to identity.)

§

Expressing a yearning (for change) {p108}

...I had witnessed my subconscious opening to express a yearning for some such deep loving-connection. Is it possible I have met my twin-soul, my twin-flame?

I have occasionally reflected upon the words of Deepak Chopra in his book "The Seven Laws of Spiritual Success". A paraphrasing of two "wisdoms" goes along the lines of: "when one offers an intention (to the universe) to have an experience, one must take care not to form an attachment to any assumed outcome," or if you like: one should learn to "ask without expecting". I am sure such words have left many a grandmother's lips, but I can nevertheless recommend finding a home for some such similar intentions, whenever *change* is desired.

§

Re eating: why does eating seem so important? (Exchanging our atoms with the universe) {p109}

Exchanging our atoms with the universe is of course exactly what we all do when eating (...etc.). Someone conducting a workshop once imparted (possibly quoting someone quite infamous): "A tree is everything-but a tree." We had then meditated on that statement for some time before agreeing: it is only in the arrangement of molecules that most things can be seen to differ, because the vast majority of the *stuff* that makes up anything, consists of the molecules which come from everything-else around – the air, the water, the digestion of other things…etc. Over-eating is sometimes considered to represent a need for security, but it might perhaps signpost instead, an even deeper need: for *change* – for growth, for expansion of the inner world.

§

Re blaming others for how we are feeling
(…the human condition) {p110}

Blaming others for how we are feeling, seems to be a behavioural response that commonly stems from an actual or perceived loss of faith/trust, regarding a key love-attachment in childhood. Therefore, what my subconscious is doing (in *Mosquitoes*), is seeking to attach the emotion originating from the past, with what is happing now, even though there is nothing happing *now* to warrant such a powerful emotional disturbance. Nowadays, my understanding is that any such love attachment is – in effect our *own* attachment: *our* connection to the source of all love and all connectedness. However, whilst I can *now* perceive things this way, (when I am in balance,) it does not mean I always experience life this way *in* the now. Like all human beings, I bear the memories of my prior suffering as shallow-buried tracks, that run just beneath the surface of my awareness, and my peace covers-over my suffering as a new-mown lawn hides a rutted landscape. At times of challenge, the peace that one may have cultured can wear thin, and one can find oneself influenced by those tracks of prior pain once again. On this occasion however, just for now (in *Mosquitoes*,) the energy that flows from my sense of celebration, would seem to be helping me return to a greener perception, and thus I ride over those ruts of my pain-past (…)

The human condition is beautiful, but can seem to be somewhat complex – the experience of being human involving juggling/wrestling with a number of mind-states, which we are not usually taught to understand. Even when such mind states are to some extent understood, their nature and tendency towards variation, needs ones' regular mindful attention in order that the suffering programmes that we – most of us – are given/agree to, do not find new purchase in our lives. Many such programmes (or "agreements") would most-often seem to take root in our psyche in the earlier years of life. They would seem to reside in what some call the "conditioned mind" – being the aspect of our thinking that operates through our subconscious. Without sufficient attention (from our "unconditioned mind"), the subconscious processes can seem to shape and reshape our perceptions of life, bringing us back to face those original experiences that gave rise to emotional-pain – in a new form: suffering. Our unconditioned mind may be said to be the place of thought/thinking, from where we perceive the here and now in the here and now. Working from within this (unconditioned) mind-space, and seeking to identify and accept that which is true (/was true,) we can strive to be free of past-pain and reprogram ourselves /make new agreements. Such a process is sometimes called the journey (back) to authenticity.

The conditioned mind itself is not our enemy. It may in fact, be a most valuable asset, for in continuously juggling the emotional symbols we hold within us, our attention turns towards the past and towards the origin, giving us the opportunity to move from suffering towards healing – via learning.

Accordingly, it is through the processing of these prior experiences, in overcoming, understanding or transcending their repetition, that we take our conscious path towards healing.

§

Perhaps "authenticity" owes its meaning as much to honesty as it does to truth. {No expansion: see page 128}

§

The mind works to bring emotions to the present, as a means of re-presenting us with experiences of the past. {No expansion: see page 132}

§

Caught up in belief systems of religious origin {p133}

I try to be on my guard against being caught-up in belief systems of religious origin. If there is a unitary presence, a singular origin, or set of divine laws that drives life, then it certainly does not need a name, and it does not need to be worshiped or be believed-in for it to be true. I accept that every religion is likely to be based on some ones' true personal experiences; I can also accept that many who have followed or practiced a religion, have subsequently had their own true experiences when reading or seeking to understand or follow their preferred texts. However, so much of the original content, has been subject to such change during the process of transference by word of mouth, or through translation, or the evolution of languages, and through the mixing and changing of cultural context – that it must give rise to the question: just what truth and whose truth do the ancient texts now purport to represent? Is it not of purer purpose to seek our own experience of life, and not to simply subscribe to the experiences of others?

Words are – as all *things* – simply signposts: metaphors. Words are assumed by many to be absolute, but words are anything *but*. Therefore, while I am open to the words of all and any religion, I take my own understanding from them. Sometimes I come across "an understanding" that fits the shape of an outstanding question I have, or I find myself given to consider a potential "new understanding" and so I set it aside for cross-comparison, reflection, reinterpretation etc., but my preference is to allow "my truth" to be shown to me, proved (or not) through my own experiences, and then I can *believe* in them.

§

When someone presents an opinion with (too) much confidence and assertion… {No expansion: see page 136}

§

We can always find cause for worry… {p149}

When life would seem to be providing all the *things* needed – when we cannot blame the world around us for withholding anything – what then is left as the source of suffering but *ourselves*; our perceptions, our prejudices, our misconceptions. In which case, do we *really* have to keep striving to accumulate every*thing* that we need, or should we instead search for the cause of the condition within us that gives us to thinking we are lacking. At what point should we start to turn our focus from what we think we need, to what we feel we need, for surely our emotions are the better signposts to healing. The mind is our ally when we are seeking truth, but it is surely the heart that leads us towards fulfilment, towards wholeness, towards Love.

At what point does one start to look at the interface between the universe and the self, or the mind and the emotions for that matter. Is it perhaps, the interface itself that is the source of the "sense of lack"? If so, should not the interface between the two – the universe and the self – be the focus for our healing? Could that interface indeed, be the best source of all healing? Or, should we be looking deeper still. Perhaps it is not in observing the interface between ourselves and the universe that we will find the most learning, but in considering why we should think ourselves separate from the universe in the first place? (And I suspect, it is not by chance that I have I firstly supplanted "healing" with "love", and then with "learning".)

§

Why have I not worked with (my unworthy child) before? {p175}

To be fair, I have worked through a number of such personal issues; things that originated in my childhood and that have been kept alive by my unwitting-agreement. Indeed, there have been a number of conditions – behaviours, outlooks, attitudes etc. – adopted by way of an identity; as a way of behaving to the world. Of course, I had not understood what I had done at the time of "agreeing" to and adopting these identities. I had been too young, and simply tried just to get through and make some sense of the world which at times seemed to be of "non-sense". When, in some way, my connection to those nearest and dearest to me had been threatened, I had been brought to respond in ways that went against my natural inclinations towards the world, and often under the direction or coercion of those few in whom I had invested my ultimate trust. Back then, those to whom I "owe thanks for all that I am and everything I have" (for that is what we are told) seemed to be presenting me with such dire ultimatums that I felt forced to choose between believing myself and my natural inclinations, or risking the loss of my perceived love-connection. To maintain a sense of these connections I had accepted the distorted perceptions, and thus adopted the identity and carried the pain associated with those untruths – in the hope that I might then retain or return to their "love".

What choice had there been? What choice is there for any such children and other such vulnerable people who have yet to form a true understanding of life and the world around them? We all want to believe those persons we most need, and if it seems necessary, we let go of our own natural inclinations and act the role that is expected of us, leading to the adoption of a self-image to suit. The above, is the basis of my current understanding of the process of social conditioning; the process that seems to take place all across in the world, and would seem to be relevant to almost everyone in some measure. This "social conditioning" works well for all, when what we adopt are those perceptions that are based on truth, but it works against all, when the perceptions being fed/forced upon us are not wholesome.

All is not lost however, for it would seem that we retain a certain aspect of Free Will throughout the process of our social conditioning. It may not be such that we can hold our own against the pressures to behave, perform, and otherwise bend towards compliance, but there seems to be some level of "inner knowing" that – regardless of strife and trauma – can arise at a later time to monitor, review and query the currently held self-images. This inner knowing can bring us new hope and empower us to take new responsibility for our experience of life – which often seems to be the key to change. When we finally reach the understanding that – indeed – we could only have ever adopted the distorted perceptions of truth "by our agreement", we are then open to the path of change.[*] We may well have been under threat – physically, mentally, emotionally – but, unwittingly, we agreed – we accepted that distorted truth. [**]

---

[*] This process represents one method of healing. There would seem to be three: i) suffering and modifying behaviour to avoid reproducing it; ii) understanding the root of the particular "untruth", understanding the process of suffering, and practicing "forgiveness"; iii) transcendence: sensing and living as the true spiritual and love-centred beings that we are, we practice "non-resistance". (But all this is for another time; for your further investigation…or another book.)

[**] I do not think that we (human beings) are inherently ignorant (which only follows after suffering) but, innocent, and curious. Wisdom from living the physical world does not come out of simple belief, but from experience. We can choose what concepts and understandings to apply in our lives because we have Free Will. Therefore, we can choose to learn, and then choose to apply/extend our learning, or we can choose not to.

Therefore, in knowing that "agreement" could only have come about because of the "un-true" action of our own Free Will, it comes within our power to *un-agree*. We can choose to change our mind: to modify, disable and release ourselves from those distorted perceptions – *now*.

The process of renewal as I describe may not be easy, but it seems that life is not meant to be *easy*; but it can be *beautiful*, and my experience is that such truth-directed, mindful effort towards one's own healing – reveals such beauty.

§

There I go again, judging myself [for being] [stuff – happens] {p177}

Sometimes stuff happens: stuff that is not so easily foreseeable, stuff that is sometimes challenging stuff: some good, some *bad*. When stuff happens, is it helpful to condemn ourselves simply for *being* in it: for instantly assuming that the end result will be "wrong", or will reflect something wrong about ourselves? What is "wrong" anyway (?) often it is just one particular viewpoint from one particular perspective.

It may happen that – on reflection – we consider the "stuff" to be something we could or should have foreseen; and if so – then fair enough; but all we need do is to learn from the experience so that next time we can take a different path.

Judging and then *condemning* ourselves for making mistakes is self-defeating and unnecessary, and if we keep repeating the same mistakes, there is no need to judge ourselves, but instead to look to another level…the "agreement" that hides beneath (/the "untruth" – see above), and the circumstances that led us to it.

§

A lack of control over my life {p187}

It may well be good, sometimes, to not feel "in control"; to feel that we do not have such complete influence over our experiences that we keep ourselves in our comfort zone. This is not to promote erratic and mindless behaviour, but sometimes, "goodness" requires that something changes. If our control means that we "keep doing what we have always done", we should not be surprised if we keep *finding* ourselves right back where we started; experiencing a similar result time and time again.

Accordingly, perhaps what makes for a good learning experience – such as a retreat – is if we cannot control all the information that goes into, and comes out of our experience, so that we have to – in some way – submit; release control.

After all, what we have been striving to do whilst *in control*, is to re-file and re-categorise information to fit it into to our memories of similar past experiences: our perceptions of what we *should* expect, our perceptions of what we *think* we should experience, our perception of who we think we should be, etc. As a consequence, all this serves to do is to give us a sense of security, whilst at the same time keeping us *trapped*; ergo: our control is what can keep us where we are, and if "where we are" is not *of goodness*…

So maybe, the goodness that comes from not being in control, is that the truthful information coming out of past experience can be perceived more authentically. Maybe, when we are not in control, the memories of past events that at times spill-out pain, *also* bring to the surface different and more-important information that allows us to see the events for what they truly represented, and not just how we have previous filed them, boxed them up – packaged them away…

§

I – we – really, can only be sure of this "now" {p217}

"Now" is all we ever really have. This does not stop the monkey mind from trying to précis the future – which it largely does based on the amalgamation of the memories of past "nows". The memories the monkey mind seeks are those that are framed by some sense of "security" and/or those that are readily accessible because of having been replayed/re-cast repetitively. The monkey mind can only offer unreliable predictions of what might come to pass, because everything is based on what has *passed* – not on the reality now/to come. Because the past is all the monkey-mind can absorb, it needs us to keep regurgitating those memories in order to feed itself.

Sometimes, the best one can do is just to be "quiet" with it – trying not to feed the hopes and fears of the monkey-mind. In this approach it is best not to counter the monkey-minds' hopes and fears; not to try and push them away – but instead to step around them – and it will run out of steam… eventually.

The monkey-mind runs out of steam because it relies on repetitive thoughts: thinking and re-thinking – worrying if you like – to keep those so-called secure memories alive, or rather, to keep them appearing to be alive. Unfortunately, it so happens that the repetitive thinking we all tend to do most of, is the type that contains the most fear-based memories, and it is these ones that provide the most motivation to seek security and "escape", or at least to avoid the pain of the past. Why (?) because the monkey mind finds most energy from those kinds of thoughts. I use the term "fear-based", but I could also write "fear-directed" because fear itself is not real. Fear is an emotion that (*simply*) asserts its feigned reality within the subconscious, as a means of bringing our awareness to those conditions that may otherwise escape us. Similarly, love-directed thought – at the subconscious level, the level of "need", the level of "fear" – is also not wholly real because the pure energy-essence from which Love is perceived is of a spiritual nature, and needs our mindful attention to fully perceive and connect with it. Thoughts of love at the subconscious level, can only be perceived at all because of the attachment we make between them and other "things"; other things that we have thought to be secure in our subconscious (through repetitive thought).*

We can *sense* such as happiness, fulfilment, success, achievement and various other such similar forms of attachment emotions, but all of these differ from the pure essence of Love – which can only be experienced with mindful connection to the source-stream of *all that is real*.

§

Free Will…and the ego: "I" {p246}

"*Free Will*" works both ways – has to work both ways. It is only by having the option to accept or reject truth, that we can either feel the warmth of its acceptance, or can suffer from its distance, until we are turned again to be beckoned by its light. Life of course can be *complicated*; it offers so many enticements towards happiness and pleasure purely from the promise/belief that

---

* I have used the term "subconscious" with respect to one stream of thinking that takes place within "mind", but it can be replaced with the term "conditioned" i.e., "the conditioned mind".

joy, love and peace are such things that can be "attracted", bought, or sold, by something other than with the currency of truth. We are constantly force-fed information, and we are led towards assembling it in specific packages of knowledge, and then we are enticed and encouraged to believe these are of value. By another process: we are given information for information-sake – by way of simple entertainment or even worse: we are given to believe that regularly and repeatedly "loosing time" to entertainment is in some way good, or is enough to bring pleasure in itself.

Yes, life can be a complicated journey; one where Free-will can take the role of the navigator and driver – which sounds right and fine, other than the fact that in the back-seat (and sometimes in the passenger seat,) sits the main protagonist: the ego; 'I'.

§

Re...*choices are like stepping-stones...* {p246}

All choices are points in time within which decisions, indecisions, actions, and inactions may be manifested. Many scientists now seem to agree on one underlying natural law: that everything is energy, and every action/interaction gives rise to an equal and opposite action/interaction – leading to the understanding, (I would suggest) that some/any "thing" can only exist when there is another expression of the same energy to balance it elsewhere. Every choice is therefore a stepping-stone, and every stepping-stone makes a difference. If we take enough responsibility in our steps from day to day, our choices, our actions or in-actions, if we try to apply our innate sense for truth with care, then the small steps would seem to make towards a big investment.

§

Giving attention to what seems real – now {p263}

If one gives attention to how things are just *now*, to how one feels and to what one is physically facing *just now*, it is clear when a decision is needed and it is easier to make a right-minded decision on what actions to take. With "worry" however, our minds get lost in a myriad of "what-if" scenarios that distract, cloud our judgement, and sap our energy. One might argue that we should think about all the various scenarios so that we can plan with them in mind, but there are so many "ifs" and "buts" that we waste energy trying to project into the future, and being so distracted – we miss the Now. If one takes over-thinking too far, it contributes to such as worry, depression, or one of many repetitive/compulsive tendencies whereby we lose all sense of the goodness in Now.

Moreover, if we are not in the Now, we miss-out the deeper experience of true joy and peace of the kind that comes (only) with the true love connection. To fully perceive/receive these experiences we have to be a part of them – not just observe them, which means we need to be where those energies exist, and they exist only in the present moment: now.

No one experiences future-joy or future-peace because it has not yet happened, and similarly one cannot experience past-joy or past-peace – because it has already passed. One may have memories of these, and likewise one may have hopes and dreams for the future, but they are only projections of thought – framed within the hypothetical construct of "future". To go further, even these thought projections of future are themselves, still most often based on the memories of experiences already passed.

We experience excitement and fun and happiness and many such-similar perceptions, and these can seem very fulfilling, but these are comparatively short lived because they require us to identify what it is lacking: and when the need or expectation is met, all that happens is the "need" it cancelled out. Sometimes we may even set ourselves a negative need (i.e., an aversion) as an expectation that we want to avoid, but the action is the same, the energy play is the same: we set up a target and if we hit the target, we "reward" ourselves with the assumed response – but for a short time only. "For a short time": because in setting ourselves up for – hypothetical – future experiences, we engage with the perception of time, and the problem with time, is that almost as soon as we reach our time-based target – it passes. In addition, the emotion we had lined up for ourselves soon passes with it, and all because we pinned our hopes to a time.

Then of course, there is "entertainment" whereby we place ourselves in a situation where our expectations – hopes and fears – can be *apparently* achieved or avoided without really trying. In fact, through various forms of media, story lines can lead us to adopt *pretend* hopes and fears that have been formed on our behalf. In this contrived semi-reality, we may find our hopes and fears fulfilled – or not; toyed with and manipulated, and to such an extent that, through drip-feeding, our sense of reality can become distorted. All of this can happen with "entertainment".

There is the argument of course, that we can use entertainment for good, to give our minds a break when we cannot control our attention enough to stop worrying, or to stop our actions if we perceive we are working too hard. Additionally, one might argue that we can use entertainment to deliver messages of worth, to educate, to reason, to teach. However, do we actually "learn" that way? Or are we simply programming or re-programming ourselves with different subconscious behaviours…and if our lessons are not based on truth – not based on knowledge gained through our own experience of truth – will they not be found wanting again in time(?)

In summary: if such true living-experiences as joy and peace are to be gained, then the best, in fact, the *only* place to start, is *now*.

§

(And finally…) "How Truth Leads to Love" {the books' sub-title}

Truth and Love are constants; Truth is the constant relating to what we call "information" whilst Love is the constant relating to what we perceive as "emotion".

Love just *is*. To enhance the experience of love in our lives, it is more a case of understanding the barriers that we would build around ourselves – that prevent us sensing the omnipresence of love – than setting out to find love.

Recognising the precedence of truth when working with information – i.e., when formulating thoughts into words, to convey e.g., an idea, meaning, or reason, simply helps us face in the direction from which love can more easily be perceived.

The fact that love is omnipresent, however, does not mean that we all perceive /feel love the same. From the many experiences we have, and the many people in our lives, the perception of love can differ greatly from one to another. This is because we each contain both an essence of that same Love energy coloured/flavoured by our unique vibration that originates from our life-purpose. This means we perceive the Love vibration – earthbound, spiritual or divine – as being in some measure more or less in-balance or in sympathy with our own.

As we proceed through life, and as we learn, our veils of separation (the attachments to "un-truth" we have previously believed were "us") can begin to fall away and thus our perception and sensitivity to truth changes and along with this – our perception and sensitivity to love.

It is because of this, that, during the process of living, loving and growing – i.e., *learning*, we can find ourselves moving into or out of relationships, undertakings etc., personal, professional, celebratory or otherwise, until… ☺

(End of Appendix II)

Appendix III
Mosquitoes in Skyros – Spiritual Extracts

Part 1 of "nucreationstory" {152}

nucreationstory: A Creation Story...

Intelligence and the void.

Consciousness that has knowing, yet is isolated, inactive,

Aware of self and of more,

Aware of others, other selves – but aware of still more,

Consciousness, as crystals suspended in the dark of night, but with no night, and no dark,

Yet, sensing of another place, another state of being; desiring to be of that state, and waiting.

Collectively waiting with collective intent,

Collectively learning how to wait and how to invite a change of state,

Knowing there is more to be known, more that must come before that which may be All,

Something other, something to be received, to be allowed, accepted,

And they wait, waiting, without time, without space, without expectation.

Then comes a vibration so faint, and it is perceived as a sound,

And it sounds as an Aum and it is accepted,

And the Aum is permitted to pervade all: and it would, And they wait.

Then comes a pinpoint, a new sensation in the void, a vibration so bright,

And it is perceived, and it enters the collective awareness,

It grows in intensity,

It is of an expansion, it is of a strength,

It is of All, but of such Oneness that it's All eclipses all else; and it's All cannot be Known,

But because it is All, it is to be accepted so that the void might be no more,

And in acceptance it is received, it is perceived,

It is perceived as Energy.

And the Energy becomes the Light in the Dark; the first and the final of the duality of all things in this new place that was once void,

And the Light shines upon and across the faces of the Selves, and They know they are Twelve.

And the Energy of the Light is felt,

It is a Good Force.

But the Light is not to be ridden but to be admitted and entered into,

And because it is that which has been awaited, the entering must be complete,

And as they of a number surrender, they dissipate in an expansion of light that carries the intelligence of the Twelve into vibrations of colour.

Yet and even then, in the force that gives expansion is present the force that is of retraction – as it would persist; as a net covering all existence – exerting the pull, back to Oneness,

And they learn what it is to be intelligence within the Light and that the Dark enables the Light and is as One.

And they learn how their intelligence as a crystal may find the Light reflected and refracted further into ever-increasing blends of colours, how as a number – in arrangements – the Light may be found directed and redirected into recurrent patterns,

And they learn – with their intelligence within the Light – that as a pattern is needed, it comes forth.

Yet, as their Intention ceases, so do the patterns return to the Light,

And even though they are within the Light – part of that Light, the Light that is of the Good-force that from the Oneness came – they learn that there must still be, so...much...more.

As the aeons pass and the expansion continues, they consider the Dark and the Light,

And when they consider only dark it becomes all-encompassing and seems to threaten the void,

And when they consider light, they find themselves within the expansion and grow with it.

And as the expansion proceeds, they come to know the patterns of light that arise from their intentions and they venture that from within the patterns – more learning might come.

And so, they consider how the Light had first come upon them: after waiting,

Waiting that was with the knowledge that there was more, but not knowing what it was,

Waiting that enabled a change, with an intention that there should be change, but permitting something not previously known to be within that change,

Not assuming what would be in that change,

Creating a space that was open to be filled with light or with void,

Intending a change without knowledge of what that change might wholly be,

Asking without assumption,

And thus they realise Faith: the allowance of a space in the knowledge of All, a space that may be filled with light – and it was.

And thus the patterns in the light caused by their collective intelligence enables that space, and into that space enters once again something of the Oneness, something of the Good-force, something in the form of Light that risks the Dark.

And so they learn that something in the nature of the Good-force is of change, and that change in part reveals something more of the nature of Oneness,

And, as if with a lowering of vibration, they observe that the Oneness gives something of its Light,

And so they form that space within the patterns within their light, And they intend change without assuming its content,

Accepting both Darkness and Light, both Oneness and Void,

And as they surrender to this – the Good-force – it enters and is received in that space.

And they behold, in the giving of its very Light, the Good-force – in a lowering of its vibration – now permits their intended patterns to continue beside and without their immediate intention.

And in that space – within those patterns that now exist without their presence – is something of the Light, the Good-force,

The Oneness giving something of its very matter: An act of Creation.

§

"Synchronicity" – the complete transcript… {187}

"Synchronicity.

Does everything happen for a reason…? Yes, of course, everything does happen for a reason.

Sometimes it is Free Will that gives rise to an action or a behaviour or a thought, but behind so many things that we feel is Free Will, is Spirit leading us on towards that which we are next to learn.

Many a time in life, we may find ourselves walking down a new path, facing a new situation, thinking we must be responsible for having made these decisions to be where we are – to find ourselves where we are; but more often than not we have been led to the position we find ourselves in so that we may be faced with that which was always going to come to us. Only when we are led away from the Light for a short time – can we turn back and see it.

It is indeed Intention that comes from Spirit – that gives rise to all thoughts and actions. The word synchronicity, therefore, can be applied to the plan that is behind all our experiences as individuals. Synchronicity is the way in which our thoughts, our intentions, our actions actually fit into the marvellous Plan there is for us as individuals: that which we should learn.

We may find ourselves making decisions which give us challenge, suffering, and torment for periods of time, but very soon down the path we find our understanding of how we came to this place where we are now and we look back and see a bigger picture: the bigger picture that is for our learning.

Spirit is there to support us always, giving us thoughts and ideas – not that we feel, see and sense them always – just to keep us heading towards the path: the path for finding our true-life purpose for this life-experience.

And of course, it is a wonderment that we may come across another individual on this earth, and – out of the blue, it often seems, they are there just on the right occasion to say things or behave in such a way that fits just-right with what we need to know or we need to hear. And, those that may not find a connection and understanding of Spirit will think 'how wonderfully co-incidental things can be' but of course, these things were never just co-incidental. They were the larger Plan of Spirit acting through another individual to work perfectly towards our own learning need.

So, synchronicity is the way in which our thoughts, our actions, our experiences fit in with the Greater Plan and the thoughts actions and experiences of others – guided also by the same Plan.

Thank you for this space. Shalom..."

§

A scene or an experience of some relaxing nature is often described, such as a walk through nature. It can feel as if one is in front of a wrap-around cinema screen – into which you then enter. Sometimes there is a short personal exploration to gather some small treasure such as an object, coloured light, or one might come across a being – human, animal, or mystical. The virtual group might then be led to a special place, where – with one's personal treasure – the group congregates, often in a circle, and around a feature such as a crystal, a well, or a fountain, or within a cave or forest clearing.

From this point, the core meditation takes place, often introducing an energetic-visual perception and moving onto an energetic-emotional perception, where powerful energy brings the potential for change. A light may beam down into the space within the virtual group, and/or the light may reveal the space to have something of a crystalline structure. The persons or situations in need of change – personal or worldwide in nature – may be visualised as entering the space and/or being bathed by the light. The group is often then encouraged towards a state of stillness for a while, to allow the intentions and the energy(s) to manifest.

The final section usually entails being talked gently out of the virtual group space and back via the scenery where the visualisation first started, often retracing the routes taken so that personal treasures, guides etc. that had been gathered on the way may be let-go of – returned.

If nothing else, such experiences are very relaxing, and sometimes – things *change*.

§

"Today I talk of Love" – the complete recording… {199}

"Today I talk of Love.

Love ultimately extends to and originates in Spirit. It is that connection which binds all souls together and acts through the Law of Duality that finds divine intention separated – in this physical plane – into two sides of the same coin: the Ying, the Yang, the woman, the man.

It is said so often that if we feel the pull of Love towards another – another sentient being, another person, an animal, indeed anything that articulates life even plants, flowers, trees – that if we feel the pull of Love, then to express Love towards anything else that expresses life, the truest expression is to enable freedom for that sentient being – for that life-form. For, in experiencing freedom every sentient being finds their true self: that connection to all that has been, and their path to what is to come.

And there need be no fear when we seek to find our authentic self, and no fear when we seek to set another free. For that which is real, will always be; that which is real cannot be lost. For the truth of all that is real emanates from spirit – as does Love.

If we feel we have come across a Love connection that is true in our lives, we need not fear walking away from that Love connection for it will remain and will pull us back. Indeed, the truest sign to us that a Love connection is based on spiritual truth is when we can let go of all the material trappings of that connection, and step away from that person – from that flower, from that animal – and observe them in their beauty.

And, if by chance we find our lives entwined again with that person, then in truth we have a Love divine.

Thank you for this space."

§

The guided visualisation: ECOS – 12 Sep 2016 {226}

"Close your eyes.

Be aware of your breathing.

Take some long, slow, deep breaths in...two...three – holding on the five... six... seven... and then out...two...three, holding-longer on the five...six... seven...eight,

And again...two...three, holding on the five...six...seven...and then out ...two...three, holding-longer on the five...six...seven... and eight, And once more (repeating the above),

And now we allow our breath to find its natural steady rhythm,

And in your mind's eye, we walk together now, out to the beach here in the bay.

We are standing in a line, hand in hand, facing the sea, facing the sunrise, We walk towards the water's edge; feeling the sand push between our toes,

We are near the water's edge now and the coolness of damp sand on our feet and the gentle sound of breaking waves fill our senses,

We are at the water's edge and the water now seeps around our toes, and we feel the pull to have the water bathe us fully,

Still hand in hand, we now walk slowly together into the sea, feeling the water rising up over our ankles, our shins, over our knees and our thighs,

Up to our waists now in the sea, we look side to side at one-another and we smile for we know we are safe and can go deeper still together,

Up to our chests, our joined-hands now immersed,

Up to our necks and we are feeling both elated and calm, both excited and focused, we have no concerns; we have no further thoughts.

The sea is warm and inviting and as we continue to walk further in, the shortest to the tallest of our number are immersed entirely and – to our wonder and delight – we find we are each encapsulated in giant bubbles of air that protect and support us, bubbles that close and meet where our hands join.

Content that we are safe and protected in this new environment, we look around now at the water, the sand, the rocks and sea life,

It is as if a whole new world exists here, under the surface; we have seen the surface from above, and we have known that there is something below, but only now as we have come together, only now, do we feel it safe to venture – under.

And, "under" is not quite as we had expected it to be,

You feel no risk, and it is much quieter than you would have imagined: there being not only little-sound but also – not much sea-life either,

And you know that there is work to be done to bring about a change; to bring about more vibrancy, to encourage life, more "living"; but what is to be done and where?

Then, ahead and to the right, you see a small archway of rocks – an opening whose position corresponds with the cove you know to be above the surface,

The archway is quite low, but the opening is tall enough to enter and it stretches far back into the cliff-face that towers above,

Hand-in-hand we enter, going through the archway to find that we are in a smooth-walled tunnel,

As we go deeper, you become aware of a change in the quality of the light, and in the colours around you.

Going deeper and deeper the arched ceiling opens up into a domed cavern where there are a series of smooth rocks and giant domed shells arranged in a circle, and in the centre is the largest scallop-like shell you have ever seen,

We form a circle – each having either a rock or a giant upturned shell that will be our seat, and as we together sit down, the quality of light changes again.

You can sense the light, you can feel it, but you are not quite sure from where it comes – until your gaze settles upon the beautiful centre shell,

In the shell sits a single beautiful pearl; creamy-white with hints of pink and blue – it is luminescent.

As you watch, you see hundreds of tiny bubbles beginning to come from underneath it, and with the light from the pearl now intensified, the bubbles increase in size and number, and begin to circulate, and as the number and circulation of bubbles further increases, so does the vibrancy of the light, and there forms a veritable whirlpool; a spiral of swirling bubbles and rippling currents of light.

The ripples of light and swirling bubbles spiral up and then out and overhead, and the pinks and blues expand to take in the greens of the seaweed and creamy yellows of the surrounding rock wall, and the spiralling light expands further overhead and behind you, until you feel surrounded and encapsulated in its swirling pearlescent vibrancy.

You sense much power, but there is no fear, for the expansion of light that you are now within brings with it yet a sense of peace and calm, and it contains the power to heal that comes from the energy of Change in All – an energy that is already without and within you; and in accepting this flow, this movement, this change – you find a new perspective: witnessing both power and calm working together, as one.

At the height of sensation, your eyes focus towards the centre and just above the point where the edge of the shell is just discernible through the ripples and bubbles, and you observe the concentrations of colours becoming darker.

And from a mixing of all colours, a deep amethyst takes form and its ripples become static to form first shadows and then shapes, and then a form emerges.

A kind face with gentle features forms and hands are offered you which your arms now extend to meet, and there comes a sensation, that all-powerful connection, the fulfilment of the faith you have held while in the state of Being.

And now – you understand...

- *That all can be done – that all must be done – and that the energy of change and the power to change circulates now within you;*
- *That the process of living is the process of change and that change involves all colours – as coming from the source of All;*
- *You understand that to enable change – it takes your acceptance,*
- *That, all is as it can only be.*

And then, just as it had arisen, the torrent of spiralling bubbles and cascading lights subside, and there, at the bottom, in the centre of the shell, is the creamy pink and blue pearl once more; seemingly untouched, unaffected.

You become aware of the group once more – seated in a circle,

You are aware that the nature of the light is now in some way different from when you had first entered the cavern,

As you stand and move out of the cavern you look for the hand of another,

And as hands come together, life-supporting bubbles come together, and together we walk back towards the shore.

Coming with you are the memories shared, and the afterglow of the peace that you absorbed now spills out from within you – mixing with the water and shedding new light on the surroundings; enabling new perceptions and new experiences within-which change can be welcomed.

Back on the shore, we come out just as we had entered: hand in hand.

Opening our eyes now to clear our vision, we give thanks to those around us who have shared this experience – this day.

Thank you."